**Diabetic LIVING**®

# diabetes daily

Zucchini Ribbons, Pasta, and Arugula, *p. 159*

**Diabetic LIVING**®

# diabetes daily

HOUGHTON MIFFLIN HARCOURT
BOSTON • NEW YORK • 2018

MEREDITH CORPORATION
*DIABETIC LIVING*® DIABETES DAILY

**Editorial Director:** Jennifer Darling
**Creative Director:** Michael Belnap
**Senior Associate Editor, Caitlyn Diimig, RD**
**Contributing Project Manager:** Shelli McConnell,
Purple Pear Publishing, Inc.
**Contributing Writer:** Bailey McGrath
**Contributing Copy Editor:** Caitlyn Diimig, Carrie Truesdell
**Contributing Proofreader:** Gretchen Kauffman
*Diabetic LIving*® **Test Kitchen Director:** Lynn Blanchard
*Diabetic LIving*® **Test Kitchen Chef:** Carla Christian, RD, LD
**Contributing Photographers:** Jason Donnelly, Carson Downing,
Andy Lyons
**Contributing Stylists:** Joshua Hake, Jennifer Peterson

HOUGHTON MIFFLIN HARCOURT

**Executive Editor:** Anne Ficklen
**Managing Editor:** Marina Padakis Lowry
**Art Director:** Tai Blanche
**Production Director:** Tom Hyland

WATERBURY PUBLICATIONS, INC.

**Design Director:** Ken Carlson
**Editorial Director:** Lisa Kingsley
**Associate Editorial Director:** Tricia Bergman
**Associate Design Director:** Doug Samuelson
**Associate Design Director:** Becky Lau-Ekstrand
**Production Assistant:** Mindy Samuelson
**Graphic Designer:** Ruby Hotchkiss
**Photography Assistant:** Emma Carlson

For information about permission to reproduce
selections from this book, write to
trade.permissions@hmhco.com or to
Permissions, Houghton Mifflin Harcourt Publishing
Company, 3 Park Avenue, 18th Floor, New York, NY
10016.

hmhco.com

Library of Congress Cataloging-in-Publication Data is
available.

ISBN 978-1-328-49770-3 (pbk)
Book design by Waterbury Publications, Inc.,
Des Moines, Iowa.

Printed in China

SCP 10 9 8 7 6 5 4 3 2 1

Pictured on front cover:
Stove-Top Chicken, Macaroni, and Cheese, recipe *p. 177*

Pictured on back cover:
Fruity Coconut Smoothie Bowls with Toasted Oats, recipe *p. 104*

# from the editors

Good for you! If you're holding this book, you've made an important step toward making shifts in your life that will ensure the well-being of you and your loved ones. A diabetes or prediabetes diagnosis doesn't change who you are, but it does mean you need to make some changes in how you care for yourself. We'll help you put the focus on your whole self—mind and body.

The first part of this book teaches you strategies for living mindfully. Start by building a support team of medical and nutrition professionals, other people with diabetes (PWDs), friends, and your family. Learning how to deal with diabetes and getting into new routines is stressful. We'll help you identify your stressors and suggest simple, achievable techniques for bringing your stress level down. An important aspect of your self-care is exercise. Discuss your fitness level and abilities with your doctor first, then start slowly with some of the exercises we've outlined. They are a good first step to becoming stronger and meeting weight loss goals.

The other piece to the diabetes-management puzzle is healthful eating. What you eat is a constant in diabetes management. If you use our strategies and recipes, eating mindfully will soon become second nature. These recipes are thoughtfully created with wholesome ingredients and the right amount of nutrients for people with diabetes. These recipes are also delicious and healthful for everyone at the table. They are a good place to start as you learn how to cook with less fat, carbs, and sodium without sacrificing flavor and satisfaction—and you don't have to give up dessert! Charts with two full weeks of menus make it easy to jump-start your new eating plan. We show you how to fill your plate healthfully with appropriate-size portions. You'll also learn how to snack to benefit your body and resist emotional eating.

Changing your lifestyle won't be a direct path. You'll struggle and take a step backward now and again. When that happens, reach for this book to get yourself back on track. Living and eating mindfully is something you can do—and we're here to help.

# contents

# how stress affects diabetes

Managing stress will be your new normal to set you in the best path to health.

The constant worry about complications, the tedious carbohydrate counting, the guilt when you skip exercise, the anger you feel because you can't eat like others. It's exhausting and stressful.

There's a term for this—it's called diabetes distress—and it can affect those with diabetes at any point in their lives.

Distress is a normal reaction to the stresses and strains of managing a progressive, chronic disease like diabetes. It's the constant sense of burden or defeat you can't seem to shake. Many things can trigger it, such as feeling deprived by being unable to eat certain foods and getting a high blood glucose reading after a healthful meal.

Plus, the stigma that comes with type 2 diabetes and prediabetes can be burdensome. "It's hard to get emotional support when the outside world's attitude is you've brought this on yourself," says Lawrence Fisher, Ph.D., of the University of California, San Francisco. This can take a toll on both your physical health and mental health.

But getting the fears and feelings out and understanding they're a normal part of having diabetes helps. Later in this book, you'll learn how to overcome stress and anxiety and combat the negative thoughts that can come with a diabetes diagnosis *(p. 14)*.

But even if you're not experiencing diabetes distress, the daily stressors of life might affect your blood sugar levels. Hormones such as epinephrine and cortisol can increase during stressful events and could encourage the liver to produce extra glucose, causing blood sugars to spike. Prolonged stress can manifest itself into physical issues as well (see "Stress Symptoms," *right*).

There are healthy ways to handle stressful situations. In this book, we'll teach you how to be more mindful and present with your feelings. Plus, you'll be equipped with 5-minute tricks to calm you down when you're starting to feel overwhelmed *(p. 26)*. These are a few strategies to try right now.

### Be More Mindful

• Keep your thoughts on the present; live where your feet are.
• Observe your thoughts. Meditate, journal, or simply stop to breathe to reflect on what's going through your mind.
• Accept your emotions without judgment. Remember that there are no right or wrong ways to feel.
• Don't dwell on the past or worry about the future.
• Take yourself off autopilot. Sometimes our reactions to situations are automatic, such as anger in traffic. Instead, be more aware of your reactions.

# stress symptoms

If you have one or more of these issues, your body may be trying to tell you about underlying, prolonged stress.

### STOMACH
• Queasiness
• Heartburn
• Abdominal pain
• Diarrhea

If you experience acute or chronic stomach distress, see a doctor to rule out a serious condition such as ulcers or heart disease.

### HEAD
• Tension headaches
• Migraine headaches

Stress is one of the most common triggers for both types of headaches.

### NECK, SHOULDERS & BACK
• Neck and shoulder tightness and pain
• Lower -back pain

Not all back pain is caused by stress. But stress makes nearly all back pain worse.

### SKIN & HAIR
• Eczema
• Acne
• Hives
• Hair loss
• Dandruff or itchy scalp

Although it's a link that's often overlooked, stress is a major trigger of skin and hair problems.

# mindful management of diabetes

Adding moments of mindfulness to your day can help you better manage your diabetes.

With the added responsibilities of managing your type 2 diabetes or prediabetes, you may feel like there's no time to slow down and relax. But doing so can help you better understand the decisions you make and the results of those choices, as well as identify the emotions you're feeling and why.

This is called mindfulness, a practice that encourages judgment-free observations of what you are thinking and feeling in the present moment.

With mindfulness, you're observing your thoughts and emotions almost from an outsider's perspective. This observation allows for reaction to what is going on and why the thoughts are happening, not just reaction to the situation.

For example, when you're checking your blood sugar, try doing so with curiosity, not judgment. Instead of thinking, *Wow, my blood sugar levels are soaring. I really blew it at that dinner party,* consider the result as simply information. That way, you can act from a place of calm instead of a place of distress. Think, *My blood sugar levels are high, but I can take a walk after the party to help bring them down.* You're not pushing away or ignoring that guilt, shame, or frustration, but you are acknowledging those emotions by labeling them, working past them, and using your energy to figure out a solution to feel better.

"We create so much suffering for ourselves when we layer judgment and failure into our diabetes management," says Heather Nielsen, a counselor and wellness coach in Portland, Oregon, and person with diabetes (PWD) type 1.

Taking out that layer and replacing it with mindfulness can ease anxiety and diabetes-related distress and improve overall well-being, according to a study published in the journal *Diabetes Care.*

In this book, we'll teach you many ways to practice mindfulness: mindful living techniques like meditation *(p. 28)* and smart goal setting *(p. 44);* combatting emotional eating habits *(p. 56)*, mindful eating practices like listening to hunger cues *(p. 58),* and much more.

Some people find it helpful to set aside time to practice mindfulness; others incorporate it into daily activity. Remember, there is no right or wrong way. Try a few of the techniques in this book to see what works best for you. Regardless of your approach, practicing mindfulness will help you control stress, pay more attention to the foods you eat, and improve your overall health.

# mindful living

# you've been diagnosed. now what?

## A diabetes diagnosis can be overwhelming. Here's how to take control.

### What Is Diabetes?

To manage your diabetes well, you first need to understand what is happening inside your body.

Type 2 diabetes has a number of contributing factors, such as excess weight, sedentary lifestyle, and genetics. An underlying factor is when the body's muscle, liver, and fat cells resist the effects of insulin, which causes a buildup of glucose in the blood. This is called insulin resistance.

Type 2 diabetes is also characterized by inadequate insulin secretion from the beta cells in the pancreas. This is called insulin insufficiency, which can be caused by genetics and sometimes by years of insulin resistance. People with prediabetes and type 2 have both insulin resistance and insulin insufficiency.

### What Happens When I Eat?

One of the most important things to understand is how food affects your body differently now that you have diabetes.

"Before you had diabetes, your body was on autopilot," says Donna Starck, RD, LD, CDE, of UnityPoint Health in Des Moines.

When you ate carbohydrate, your blood sugar would rise and your pancreas would respond with the right amount of insulin, a hormone that allows the body's cells to receive and use glucose for energy.

With diabetes, your body requires assistance. This is because your body isn't making any insulin, isn't producing enough insulin, or can no longer properly use the insulin it produces. This is what happens when a person with type 2 diabetes eats carbohydrate:

**One of the most important things to understand is how food affects your body differently now that you have diabetes.**

- ▶ Food goes down your esophagus and into your stomach.
- ▶ The digestive system quickly breaks down carbohydrate into glucose.
- ▶ Glucose enters the bloodstream.
- ▶ The pancreas releases insulin in response to a buildup of glucose in the bloodstream.
- ▶ Insulin tries to attach to the body's cell receptors, but it is unable to bind to the receptors properly.
- ▶ Glucose cannot enter the cell and continues to build up in the bloodstream.
- ▶ The pancreas continues to release insulin in an effort to lower blood sugar. Thus, many people with type 2 diabetes have very high levels of insulin circulating in their bloodstreams.

**Blood sugar checks provide insight into how food, stress, exercise, and other factors affect blood glucose levels.**

## Manage Diabetes Mindfully

The progression of type 2 diabetes is managed by eating healthfully, exercising, monitoring your blood sugar, and taking medication. Just as important: taking care of your mental health.

## Eat Right

A large part of managing diabetes is being mindful of what you eat. What you eat directly affects your blood sugar levels. Foods that contain carbohydrate have the greatest impact on your blood sugar. In this book, we'll show you how to eat mindfully by planning meals, reading labels, listening to hunger cues, thoughtfully filling your plate, and more.

## Move More

Exercise has many benefits in diabetes management: Among them are helping to lower blood sugar levels, bringing down your A1C, improving circulation, and decreasing stress. Aim to get 30 minutes of moderate activity five days each week—anything from a brisk walk to swimming to cycling. Or try our workouts starting on *p. 32.* The American Diabetes Association (ADA) also recommends getting up and moving every 30 minutes— try marching in place, stretching, or doing side lunges.

## Monitor and Adhere

In this book, we'll focus on eating right and moving more. For many people, it's important to check your blood sugar a few times a day and to take the medications your doctor prescribes.

Blood sugar checks provide insight into how food, stress, exercise, and other factors affect blood glucose levels. Check several times a day and make those checks count. Here are mindful ways to check:

▶ Rotate fasting checks before meals, after meals, before bed, and during the night to limit the number of test strips you use each day.

▶ Check just before you eat and one to two hours after to learn how a meal or snack affects your blood glucose levels.

▶ Note how you feel before and after eating. For example, if a large breakfast of sausage, eggs, and toast leaves you sluggish, drop the sausage in favor of a small piece of fruit. If stress causes your blood sugars to spike, find ways to decompress (we'll show you how on *p. 26).*

## Stress Less

Diabetes can stress you out (to say the least). But managing that stress is vital to diabetes management because it can have serious effects on your blood sugar. Hormones, such as epinephrine and cortisol, increase during stressful events, encouraging the liver to produce extra glucose while also increasing insulin resistance. Learn how to identify and combat stress starting on *p. 24.*

# build your support network

Surround yourself with a team of diabetes experts to keep your health on track and with family, friends, and other PWDs for emotional support.

## Your Health Care Team

Every PWD should see a primary care provider (PCP) for general checkups. Developing a relationship of trust and openness with your provider will lead to better management. Your PCP will oversee all aspects of your diabetes care and refer you to specialists when necessary. Look for a PCP who makes you feel comfortable and regularly works with PWDs.

Perhaps the most important member of your team is a certified diabetes educator (CDE), who will serve as the primary source of support and education. A CDE may be a nurse, dietitian, pharmacist, social worker, or other professional who is knowledgeable in diabetes management. He or she will work with you to devise an individual plan and give you the tools to manage diabetes, such as setting up a food plan, teaching you when and how to test blood sugar levels, and helping you cope with stress. Ask your PCP for a referral or visit diabeteseducator.org to find an educator near you.

## You may also see:

- Endocrinologist
- Optometrist or Opthalmologist
- Dentist
- Registered dietitian nutritionist (RD or RDN)
- Pharmacist
- Podiatrist
- Exercise specialist
- Mental health professional

## Support Network

Managing diabetes can be overwhelming, time-consuming, and stressful. But having people around to support your efforts helps. Even better—finding people going through the same thing. Getting together with other PWDs can make a big difference in how well you take care of yourself. Studies have shown that people who participate in activities with others have better control of blood sugars, better quality

## digital support

The diabetes online community (DOC) is a great place to meet others with the disease and form connections. Here are a few of our favorite online groups:

- DiabetesDaily.com
- DiabetesSisters.com
- TuDiabetes.org
- EsTuDiabetes.org
- The Diabetic Living® Facebook page: *facebook. com/diabeticliving*

Join diabetes Twitter chats like Diabetes Social Media Advocacy #DSMA, Diabetic Connect #DCDE, and Health Care Social Media #HCSM

of life, and less depression than those who don't. "The research about diabetes, and chronic illness in general, clearly indicates that support from others enhances self-care," says John Zrebiec, M.S.W., CDE, director of behavioral health services at the Joslin Diabetes Center in Boston and *Diabetic Living* adviser. "This is likely because it is a natural response to being able to share the burden."

## 4 Ways a Support Group Can Help You

**1. Feel Connected** Identifying with a group relieves the feeling of isolation that often comes with diagnosis. No matter how helpful friends and family are, they still can't fully understand what it's like to live with diabetes. Spending an hour with other people who deal with the challenges of diabetes can help you feel less alone.

**2. Overcome Self-Blame** Getting together with others can help you get over the shame that many PWDs experience. You'll see that everyone developed the disease for a number of different reasons.

**3. Gain a New Outlook** Other people can offer fresh perspectives on something that may be troubling you, such as starting insulin. Or maybe you have questions about packing a healthful lunch. Someone else may have a great tip.

**4. Learn Acceptance** Hearing other people talk about similar struggles with diabetes helps you break through whatever is holding you back and jump into action. You might become more compassionate with yourself.

### support-group etiquette

Ready to attend a support group for diabetes? Here are tips for minding your Ps and Qs.

**DO** open up and share stories about yourself, including challenges you're facing and successes you've enjoyed.

**DON'T** monopolize the conversation.

**DO** offer support to others in the group.

**DON'T** judge what others say or share their medical information with people outside the group.

**DO** ask questions, however minor they might seem, because chances are you're not the only one with those issues.

**DON'T** focus only on the negatives of living with diabetes.

Find a support group through your diabetes educator, local hospital, or diabetes organization, such as the American Diabetes Association *(diabetes.org)*. Before settling on one, attend a few meetings to make sure it's a good fit. Rule of thumb: The conversation should be positive and helpful. Constant complaining from others won't encourage you to take positive action toward managing the disease.

# get family on board

Living with diabetes on your own is hard. Uncooperative family and friends can hinder diabetes management. Whether it's your sister complaining about you ditching your weekly pizza dates or your spouse micromanaging everything you put in your mouth, you can use various strategies to help loved ones be more helpful and less damaging.

## 3 Ways to Help Friends and Family "Get It"

**1. Educate**  Many people are confused about what diabetes is and how to manage it, and they often make comments or recommendations based on unreliable, inaccurate, or unrealistic information. Invite friends and family members to a diabetes education or support group. Ask your spouse or partner to join you at a doctor's appointment or CDE visit to get credible information firsthand. He or she is more likely to listen to info coming from an authoritative figure.

**2. Request Specifics**  A direct request detailing how family can help is often best. Some examples: provide a shopping list of healthful foods to keep on hand; ask for reminders for medication or glucose testing schedules; get help with stress management techniques, such as regular massages (stress can elevate your blood glucose and trigger the urge to eat when you're not hungry). Ask someone to take on a chore so you can go for a walk.

**3. Make It a Family Affair**  Explain how eating better and moving more can benefit everyone. Try a new recipe together. Take up a new physical hobby as a family, such as kayaking or biking. At a restaurant, share a meal. Better yet, suggest outings that don't center around food, such as a trip to a museum or a Sunday afternoon visit to your nearest park. And remember: If family or friends continue to blow off your requests and disregard what's best for you, it's OK to explain that you may have to limit contact to stay healthy.

## 7 tips for loved ones

(Feel free to copy and give to a family member!)

**1. AVOID BLAME AND SHAME.** PWDs have a lot to handle, and they need your support more than anything. Blaming only adds to stress.

**2. LISTEN** to the PWD's wants and needs.

**3. LEARN ABOUT DIABETES** and how it can affect the body and emotions.

**4. JOIN THEIR NEW HEALTHY LIFESTYLE.** Try to eat like a PWD and exercise together.

**5. PROVIDE HELP.** Ask what the PWD needs. For example, help make a healthy dinner or offer rides to the pharmacy.

**6. BE A CHEERLEADER.** Encourage PWDs and remind them they're doing a good job.

**7. PROVIDE ACCOUNTABILITY.** For example, you can offer to hear a weekly update on goals and act as a sounding board for new strategies.

## how to model a healthier family

If words fail, lead by example.

◗ Invite loved ones to medical appointments to help them understand the seriousness of the disease.

◗ Live your life in a healthful way: Limit alcohol intake, stay active, eat well, and don't smoke, .

◗ Help everyone focus on other health goals that make managing diabetes even more worth it. Some examples are improving your tennis game and keeping up with the grandchildren.

◗ Ask loved ones to join you on your journey: What's good for me is also good for you.

◗ Keep tempting foods out of the house. If you buy it, you'll be more tempted to eat it.

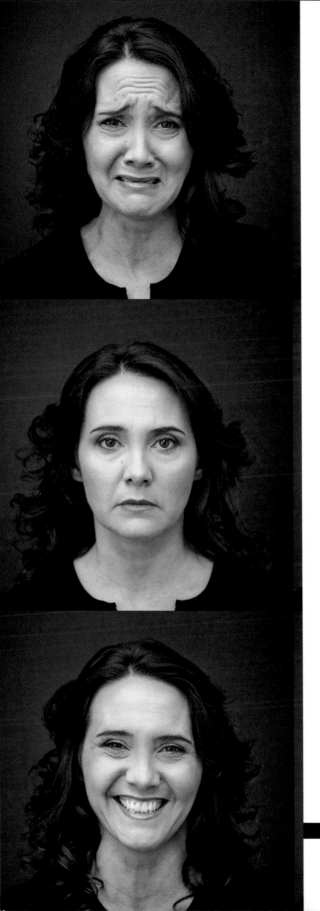

# how stressed out are you?

Stress can have negative effects on your diabetes management. Take our quiz to find out if stress or anxiety is hindering your health.

**On any given day, which best describes the internal "chatter" in your mind?**

**A.** I feel generally optimistic. Every day presents another opportunity for adventure.

**B.** I tend to worry, and when something goes wrong, it's all I can think about.

**C.** I frequently find myself worrying and imagining worst-case scenarios.

**D.** I sometimes feel so overcome by anxiety that it's difficult for me to leave the house or maintain relationships.

## At the holiday office party, which description best fits you?

**A.** I look forward to it all year—I love any occasion to mingle.

**B.** I need a while to "warm up" and much prefer small gatherings.

**C.** I only go if I must, and I remain on the sidelines until I can make an early exit.

**D.** Even the thought of being around that many people makes me break out in a sweat.

## How often do you experience headaches, tightness in your chest, neck pain, or muscle tension?

**A.** Only occasionally.

**B.** Any time I get overwhelmed, such as when I'm facing a deadline, I have a presentation to make, I'm late, or I have too many obligations to fulfill.

**C.** One or more times a week.

**D.** I struggle with these symptoms on a daily basis.

## Which nighttime scenario best describes you?

**A.** I'm asleep before my head hits the pillow.

**B.** I can usually fall asleep within 15 minutes.

**C.** I tend to dwell on past mistakes or worry so much it's difficult to fall asleep.

**D.** I toss and turn every night and am lucky to catch four or five hours of shut-eye.

## How often do you find yourself unreasonably—as in excessively or without an apparent cause—irritable?

**A.** Rarely.

**B.** Every now and then.

**C.** Weekly.

**D.** I can lose it at the drop of a hat.

## how did you do?

**MOSTLY A'S** Congratulations, you're as cool as a cucumber. Keep up the good work!

**MOSTLY B'S** You may have a tendency to worry, but you're not in the red zone. Deep breathing, meditation, or a yoga session can help keep stress at a minimum.

**MOSTLY C'S** Your stress is severe enough that it sometimes interferes with your daily life. Consider trying cognitive-behavioral therapy with a professional to learn techniques to stop anxiety in its tracks.

**MOSTLY D'S** Your stress has reached an unhealthy level. It would be a good idea to seek professional help. Anxiety is highly treatable; there are plenty of methods to help you beat stress, stay positive, and get the most out of life.

# stop the stress

Find your calm with these tips and strategies to manage stress and anxiety.

You're packing for a family trip that you've been looking forward to for months. Yet the week before, your heart races, your stomach is in knots, and you lie awake at night, worried that you forgot to pack your meter or your hotel won't be in a safe neighborhood. By the time you're boarding your plane, you're exhausted.

This type of worry isn't garden-variety stress. It's anxiety—and most people don't realize there's a difference between the two.

"Stress stems from something actually happening that is stressful, while anxiety is anticipating that something in the future will go wrong," says Jenny Taitz, Psy.D., a board-certified clinical psychologist in New York City.

About 18 percent of Americans suffer from an anxiety disorder, according to the National Institute of Mental Health, And if you have diabetes, you're more likely to be diagnosed with a mental disorder, according to the American Diabetes Association.

Anxiety is a natural part of our body's fight-or-flight response. When we encounter a threat (real or imaginary), we feel stress, which triggers the release of adrenaline and cortisol. These hormones are meant to prime the body for action by accelerating heart rate, tensing major muscle groups, and thickening blood, but they can potentially wreak havoc on your blood glucose levels.

In small doses, this heightened awareness can be a good thing. "Anxiety can be a signal to pay attention, marshal our resources, and make changes where necessary," says David Sack, M.D., a board-certified psychiatrist and CEO of Elements Behavioral Health, a network of addiction treatment centers. "But when we can't turn off that anxiety, and worry is all we experience, then anxiety has become a problem."

Feeling overwhelmed by worry and irrational fears to the point that your everyday life is affected may indicate you have a diagnosable anxiety disorder. The mental toll can be devastating, especially for PWDs.

"People will eat junk foods because they can activate pleasure centers in the brain and temporarily relieve stress," says Mark Heyman, Ph.D., a clinical psychologist in San Diego who specializes in diabetes and also has type 1 diabetes. "People may also engage in avoidance behavior—they won't be physically active or they avoid diabetes self-care."

And it's not all in your head. Anxiety can manifest in intense physical symptoms, including dizziness, digestion issues, headaches, high blood pressure, and even tingling in the arms and face. Fear and worry regarding these physical symptoms can actually increase anxiety, triggering cycles that are difficult to break out of, Taitz says.

Whether you're occasionally overwhelmed by anxiety or it's truly paralyzing your day-to-day life, simply wishing you felt in control won't give you much relief. But there are ways to cope. Read on to learn how.

## Lighten Your Load

Anxiety can rear its ugly head when we're going through major life changes, like being diagnosed with diabetes. Here's how to deal with the negative emotions that can come with a type 2 diagnosis or when dealing with diabetes burnout—the overwhelming frustration and fatigue that comes from managing a chronic condition.

**Educate Yourself** "The more you learn, the more empowered you'll feel," says Paula Wilkerson of Albany, New York, who was initially terrified by her diagnosis. "Now I know the diagnosis doesn't mean life is over. You can begin an even better life that includes taking better care of yourself and understanding your body," she says.

**Challenge Your Thoughts** When we feel anxious, we tend to default to "what if" thinking, which catapults us directly to the worst-case scenario: *What if I forget my medications? What if there are no healthy options on the menu? What if my coworkers act differently around me if I tell them I have diabetes?* Instead of letting these catastrophic thoughts repeat in your head, try identifying and addressing them, says Marla W. Deibler, Psy.D., a clinical psychologist and executive director of The Center for Emotional Health of Greater Philadelphia in Cherry Hill, New Jersey. "Ask yourself, 'Is that really likely to happen?' or 'If it does happen, could I handle that?'" You can try digging emotionally deeper, too—like a therapist might—by asking yourself, "If something bad does happen, what might that mean for me?"

**Open Up to Family and Friends** Rather than shutting out people who care, invite them to support groups. Involve family and friends in your diabetes care. Let them know how you're feeling. Tell them that if you seem angry sometimes, it may be due to your own frustration. Getting loved ones involved will help them understand diabetes and also keep you from feeling isolated.

**Set Realistic Goals** Unattainable objectives set you up for disappointment. Set small, achieveable goals. Do the best you can and accept that you won't hit 100 percent every time.

**Focus on the Positive** Rather than dwelling on the prospect of developing complications someday, consider the healthful behaviors you're learning and how those new habits will help you lose weight or boost your confidence and keep you from developing complications.

**Get Involved** Volunteer for a diabetes-related event. "These activities are therapeutic and encourage positive thinking, instead of the 'poor me, not me' mantra," says Karmeen Kulkarni, RD, BC-ADM, CDE. "Being around people who have diabetes will help you share your feelings, plus you may pick up tips."

**Get Help When Needed** If you try these strategies and still feel that your anxiety is weighing you down, you may benefit from the help of a therapist. It's tough to admit you need help, especially when stigmas continue to be attached to mental health. "But asking for help isn't a sign of weakness or of personal failure," Taitz says. Therapy has a high success rate of treating anxiety. In some cases, antidepressants or antianxiety medications can be helpful on your journey to recovery. Consider it no different than medicine you'd take to treat a physical ailment like diabetes.

# 5-minute stress busters

These 15 mental makeovers will help you find your happy—fast.

**1. Try a moment of mindfulness.** Practice this form of meditation, in which you focus on the present moment during everyday routines. Before starting your day, turn off your phone and make a cup of green tea. Use all your senses: Feel the warmth in your hand, the steam on your nose, the liquid in your throat. You can do the same while preparing dinner: Take notice of the sounds of your knife cutting vegetables, the feel of the knife in your hand, the rhythm of the slicing, the vibrations of the cutting board, and the scent of the vegetables releasing their juices.

**2. Escape into a book.** Research has found that silent reading slows your heart rate and reduces muscle tension within six minutes.

**3. Get outdoors.**
**Minute 1** Find a spot where you connect with nature—a patch of grass in the backyard or a quiet window to look outside.
**Minutes 2–3** Observe and focus on the natural world around you until something catches your eye. Take deep, calming breaths.
**Minutes 4–5** Think about how that one element of nature reflects something about you and say or write down your conclusion. It doesn't have to be profound: "The cardinal is red and that's my favorite color" can do the trick.

**4. Snag some exercise endorphins.** Even brief bursts of exercise can help reduce blood pressure and cholesterol, research has found. Try this quick routine a couple times a day or when you're feeling overwhelmed.

| ACTIVITY | TIME |
| --- | --- |
| Warmup: March in place | 60 seconds |
| Squats | 30 seconds |
| Lunges | 30 seconds |
| Plank | 30 seconds |
| Squats | 30 seconds |
| Lunges | 30 seconds |
| Plank | 30 seconds |
| Stretch | 60 seconds |

**5. Open your ears to music therapy.**
**To Calm Down** Play the nature-inspired music of your choice, suggests Judi Bar, yoga program manager at the Cleveland Clinic's Wellness Institute. Don headphones, close your eyes, and, if you can swing it, lie down and cover your eyes with a rice-filled eye pillow warmed a bit in the microwave. "To fully immerse yourself in the music," Bar says, "focus on listening to individual notes or a nature sound in the background for three to five minutes."
**To Rev Up** Borrow your kid's or grandkid's toy drum. (No

one's looking!) "Drumming can release endorphins—those natural feel-good chemicals," says Allison Gemmel Laframboise, a yoga and drumming teacher at Kripalu Center for Yoga & Health in Stockbridge, Massachusetts. To get started, drum to the rhythm of a spoken phrase, like "I eat peaches. I eat peaches. I eat peaches." Then lose the phrase and focus on the sound and feel of the pattern.

**6. Turn off your phone.** Or put it on silent mode. Those emails can wait. Just be present in your physical space for a few minutes.

**7. Take a whiff.** Try inhaling the scent of calming essential oils such as frankincense and lavender for a few seconds to fend off anxieties.

**8. Wet your wrists.** Place your forearms under cold running water for 60 seconds while breathing deeply. Your wrists have a large number of small blood vessels, and the cold water helps cool and calm you, according to Julie Rosenzweig, Ph.D., a psychotherapist in Lake Oswego, Oregon.

**9. Play with your pet.** It's virtually impossible to stay stressed when you're rubbing your dog's belly or dangling string in front of your cat.

**10. Get a good laugh.** Whether it's shared with a friend or in reaction to a funny video, mirthful laughter increases circulation, decreases hypertension, stimulates the immune system, stops the release of stress hormones, and increases feel-good hormones, research shows.

**11. Color yourself calm.** Filling in a pattern can ease anxiety more than drawing on a blank page, so get a geometric coloring book, says Donna Betts, Ph.D., president of the American Art Therapy Association.

**12. Call a friend.** Talking to someone who will listen, like a close friend or family member, can help you unpack any problems you might be facing.

**13. Do someone else a favor.** Becoming a problem solver instead of being a problem sufferer can help put your stress into perspective. It might also encourage that someone else to lend a hand if you ever get caught in a tight spot.

**14. Take it to the bedroom.** Research shows that the endorphin release that comes from sex calms the body long after the deed is done. And let's be frank: partner optional.

**15. Just leave.** Don't be afraid to physically remove yourself from a situation that feels stressful. Let the overcrowded bus or elevator leave without you.

# the power of meditation

Even if you can't picture sitting perfectly still or completely quieting your brain, you can meditate—and tap into the practice's many health benefits.

Meditation doesn't directly burn calories and cut carbs. Instead, it can help you refocus your mind so that it can become easier to stick to a health plan. And that can decrease stress levels, leading to a healthier mind and body.

## Commit to Calm

If you find yourself worried about how diabetes may affect your future, meditation can help dispel that anxiety. "Meditation is a generalized de-stressing technique that releases you from your thinking machine, from that restless voice inside your head that never lets up except when you're asleep or unconscious," says June Biermann, author of *The Diabetic's Total Health and Happiness Book*. "What we particularly like about meditation is that if you give it a try, it can bring you a wonderful respite from that problem you carry around all your waking hours—your diabetes. If you practice meditation consistently, it can change not just your physiology but your entire life."

It takes time for meditation's benefits to begin showing dividends. Your blood pressure isn't going to drop because you tried meditating once for 20 minutes. For the actual benefits of meditation to take hold, the practice needs to be recurring. Find the best method for you and continue practicing—the more you do it, the easier it will be to find your Zen.

## What Is Meditation?

The primary purpose of meditation is to declutter the mind. "You realize you are the boss of your own mind. You become a little more patient. You have the ability to bring yourself back to the moment," says Barb Schmidt, best-selling author of *The Practice: Simple Tools for Managing Stress, Finding Inner Peace, and Uncovering Happiness*.

There are many, many ways to meditate. And lucky for your busy schedule, research shows meditating just five minutes a day, five days a week is enough to lower stress and even enhance the connections you feel with others.

**Find the best meditation method for you and practice— the more you do it, the easier it will be to find your Zen.**

And those few minutes a day are worth it. You'll enjoy life more while managing the constant juggling act. "Practicing meditation and being more mindful allows you to be more present for your family, your job, your workout—everything," says psychologist Elisha Goldstein, Ph.D., author of *Uncovering Happiness: Overcoming Depression with Mindfulness and Self-Compassion*.

## How Do I Meditate?

All forms of meditation work in a similar way: You choose something to focus on—your breath, an image—and when your mind wanders, you gently bring it back. The key is finding a style that works for you. Here's a snapshot of four types. Take your pick or ask your diabetes support group leader to bring in an expert on meditation to teach basic skills. Meditation has even entered the 21st century with smartphone apps, which offer electronic reminders to remain calm and balanced throughout the day.

## Mindful Meditation

Mindfulness is about being aware of your thoughts, emotions, and environment in a nonjudgmental way; you're staying present and observing everything you're thinking and feeling. It's about accepting your feelings and thoughts as they are. You can do this anywhere: at home, in the office, on hold with customer service. Begin by focusing on your breath. Each time your mind drifts, bring your attention back. Don't criticize. Instead of thinking, *I'm so bad at this,* think, *Aah, welcome back.*

## Mantra Meditation

This technique involves choosing a mantra—typically a one- or two-syllable sound or word that you silently repeat to yourself. Sit in a comfortable position and begin silently repeating your word. "Om" is a popular one, but choose any word or sound that you like. As you become more practiced, you may make your mantra a quality you'd like to have more of: patience, compassion, joy.

## Walking Meditation

This is basically an on-the-go form of mindful meditation, but instead of focusing your awareness on your breath, become aware of the sensations of walking. Start by practicing in your backyard. Eventually you can move to somewhere calm like a nature preserve, then start weaving it into your daily life: walking mindfully across the parking lot to your office, while shopping, or to meet a friend. Start in a standing position, noticing how your feet feel. Do you feel pressure where your feet are in contact with the ground? Start walking, paying attention to how your weight shifts from one side of your body to the other. Notice how it feels as you lift your foot, place your heel down, prepare for your next step. Continue walking. Any time your mind wanders from focusing on how you're walking, gently bring it back.

## Guided Meditation

Using this method can be incredibly beneficial for new meditators. It's based on the theory that your body can respond to imagery as it would to a genuine experience. (Need proof? Imagine yourself sucking on a lemon right now. Did you pucker?) With each breath, imagine yourself inhaling IN relaxation and exhaling OUT tension. As your body relaxes, picture yourself at the beach or another calming, pleasant place. Imagine the scene in detail, using all of your senses: Feel the sun's rays warming your skin and the sand between your toes; listen to the waves crashing; see the bright blue sky; smell the saltwater. Guided meditation can be done in person with a trained practitioner or using recordings, readily available online and through mobile apps.

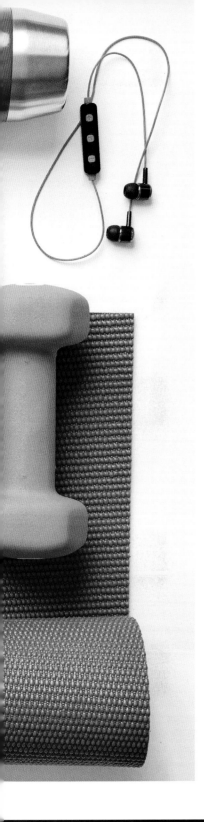

# mindful fitness moves

Regular physical activity burns calories, but it also improves insulin sensitivity and blood glucose numbers, lowers the risk for heart disease and stroke, improves sleep, relieves stress, improves flexibility and balance, and even more. A mix of aerobic exercise and strength training works best.

## fitness health

▶ Consult your doctor before starting any exercise program.

▶ It's smart to wear a medical alert tag in case of an emergency.

▶ Always carry your meter and emergency glucose tabs.

Better Work Flow

# aware in the chair

Try these quick moves throughout the day to break up sitting time.

by Robert Powell, Ph.D., CEP, CSCS, CDE

Staying active is hard when you have a job or lifestyle that requires hours of sitting. Too much sitting is associated with poor health and reduces muscle strength and flexibility. Plus, when you have diabetes, too much sitting time reduces insulin sensitivity, which negatively impacts blood sugar control. Fortunately, simply breaking up sitting time can improve your diabetes management, research says. In fact, the American Diabetes Association now recommends breaking up sitting time every 30 minutes to help manage blood sugar levels. Follow these on-the-job training tips to help manage yours. For best results, perform each activity every day or alternate activities different days of the week. (Note: These activities are not considered a replacement for additional structured exercise regimens.)

## Better Work Flow

Improve your overall health by simply getting up from your chair and walking around the office.

**How to Do It** Step away from the desk and spend a minimum of 3 minutes walking around the office, outside the building, or in the parking lot. This can be done in a longer session (10 minutes or more) or in accumulated bouts (3 minutes or more) throughout the day.

**Benefits** Improves blood flow, lowers blood sugar, lowers blood pressure, and burns calories.

**Mindful Tips** Walk to a specific point and back. Too busy? Use this time to drop off documents or have a walking meeting. Make getting out of your chair to perform a daily task your new habit.

**Progression** Increase the amount of times per day that

you get up and move from your desk. Use a pedometer or tracking device to challenge yourself with a progressive step goal.

## Solid Work Support

Improving lower-body strength is vital to support daily activities. Make getting in and out of your chair easier with body-weight squats.

**How to Do It** If desired, use your desk, office doorway, or wall for extra stability. Use your chair as a depth guide by slightly lowering and touching your chair (be careful that the chair does not move out from under you). A) Stand straight with your feet slightly wider than hip width apart. Keep your back rigid. Bend at the knees and hips; lower until you start to feel your heels raise, your back round, or your thighs are parallel to the floor. Stop sooner if you feel pain or instability. B) Next, extend your hips and knees at the same time to return to standing. Hold your arms out in front of you to help with balance and keep your chest from dropping forward. Repeat 10 times or as many times as you can (repetitions). Pause for 1 minute and repeat the sequence (set). Do 1–3 sets.

**Benefits** Improves muscular strength and endurance in the major leg muscles (butt, hips, and thighs), which increases ability to do daily tasks.

**Mindful Tips** Breathe as you raise up. If your knees or back hurt near the lowest depth, stay just above that point of pain.

**Progression** Lower farther until your thighs are parallel to the floor. As you get stronger, increase the number of repetitions per set.

The Help Desk

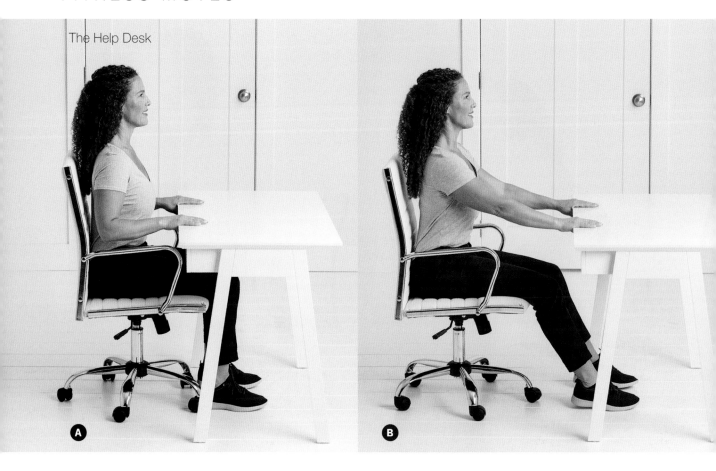

## The Help Desk

Use your desk and work chair (if you have wheels) to strengthen your upper body.

**How to Do It** A) Sit with your body 1–2 inches away from the desk. Grasp the edge of your desk with both hands (palms up if your desk is lower than your elbows; palms down if higher). Push your body away from the desk until your arms are fully extended. B) Return to start by pulling your body back toward the desk. Repeat until too tired to perform full movements. Rest for 1 minute and repeat. Do 1–3 sets.

**Benefits** Improves muscular strength and endurance in the upper body. Pushing works the chest, shoulders, and triceps. Pulling works the back and biceps and improves grip strength.

**Mindful Tips** Feel yourself push with your chest and triceps as you extend your elbows; conversely, engage your back by pulling your shoulder blades together as you pull forward.

**Progression** Increase the amount of times (repetitions) you perform each set. Increase the speed of movement.

## The Tight Agenda

Sitting a majority of the day can cause tight muscles and limit range of motion. To help preserve flexibility, perform the following exercises.

**How to Do It** Stretch the lower back and the back of your hips and thighs. A) If sitting, stick your legs straight out in front of you. If standing, start with feet together and flat on

## The Tight Agenda

the floor. Slide your hands down the front of your thighs until you feel a slight stretch in the backs of your legs or lower back. Hold for 20 seconds and slowly return to start. Do this stretch 3 times.

B) Sit tall in your chair (or stand tall) and gaze forward. Stretch your arms over your head and interlock your fingers, reaching as high as you can (stretching the shoulders, arms, and spine). Lean slightly left, then right, and then slightly back (extend the lower back). Hold each position for 20 seconds. Do this stretch 3 times.

**Benefits** Stretches the muscles that are affected while slouching in a chair with your knees and hips constantly in a flexed position.

**Mindful Tips** Make sure you're stable when standing. Only stretch to slight discomfort to avoid overstretching and injury. Remember to breathe regularly.

**Progression** Hold the positions longer or perform more sets.

### no wheeled chair?

You can do wall push-ups to work your chest. Also, work your back by grasping the inner part of a door frame, leaning slightly back, and pulling your body toward the door. Breathe out while you push away from the wall; breathe in while you pull forward from the door.

Downward Dog

Cow and Cat Poses

# greet the day

## Start your morning right with yoga and Pilates moves anyone can do.

by Robert Powell, Ph.D., CEP, CSCS, CDE

Incorporating range-of-motion exercises, like those performed in yoga and Pilates classes, can help increase flexibility and core strength. This will in turn improve activities of daily living and reduce risk for injury. Yoga and Pilates have shown to be effective in lowering blood sugar and blood pressure levels. Perform these exercises in the morning as a great way to start the day. Grab a mat or find a comfortable spot on the floor and get started!

### Downward Dog

A) Get down on all fours, palms shoulder width apart, elbows extended, and toes tucked under (knees and feet together). B) Slowly raise your knees off the floor, bracing yourself with your hands and feet. C) You should create a "V" with your body. Hold for 10–30 seconds. D) Lower yourself back to the floor by bending the knees and returning to start. E) Rest for 1 minute. Perform 3 times.

**Benefits** Stretches the entire back part of your body to maintain and improve range of motion and posture.

**Mindful Tips** Focus on engaging the core and feeling a stretch in the shoulders and backs of the upper and lower legs. Try to press your heels toward the ground. Exhale as you raise yourself up and breathe throughout the hold.

**Progression** Increase the time in the V position or decrease the distance between your hands and feet by flexing hips and creating a steeper/tighter V shape.

### Cow and Cat Poses

A) Get on your knees, allowing shins and tops of feet to rest on the floor. Lean forward, placing hands directly under shoulders and hips above knees. For Cow Pose, drop your stomach toward the floor (back swaying down) as you inhale. Look up while lifting chin and opening chest, dropping shoulder blades down to create distance between shoulders and head.

B) Transition to Cat Pose, pulling stomach in as you exhale, arching your back like a cat. At the same time, drop head slowly toward the floor, bringing chin toward chest. Repeat the Cow to Cat Poses for 10–15 repetitions.

**Benefits** Improves the range of motion in the core and teaches you how to engage the core, strengthening it.

**Mindful Tips** Focus on engaging the core throughout the transitioning of poses.

**Progression** Increase the reps or the amount of sets you perform. Increase the range of motion (stretch) to improve mobility.

Pilates Crisscross

Pilates Leg Circles

## Pilates Crisscross

A) Sit with your legs straight out in front, feet slightly wider than hip width. Sit up straight, spine neutral, with your arms straight out to your sides parallel with your shoulders. B) With the core engaged, slowly twist your torso to the right, drawing your left arm toward your right leg (do not reach with arms). Continue to twist as far as you can while simultaneously bending forward at the hips to draw your left hand toward your right foot. Pause and perform 3 slow, short pulsating motions at the hip (like your hand is sawing into your foot). Slowly reverse the movement back to start. Perform the same pattern on the left side. Repeat 5 times on each side. Rest 1 minute and repeat on each side 2 more times.

**Benefit** Improves strength and flexibility in the core.

**Mindful Tips** Engage your core to maintain your posture in the starting (central) position. Twist as far as you can without causing pain or your hips (buttocks) to raise off the floor. Breathe out during the twist and forward movement; pause to breathe in and then breathe out as you return to the central position.

**Progression** Increase your range of motion as you get more flexible. Increase the number of sets.

## Pilates Leg Circles

Lie on your back with your legs extended, arms at your sides. Engage your core by pulling your abs inward toward the spine. Draw left leg up so it is bent with left foot flat on the floor for stability. Slowly raise your right leg up until it is perpendicular to the floor (or as far as you can). In a clockwise pattern, slowly make 5–10 small circles with your raised leg and then reverse the motion counterclockwise 5–10 times (or until your leg tires and starts to drop). Alternate legs. Rest 1 minute and repeat 2 more times.

**Benefits** Improves strength and flexibility in the hips and knees while strengthening the abdominal region.

**Mindful Tips** Engage the core, not allowing your body to lean to one side or the other. Breathe throughout the rotations. Use your core, floor leg, and arms for stability.

**Progression** Increase the amount of rotations per set. Create a larger circle with legs.

Standing Side Crunch

Good Mornings

A

B

A

# standing core

## Work your core without ever getting down on the floor.

A strong core is essential to provide stability and protect the back and torso when doing everyday activities, helping to reduce the risk of lower-back pain, hernia, and falls. The body's "core" includes the abdominals, lower back, hips, upper thighs, and upper torso. By doing these exercises in conjunction with a regular exercise plan, PWDs can increase core strength and range of motion and better manage their blood sugars.

### Standing Side Crunch

A) Stand with knees slightly bent and feet hip width apart. Hold a dumbbell or resistance band at your side (or a soup can). B) Slowly bend at the hips on your right side, lowering the dumbbell toward the floor to mid thigh level. Engaging your left side, pull your body back to the starting position. Aim for 10–15 repetitions. Next, perform the same movement on the left side. Note: If using a resistance band, step on the band with your right foot, making it taut enough to provide resistance.

**Benefits** This move works the side (oblique) abdominal muscles that aid in bending to the sides and stabilizing your spine when you are carrying objects at your side (suitcase, groceries, etc.).

**Mindful Tips** Pull your stomach muscles in to support the spine. Stop prior to knee level if you feel pain in the back and/or hip or if you start to lose stability.

**Progression** Perform more repetitions per side until you reach the 10–15 repetition range, then increase resistance weight. Or bend farther down the side of the knee. Increase the number of sets you perform or reduce the rest period between your sets.

### Good Mornings

A) Stand with feet shoulder width apart and knees slightly bent. Hold a dumbbell (or grocery bag with items) with both hands in front of you with your arms straight. B) With your abs and lower back engaged, slowly bend forward at the hips and lower until you're parallel with the floor.

Standing Crunches             Wall Planks

(As you lower your weight, move hips slightly backward and keep knees stiff.) Slowly raise yourself back up by extending the lower back and hips while bringing your hips slightly forward to the starting position. Aim for 10–15 repetitions. Rest 1 minute and repeat 2 more times.
**Benefits** Works the lower back, glutes (butt), and hamstrings.
**Mindful Tips** Be sure to keep spine rigid. Do not round at the shoulders. Stop if you feel too much strain on the back side of the body (particularly the lower back).
**Progression** Increase the range of motion (goal: parallel upper body). Increase the weight to add more resistance.

## Standing Crunches

A) Drape a resistance band over the center of a door; close the door. Grab the band with both hands, standing about two steps from the door. Slightly bend the knees and engage your abs by pulling them toward your spine.
B) Bend forward at the hips by pulling your elbows toward your waist, creating an abdominal crunch motion. Aim for 10–15 repetitions. Rest for 1 minute. Repeat 2 more times.
**Benefits** This move works the front of the abdominals that aid in core stability and spine stabilization.
**Mindful Tips** Breathe out when crunching and breathe in when returning to standing. Keep abdominals engaged.

**Progression** Increase the resistance by standing farther from the door. Increase the number of sets or reduce the rest period between your sets.

## Wall Planks

Stand with forearms and palms resting on the wall and slowly step back, creating a diagonal line. Engage your core (lower back, front abs, hips), keeping your body aligned. Hold this position for 30 seconds or until you break form. Rest for 1 minute and repeat 2 more times.
**Benefits** This move provides static strength and endurance of the entire core, which will help to protect the spine from injury.
**Mindful Tips** Keep your torso straight and rigid. Breathe throughout the hold.
**Progression** Hold for 60 seconds or as long as you can. Make it harder by stepping farther from the wall. Increase the number of sets you perform the exercise.

---

### what you'll need

▶ Resistance band

▶ Dumbbell weight (or household items and a grocery bag)

▶ Doorway

▶ Wall

The Routine

# walk wisely

## Pump up your treadmill workout.

by Robert Powell, Ph.D., CEP, CSCS, CDE

Treadmill walking is a great way for PWDs to improve blood sugar, lose weight, gain energy, and reduce risk for cardiovascular and diabetes complications. Maximize your health benefits with our treadmill training program—designed to reduce boredom and help you conquer any terrain that life throws at you.

## The Routine

▶ Alternate the three interval stages—Slow and Steady, Chase with Pace, and Conquer the Climb—throughout your time on the treadmill.

▶ Beginners should start with the Slow and Steady pace and spend most of their time there by returning to it between the other two effort levels.

▶ For a longer workout, perform more rounds of each stage.

▶ For a more intense workout, alternate the stages randomly and spend more total treadmill time in the moderate- to high-intensity stages.

**Progression Pointer** Based on individual fitness levels, you may need to start with 15 minutes and build to the recommendation of 30 minutes.

**Warm-Up** Before starting the routine, walk on the treadmill for 5–10 minutes (5 minutes if you are new to exercise;

10 as you become more fit) at 0% grade. Choose a light walking speed that does not tire you. Slowly increase the speed until you're breathing harder but can still talk. This speed will be similar to your Slow and Steady speed stage. Slow back down for a minute to catch your breath before starting.

**Stage 1: Slow and Steady**
Choose a speed slightly faster than your warm-up speed. You should be able to walk comfortably for an extended period (2 or more minutes) without getting out of breath, similar to a brisk pace. Aim for 2 or more rounds at this stage. Progress to more over time.

**Benefits** Helps lower blood sugar, increases calorie burn, and increases oxygen uptake and delivery to the working muscles to improve fitness.

**Mindful Tips** This will be your light-intensity and active-recovery pace. Be sure that the speed is slow enough that you can catch your breath between the more intense stages.

### what you'll need

▶ Treadmill

▶ Comfortable clothing

▶ Supportive shoes

Lower-Leg/Calf Stretch

Hamstring Stretch

Quad Stretch

### Stage 2: Chase with Pace

Choose a speed that is 1–2 miles per hour faster than your Slow and Steady pace for 1–2 minutes. Aim for 2 or more rounds of this stage. Progress more over time.

**Benefits** Uses more glucose for energy and increases cardiorespiratory fitness.

**Mindful Tips** This is your moderate-intensity pace. You should be able to talk briefly (but not sing).

### Stage 3: Conquer the Climb

Choose a speed that is 0.5 to 1 mile per hour faster than your Slow and Steady pace and increase the treadmill incline by 1–2% or a grade that you can walk for 30 seconds to 1 minute. Aim for 2 or more rounds at this stage. Progress to more over time.

**Benefits** Uses more glucose for energy, increases fitness, and improves ability to walk up hills, steps, etc.

**Mindful Tips** This is your high-intensity pace. Your breathing rate should be elevated enough that you have difficulty speaking.

### Cooldown

With the treadmill at 0% grade, walk on the treadmill for 5–10 minutes. Slowly reduce the speed until you come to a stop. Finish with the Stretch the Effort routine.

## Stretch the Effort

### Lower-Leg/Calf Stretch

Stand with your hands pressed into the wall or treadmill handrail. Take 1 or 2 steps back with your right leg. Bend at your left knee to lower your body, keeping your right heel in contact with the floor to stretch the right calf muscle. Hold for 20 seconds and then alternate legs. Repeat 3 times.

### Hamstring Stretch

Stand with feet together. Slide your hands down the front of your thighs until you feel a slight stretch in your back legs, hips, and lower back. Hold for 20 seconds and slowly return to standing. Perform 3 times.

### Quad Stretch

Stand with feet together. Keeping thighs together, bend your right leg backward toward your buttocks and grasp your right foot with your right hand. Pull back until you feel a stretch in the front hip and thigh. Hold for 20 seconds. Switch legs and repeat. Repeat 3 times. If you have trouble balancing, lie down on your side with legs stacked and grab your foot to flex your leg back as far as possible.

**Benefits** Improves flexibility of your lower body.

**Mindful Tips** Only stretch to the point of slight discomfort. Breathe regularly during each stretch.

# setting weight loss goals

If you aim to improve your overall health, losing weight will naturally follow.

There's a reason you want to lose weight; you just need to identify it. Will it help your self-esteem? Allow you to live longer? Make it easier to play with your grandkids? Take a vacation to a new place?

Weight loss provides many health benefits for PWDs: better blood glucose control, less need for medication, lower risk for cardiovascular disease (PWDs are more likely to have heart issues), and simply feeling better! And you don't have to lose a ton of weight to reap the health benefits. Studies show all you need to lose is 5 percent of your body weight to improve insulin sensitivity. For a 300-pound person, that's 15 pounds.

Think about your long-term goal. Then choose a smaller habit to help you reach it. General goals like "become healthier," "lose weight," and "eat more fruits and vegetables" are rarely effective. To be successful, you need tangible, trackable objectives. Think of goals as behaviors that lead to weight loss—not the number of pounds you lose. Focus on the process. What healthy habits will you develop for long-term success? For example, instead of "eat more vegetables," maybe your goal will be "fill half my dinner plate with vegetables."

## Follow our 6-step guide to set yourself up for success.

### Identify, Then Overcome

**Step 1: Identify Your Roadblock** Humans are incredibly good at identifying foods that are packed with calories, a trait that evolved during the Ice Age. This isn't so helpful now, when grocery stores stock freshly baked goods like donuts every day. Being aware that it's natural to desire sugary sweets and fatty foods is the first step—this allows you to make a change. So now you need to figure out what vices you're subject to: Are you eating out too much? Spending hours on the couch every night? Not eating enough low-carb vegetables? For now, pick a roadblock you'd like to tackle and work from there.

**Step 2: Find Out Where You Stand** Identify what you've been eating and how you've been exercising. How many nights a week do you snack, and what do you snack on? How often do you go for a walk? Write down your recent habits and then come up with solutions such as replacing potato chips with baby carrots and going for a walk after dinner before watching TV.

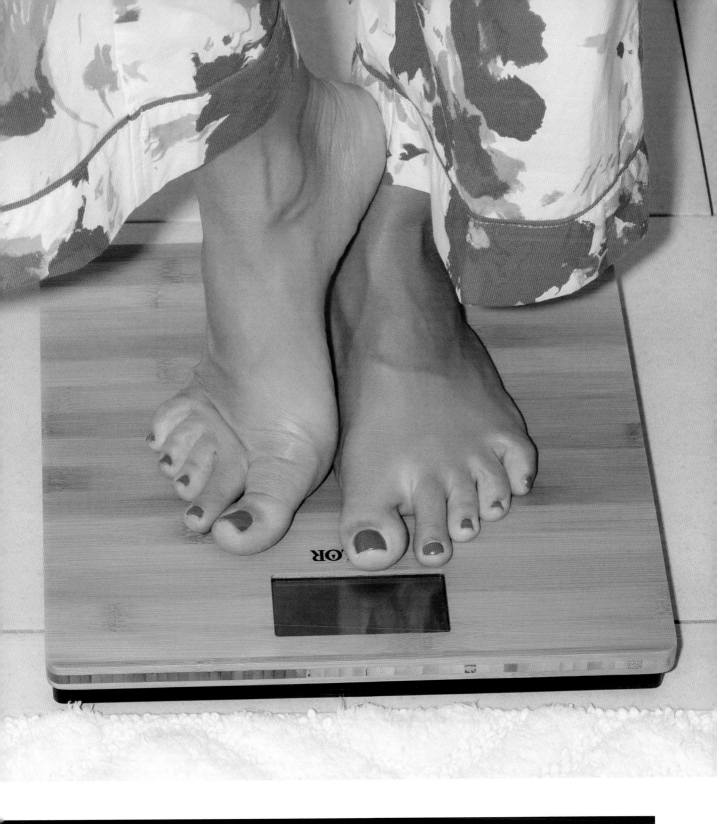

## when to weigh

Periodical reminders are essential on this journey. You might not see results every day, but the more you weigh yourself, the more mindful you will be of your goals. A study at Cornell University found that dieters who didn't weigh themselves at least once a week started putting on pounds. Tip: Step onto the scale on the same day and time each week for consistency.

**Step 3: Keep a Journal** Keep track of what you eat, when you eat it, and where you eat. This can be a good motivator when you stay on track or a firm reminder when you stray. Try food and exercise logging apps such as mySugr and Lose It!

**Step 4: Bask in the Little Victories** Be mindful of the small decisions you make every day, like taking the stairs instead of the elevator and gardening instead of bingeing on a TV show. Reward yourself. Maybe you'll celebrate exercising five days in a row by buying yourself a bouquet of flowers or enjoying a quiet reading hour.

## get smart

Write down goals to increase your likelihood of success. You can home in even sharper on a target with the action-oriented SMART goal method. Here's how:

**SPECIFIC** Write your goal clearly and detailed (e.g., I will walk five blocks every weekday morning right after the kids leave for school.).

**MEASURABLE** Make your goal objective so you can say you've met it 100%, 40%, or whatever level.

**ACHIEVABLE** Are you likely to achieve this goal?

**REALISTIC** Is it possible to achieve this goal with the resources you have?

**TIMELINE** Determine when you will perform your action and when you will assess your results.

**Step 5: Share Your Journey** Getting friends and family involved can help keep you accountable. This can be as simple as posting on Facebook or sharing your achievements over a meal. Support from loved ones can make success that much sweeter. They might decide to join you!

**Step 6: Keep Going** Once you feel that you've successfully integrated a life change, make another small change. If you've managed to remove snacking from your nightly routine, maybe it's time to take a nightly walk. Once you start doing this, each change will become a normal part of life, like brushing your teeth every morning and going grocery shopping each week.

## Taking a Mindful Approach

You can plan and plan, but sometimes our emotions and social traditions can get in the way. That's why it's important to stay in tune with your body and feelings and to recognize why you may be straying from your plan.

Most of us want to believe we can handle our feelings. We're grown-ups, right?

Well, yes—but no. The coworker who shifted the blame, the mother you miss whenever you see pink peonies, the combative teen who took the place of that sweet toddler—it can all add up to an urge to bake a batch of Grandma's cookies.

The truth is once you understand the feelings in that pan of cookies, you can look for healthier ways to soothe yourself.

As a case in point, Diane Robinson, Ph.D., describes a veteran who had a long-standing ritual of slipping toffee candies in his pocket every morning, which was pushing his weight and glucose readings out of range.

They talked about alternatives, and he decided to try sugar-free candies. "But that didn't really fly," Robinson says.

Next she asked why he wanted to improve his health. He began to talk about playing with his dog and grandkids and about the yardwork he used to enjoy.

They decided he would place pebbles in his pocket instead. "He still had his ritual. But now it was pebbles representing the dog, the grandkids, and the garden," Robinson says.

"He started to respond to something much deeper when he would touch the pebbles. And that worked."

Think of your not-so-healthy traditions. For example, do you make the same breakfast every Sunday morning that your dad did? As delicious as that sausage and egg biscuit is, it could throw your glucose levels into a tizzy.

Being aware of why we do things can help us find ways to convert bad habits into good ones. Robinson suggests making one small change every week. At the end of one year, your health will have improved in 52 ways, and plenty of them will become good choices you don't even need to worry about any more. You can still have a breakfast sandwich, but start a new tradition and use whole wheat bread with egg, avocado, and tomato.

## outthink your barriers

Life coach Meshell Baker lends her advice for pushing past roadblocks:

**REFRAME NEGATIVE THOUGHTS.** Instead of thinking, *I can't,* ask yourself, *How can I make this happen?*

**KEEP YOUR EYES ON THE PRIZE.** "When you see people who have big results you want, ask yourself how you will incorporate a habit into your life to get the result you want."

**TEMPTED?** Wait 20 minutes. Feelings often dissipate.

**HAVE A TIMEOUT.** Put temptation on hold by calling a friend or reaching for a podcast.

**TRIED EVERYTHING?** No, you haven't. "You simply haven't found what works for you." Keep going. You'll find your way if you stay with it.

# mindful
# eating

# what is mindful eating?

Brainpower, not willpower, is the real secret to sticking to your meal plan.

The way you think about food is directly linked to how much you eat. If you fully concentrate on your meals and enjoy the taste of each bite, you're more likely to eat only when you're truly hungry, stop when you're satisfied, and enjoy your favorite foods without eating too much.

Research shows that this strategy, known as mindful eating, works—and it works well.

"Mindful eaters consume fewer calories because they really savor their food," says Susan Albers, a clinical psychologist at the Cleveland Clinic and author of *Eating Mindfully*. "They feel satisfied sooner than people who eat when they're distracted." Unfortunately, we often eat on autopilot. We grab breakfast as we're heading out the door, eat lunch at our desk, and have dinner in front of the TV. We don't really register how much we're gobbling, consuming hundreds of extra calories a day. And all those extra calories pack on the pounds and make managing blood sugar levels more difficult.

**Mindful eaters are adept at recognizing their body's hunger cues. They've learned what real hunger feels like, and when their system signals them that they need to eat, they do.**

Mindful eaters, on the other hand, are adept at recognizing their body's hunger cues. They've learned what real hunger feels like. When their system signals them that they need to eat, they do.

You, too, can eat more mindfully to drop pounds. Here's how.

## Find Your Satisfaction Sweet Spot

"Think of fullness on a scale of 1 to 10," says Jean Kristeller, Ph.D., a professor emeritus of psychology at Indiana State University and author of *The Joy of Half a Cookie.* "People often shoot for a 9 or a 10 but are usually satiated much sooner, at about a 6." To determine when you've hit the satisfaction point, "put down your fork for a few moments several times throughout your meal to gauge where you are at and whether you still feel hungry," she advises.

## Get to Know Your Body

"True hunger comes with definitive signals: Your stomach feels empty, it growls, you can't concentrate, you feel irritable, and you yearn for food in general, not something specific like chips or cookies," says Jean Fain, a psychotherapist at Harvard Medical School and author of *The Self-Compassion Diet.* If a nutritious dinner like grilled chicken with steamed broccoli sounds pretty amazing, chances are you're truly hungry and need to eat something. If it doesn't, figure out what the real problem is—boredom? loneliness?—and deal with it. But remember: You may need to stick to an eating schedule to prevent low blood sugar if your diabetes medications could cause hypoglycemia. Other times, you may need to eat even if you're not hungry—such as snacking because your meal is going to be delayed or it's your scheduled lunch break at work, and if you don't eat now, you'll be ravenous later. Even during these times, listen to your body's hunger cues and take the time to truly enjoy your food.

## Be a Food Snob

Mindful eaters are picky about food—in a good way. They pass up things that don't bring them pleasure, Kristeller says. At a cocktail party, for instance, they will skip the deviled eggs and savor the coconut shrimp instead. "[Mindful eaters] see no point in eating foods they consider mediocre," Albers says. "There's no payoff."

**In a study, diners who ate a meal in 22 minutes consumed 88 fewer calories than those who consumed the same food in 9 minutes.**

## Take Your Time

Instead of inhaling your dinner, sit at the table while you eat and make the meal last at least 20 minutes. In a study at Texas Christian University, diners who ate a meal in 22 minutes consumed 88 fewer calories than those who consumed the same food in 9 minutes. When you eat slowly, it's easier to read your body's hunger and fullness signals. But it's often not possible to linger quietly for nearly half an hour over every meal. So try this easy compromise: Turn off the TV, hide your cell phone, and set aside just 3 minutes to savor the first few bites of your meal or snack. That small amount of time is enough to help your brain register pleasure and the beginning of satiety.

## Come to Your Senses

Employ all five senses—not just taste—when you eat. "This gives you more pleasure from your food, so you end up being more satisfied," says Lillian Cheung, a Harvard School of Public Health lecturer and coauthor of *Savor: Mindful Eating, Mindful Life*. Stop eating on autopilot and relish each bite. Look at the colors on your plate and inhale the aroma. Listen to the sizzle of that stir-fry or the crunch of the carrots. Enjoy the texture of that creamy Greek yogurt.

## Never Deprive Yourself

"Typically, when we experience the urge for an unhealthy food, we try to ignore it, which causes stress," Albers says. And stress triggers the release of the hormone cortisol, which encourages the body to store fat and causes blood sugar spikes. Instead of trying to fight a craving, acknowledge it. Then think for a moment: Am I hungry? Do I really enjoy eating it? Is it something special that I don't get to have all the time? If you can answer yes to these questions, go for it, Albers says.

# are you an emotional eater?

Feeding your emotions can affect your diabetes management and overall well-being. Take our quiz to find out if your feelings could be influencing your food choices. Then learn ways to cope.

## What's your most common cue to eat?

**A.** My stomach growls.
**B.** The clock says it's mealtime.
**C.** I feel bored, restless, unhappy, or lonely.
**D.** Eating is my go-to form of stress relief and comfort.

## Which best describes your overall attitude toward food?

**A.** Food is the body's fuel, and I eat to keep going.
**B.** I enjoy good food, and it's even better shared with loved ones.
**C.** I have many positive memories involving food, so I eat in part to re-create those feelings.
**D.** For me, food equals love, warmth, and companionship.

## When something doesn't go your way, what's your first thought?

**A.** I'll get 'em next time.
**B.** I wish it had been different, but it will work out in the end.
**C.** I need to meet my BFF for drinks and dinner.
**D.** When can I get out of here and hit a bakery?

## Think about the language you use to describe food. How often do you use emotion-charged words such as decadent, indulgent, love/hate, obsessed, sinful, guilt, joy, and craving?

**A.** Almost never; I mainly eat because I have to.
**B.** Only in relation to a truly outstanding meal.
**C.** Often. For me eating is always an emotional experience—sometimes good, sometimes bad.
**D.** Regularly. I constantly think about food and feel stressed if I can't eat as planned.

## The last time you experienced a significant disappointment, how did you cope in the hours just afterward?

**A.** I cried and processed with my friends.
**B.** I treated myself to a fancy dinner to cheer myself up.
**C.** I binge-watched Netflix while eating lots of salty snacks.
**D.** I polished off a carton of ice cream before I could even register what was happening.

## How often do you feel out of control when it comes to eating?

**A.** I don't even understand the question!

**B.** I've sometimes had to walk away from the table in order to stop eating.

**C.** I've completely zoned out while overeating more times than I care to admit.

**D.** I often find it difficult to stop eating, even when I'm full or don't like what I'm eating.

## What is your emotional state after you eat?

**A.** I feel satisfied.

**B.** I feel a little sad the meal is over.

**C.** I often feel guilty.

**D.** I sometimes feel so guilty and overwhelmed that I can succumb to despair.

## add up your score

**A = 0 points; B = 1 point; C = 2 points; D = 3 points** Find your score below to see where you fall on the emotional eating spectrum.

**0–6** Oh, you stoic, you! You have a utilitarian attitude toward food—you eat to keep your energy up. Currently you are not an emotional eater.

**7–12** Food is connected to emotion for you, but as long as you keep your meals healthful and stay tuned in to your emotional state, you should be OK.

**13–17** There is a strong connection between eating and positive emotion for you—take care not to let it go too far. Focus on healthful foods and portion control. If you feel stressed, bored, or sad, try calling a friend, meditating, or going for a walk instead of reaching for the chips.

**18–21** Chances are high you're using food to feed your feelings and not your body. Consider seeing a counselor or dietitia to explore your relationship with food. Practicing mindfulness can reveal what's at the root of your emotional eating.

# stop feeding your feelings

Do you overindulge in unhealthful foods when you're happy and celebrating or sad and sulking? There are ways to break the cycle.

Whether you're celebrating that promotion at work or sulking in front of the TV after a fight with a loved one, it's easy to turn to food for comfort.

But does it work? Not well, experts say.

The immediate positive effects of emotional eating may be a distraction, a boost in the brain's feel-good chemicals, more energy, and satisfaction from a fun food. However, just 30 minutes later, emotional eaters tend to rate themselves as feeling more guilty and more dissatisfied with themselves, says Brian Wansink, Ph.D., author of *Slim by Design: Mindless Eating Solutions for Everyday Life*.

Once the distraction and calming effects of eating wear off, toxic emotions of guilt and shame often replace them. The long-term effects include lower self-esteem, a lack of trust in one's body, and intrusive thoughts about food and weight, says Deborah Kauffmann, RD, LDN, a Maryland-based nutrition counselor for emotional eaters. And don't forget that unplanned eating often causes a jump in blood glucose.

And the more often you eat for comfort, the more likely it will develop into a habit. "The first time you grab a croissant at your coffee place, it may be a choice—though the fifth time, you may barely deliberate," says Jennifer L. Taitz, Psy.D., a licensed clinical psychologist in New York and Los Angeles and author of *End Emotional Eating*. Habits are hard to break because the habit-forming part of the brain allows us to act without much effort. So if you often soothe hurt feelings with a buttery croissant or a creamy milk shake, you're likely to do it automatically. And if this becomes your standard way of dealing with emotions, you might begin to confuse emotional discomfort with physical hunger, she says.

Stress also can lead to an increase in the appetite-stimulating hormone ghrelin. Even the specific food you desire may be deep-rooted in your brain. People reach for foods that made them feel good in the past, like Mom's pasta or a box of cookies.

## 43

PERCENTAGE OF AMERICANS WHO SAY THEY OVEREAT OR EAT UNHEALTHY FOODS TO MANAGE STRESS.

Source: American Psychological Association

Luckily there are ways to break this vicious cycle. Try the following strategies to end the pattern of reaching for food feeling when in a mood:

**Keep a Log** Tracking food and identifying your mood while eating is eye-opening. "Many times people have no idea that they turn to food when feeling lonely or frustrated," says dietitian Cathy Leman, RD, LD, a Chicago-area nutrition counselor. The type and amount of food may be astonishing once you see it in writing. If you track your blood glucose levels in the same log, you may find additional motivation to learn better stress-management techniques.

**Learn to Manage Your Emotions** Your log will help you identify and name your emotions, which paves the way for dialogue or self-reflection about the situations that trigger the strong emotions.

**Develop a Keen Sense of Your Values** "In the moment, we forget what matters," Taitz says. Knowing what's important helps you choose appropriate actions. For example, keeping a photo of his kids nearby can help a truck driver remember what's in his heart when his mind screams drive-through.

**Develop Nonfood Coping Skills** Eating emotionally expresses and reinforces that we don't have the skills to cope in healthful ways. Regularly soothe yourself without calories. Try deep breathing or a 5-minute jumping-jack break, relax with a warm bath or a cup of tea, or write your thoughts in a journal. Learn to talk to yourself the way you would talk to a friend—with kindness and thoughtfulness.

**Push the Pause Button** Putting time between the urge to eat and actually eating lets you remember your values and nonfood coping skills. Tell yourself, for example, that if you still feel the need to eat after the timer goes off in 15 minutes, you'll allow it. You'll likely notice that the intensity of your craving fluctuates and dwindles to a manageable level.

**Remove Temptation** If you reach for ice cream or cheesy potato chips in moments of despair, banish them from your house.

**Get Help** Calling a friend may be enough. But if emotional eating is a continuous problem or hurts your emotional or physical health, seek a therapist skilled in helping to conquer unhealthful eating behaviors.

# how hungry are you really?

Next time you're thinking about eating, pause and use this guide to figure out if you're actually hungry.

Hunger only drives about three-fourths of the food choices we make. Habit, mood, stress levels, and whether we're socializing influence the rest, says Ellen Albertson, Ph.D., RD, a psychologist and founder of *smashyourscale.com.* While the occasional "I'm not hungry, but I'd love dessert" rationalization is OK (and expected), understanding hunger cues keeps mindless eating in check. In fact, the ability to recognize real hunger is one of the biggest hallmarks of naturally slender people (those who remain at a healthy weight without dieting), says 2015 research from the Cornell Food and Brand Lab.

## Starving and Ravenous?

At this point, you likely have a headache or feel shaky and light-headed, which could be signs of hypoglycemia, or low blood sugar. Try to avoid this heightened hunger. "When you put off eating until you're famished, you're more likely to eat anything and everything you can get your hands on—and do so quickly—which primes you to overeat," says Michelle May, M.D., founder of Am I Hungry? Mindful Eating Programs. That overeating can cause a big surge in your blood sugar levels. "But you don't need more food than usual," May says. To avoid overeating, take a few bites of something that takes the edge off, then pause. "This gives you time to think about what—and how much—to eat."

## Noticeably Hungry?

Right now, the physical symptoms of hunger—like hunger pangs, growling, or a hollow feeling in your gut—are on full display. You may be having problems concentrating, and your mood might also be going south—you're starting to get "hangry." This is the ideal time to eat. "You're less likely to overeat and food tastes better when you're at this level of hunger [than if you're ravenous]," says May. "If your urge to eat came out of nowhere, it may simply be a craving. True hunger tends to come on gradually, whereas a craving hits suddenly." Not sure you're really hungry? Wait a bit. Hunger won't go away until you eat.

## Slightly Hungry?

When you're kind of hungry, the muscular walls of your stomach start to contract, perhaps causing a rumble. This is simply a sign that you should start planning to eat soonish. Drink some water and see if you're still hungry in 15 minutes. However, there are times you'll want to eat now—like family dinnertime. So remember: If you're just a little hungry, you only need a little food.

## Not Hungry or Full?

If you're content, why reach for food? Do a quick self-check. Are you just following a script? For example, are you eating lunch at noon because that's when you usually do? "People who follow scripts are less likely to tune in to internal hunger cues," says Brian Wansink, Ph.D., author of *Slim by Design*. If that's the case, recognize that you want to eat but you're not really hungry. "Don't say, 'I can't have it.' Instead, acknowledge that you're not actually hungry." Of course, if eating on a schedule is part of your diabetes management plan, don't change without discussing it with your health care provider.

## Pretty Full?

You can feel the food in your stomach—but it's not like a balloon ready to burst. This is the best time to stop eating. To tune in to your internal stop-eating cues, pause periodically throughout your meal to check your fullness. "Put your fork down, drink some water, and really feel your stomach," says May. "If you comfortably sense the food in your belly, stop. You can always eat more later if you need to."

## Overstuffed?

Are you super focused on how uncomfortable your belly is right now and how stretched it feels? Feeling sluggish? You ate too much. Move away from the table! Regularly overshooting and eating to this overfull state can wreak havoc on your blood sugar levels and the scale. So slow down, chew your food thoroughly, and put your fork down between bites, says May. Serve yourself smaller portions and do it from the stove—not family-style. Getting up for a second helping forces you to tune in to your fullness.

# assembling a mindful plate

## Be more mindful of what you eat from purchase to plate.

With the convenience of grocery delivery and frozen meals, it is easy to become rather disconnected from your food. When was the last time you thought about where your food came from (beyond the grocery aisle)?

Food terms like "organic," "sustainable," and "locavorism" seem trendy, but behind the catchphrases lurk some concepts that lead to more mindful, healthful eating. Whether it's growing your own vegetables or strolling the local farmers market for seasonal produce, you have plenty of opportunities to gain a better understanding of where your food comes from. The next time you have an apple in your hand, pause and think about all the people it took to get that apple to your local grocer. When buying produce or meat, ask yourself questions such as How was this grown? Where did it come from? How was this animal raised? Asking these questions will help you build a deeper appreciation for your food. You may even notice your grocery cart will begin to look different.

Then start cooking! Make it fun by trying new recipes. Not the cook in your household? Take time to appreciate the hard work your loved one put into making a meal. Ask about the process and ingredients.

Expressing gratitude toward your food and all the people who helped get it on your plate may just change your attitude toward eating, creating a more mindful, enjoyable experience.

### Arrange Your Plate

Get your eating on track with the Plate Method. This visual guide gives you built-in portion control that helps you easily compose healthful, balanced meals for better blood glucose control and weight management.

We tend to eat what's in front of us. So portion control is easier when you start with a smaller dish. We recommend a 9-inch plate. If your dinnerware is larger, fill just inside the rim. A shallow-rimmed bowl is also a good option as long as it's 9 inches wide.

## Divide your plate into sections and fill it as follows:

**½ Nonstarchy Vegetables**  Fill half your plate with raw or cooked vegetables such as broccoli, green beans, cauliflower, cucumber, peppers, salad greens, asparagus, zucchini, and tomatoes. You'll get plenty of nutrients without spiking your blood sugar.

**¼ Protein**  Choose a lean meat, like poultry, lean beef, fish, or pork, or a nonmeat protein such as tofu, eggs, cheese, or nuts. If you carb count, track the amount of carbohydrate in vegetable proteins such as beans and lentils, too. If carb counting isn't your strategy, that's OK. You can build a balanced plate without tallying each gram of carbohydrate.

**¼ Starch or Grains**  Choose a serving of bread, tortilla, pasta, rice, beans, or starchy vegetable, such as potatoes, corn, or peas. Choose whole grains and beans to give meals a fiber boost.

**On the Side**  As calorie and carb counts permit, add a serving of low-fat milk or yogurt and a side of fruit to your meal. Choose fresh, frozen, or canned fruit without added sugars.

FILL ¼ WITH STARCH OR GRAINS

FILL ½ WITH VEGETABLES

FILL ¼ WITH PROTEIN

## Measure the Height

Avoid the trap of piling food too high on your plate—that defeats the purpose of creating a well-balanced meal. Nonstarchy vegetables should be the tallest section. Even if you've organized your plate correctly, extra calories and fats can sneak in if food is stacked too high. How high should it be? See What to Eat.

## Calculate Combos

You don't need a plate to implement the plate method. When cooking casseroles, soups, and chowders, think of each of the ingredients separately. For example, chili traditionally has meat, beans, tomatoes, onions, and peppers. These ingredients cover each aspect of the plate method. Consider that the greatest portion of food should be nonstarchy vegetables. The starchy portion and protein portion should each be about half the amount of veggies. For servings heavy in carbohydrate, such as tuna casserole and pasta dishes, remember that 1 cup accounts for about 30 grams of carb.

## Go Easy on Extras

When using items like salad dressings, sauces, and spreads, choose lower-fat versions and keep the servings skimpy.

## Choose Smart Sides

When dining out, don't be afraid to ask for substitutions. For example, if grilled chicken breast comes with corn, mashed potatoes, and a dinner roll, which are all starches, ask to swap two of them for steamed or sautéed vegetables. Your blood sugar will thank you.

## Make Fair Trades

When calculating fruit, milk, and starch servings, feel free to trade one for another. For example, if you want two pieces of bread for a sandwich, skip the milk or fruit that meal. The fruit, milk, or starch serving can also be traded for a cup of broth-based soup or even ½ cup low-fat ice cream for dessert.

# shop with intention

It's easy to mindlessly fill your grocery cart. Instead, take time to think about what you're buying and how it fits into a healthful meal plan.

## Have a Plan

▶ Plan your week's meals and snacks before you head to the market. Use our weekly meal plans on *p. 80–83* to generate your grocery list.

▶ Maintain your pantry. Replenish healthful staples as your supplies run low so you always have go-to items for quick meals and healthy snacks.

▶ Organize your list by the way your grocery store is laid out so you can avoid wandering around the store and walking by tempting treats.

▶ Use a grocery app on your phone or tablet to make preparing and updating your shopping list a snap.

## Stick to Your List

▶ Don't shop when you are hungry or stressed. You'll be less likely to grab indulgent comfort foods and treats if you shop after you've eaten and at a time when you are relaxed.

▶ Focus on your list and buy only the foods you came for.

▶ Shop without kids if possible. Supermarkets display foods with added sugars, refined carbohydrate, and high fat content at kids' eye level for a reason. You will meet your family's health and nutrition goals more easily without enduring pint-size protests.

## Dairy

▶ Avoid flavored milk products with added sugars.

▶ Be selective with yogurts. Yogurt contains lactose, a naturally occurring sugar, so don't expect to find options with zero grams of sugar. Just avoid added sugars, which are different than naturally occurring ones, by checking the ingredients list. A few added sugars are sucrose, cane sugar, dextrose, and high-fructose corn syrup.

▶ Almond milk and soymilk are dairy alternatives.

▶ Choose light or unsweetened varieties to cut calories, carbohydrate, and added sugars. Remember that nondairy milks other than soymilk do not provide much protein.

▶ When choosing spreads, opt for 60% vegetable oil spread in tub form.

▶ Choose reduced-fat cheese or smaller amounts of regular cheese. The fat-free versions lack flavor and produce undesirable results in recipes.

## Whole Grains

▶ Opt for foods that contain 3 grams or more of dietary fiber per serving.

▶ Choose 100% whole grain products when possible. Look at the ingredients list and make sure the first ingredient listed is a whole grain, such as whole wheat flour, brown rice, or barley.

▶ Packaged tortillas, wraps, breads, and buns often contain high amounts of sodium. Compare brands and choose one that is whole grain and lower in sodium.

▶ Don't purchase gluten-free items unless you have celiac disease or diagnosed gluten sensitivity. Many gluten-free grain products are higher in fat and calories and sometimes carbohydrate compared to the gluten-containing foods they emulate. They are also frequently lower in vitamins and minerals, such as folate and iron.

▶ Don't limit yourself. Many tasty whole grains, such as quinoa, sorghum, farro, and wheat berries, are full of good-for-you fiber.

▶ Store whole grains in airtight containers in a cool, dark place. Most will last up to 4 months in the pantry or 8 to 12 months in the freezer.

## Vegetables and Fruit

▶ For best quality and flavor, choose fresh vegetables and fruits that are in season. Plus, in-season produce costs less than out-of-season options.

▶ Eat the rainbow. Select an assortment of colorful vegetables and fruits. Each color family—including white and brown—offers a wealth of nutrients. We'll show you how on p. 66.

▶ Precut vegetables and fruits are a good option when you're pressed for time—they require no prep. Plus, purchasing only as much as you will eat helps to avoid waste.

▶ Stock up on frozen vegetables and fruits; they are just as healthful and cost less than out-of-season fresh produce. Avoid frozen vegetables that contain added sauce, which is high in sodium and fat. Look for fruit that is unsweetened and frozen without juice or syrup.

▶ No-salt-added canned vegetables, no-sugar-added canned fruits, and fruits canned in their own juice are also nutritious alternatives to fresh vegetables and fruits.

## Meat and Seafood

▶ Choose fresh meats that haven't been enhanced with a salt solution, tenderizing solution, or marinade; these meats tend to be high in sodium. Check the labels.

▶ Select packaged meat with the latest freshness date, especially if you are planning on eating it later in the week. If you find meat with a close freshness date at a discount, buy and freeze it as soon as you get home.

▶ Buy lean, low-sodium varieties of turkey, chicken, beef, and ham deli meats rather than cured meats like salami and summer sausage. Watch portion sizes to avoid excessive sodium.

▶ Avoid breaded chicken and fish products. They are high in added sodium, and the breading is not made from whole grains. You're better off coating plain meat when you get home so you can control the content of the coating. If you do select a breaded meat, be sure to count the carbs in your meal plan.

▶ Many fish varieties provide heart-healthy fats. Avoid frozen fish with added sauce. Buy canned fish packed in water and choose a lower-sodium brand.

▶ Loin cuts from beef and pork and skinless chicken and turkey breasts are the leanest options of all the cuts.

▶ Buy low-fat ground meat—ideally above 90% lean for both beef and turkey (95% lean is ideal!).

# how to read package labels

Learning to read food labels will help you make smarter food choices. Labels are a great tool for counting calories and carb and fat grams. Here's a look at an updated label.

## 1. Serving Size
All serving sizes are noted in common household measures (1 cup) or the number of items (8 crackers) as well as a weight. Be careful—some packages have more than one serving.

## 2. Calories
Calories are key to maintaining or losing weight. The calories noted are for the serving size listed. Pay attention to how much of the food you normally eat and translate it into the serving size to calculate how many calories you'll consume.

## 3. Total Fat
This is the sum of all types of fat. The total fat may also be broken into different types (trans fat, saturated, monounsaturated, and polyunsaturated). Limit trans and saturated fats, which are harmful to the heart.

## 4. Sodium
The amount of sodium found in one serving of the food is listed on the label. Limit sodium intake to 2,300 milligrams total per day or a level indicated by your health care provider. Sodium content can vary among brands.

## 5. Total Carbohydrate
When counting carbs, the "total carbohydrate" level is more important than the amount of "sugars." The total carbohydrate is the sum of the sugar, sugar alcohols, starch, and fiber in the food, which may be listed under the total carbohydrate label.

## 6. Dietary Fiber
This is the sum of all fiber, insoluble and soluble. Insoluble fiber is not digestible. Some fibers remain gummy and thick when digested, helping you feel full. For foods with more than 5 grams of fiber, subtract half the grams of fiber from the total carbs to get your carb count.

## 7. Sugars
The "sugars" on the label include all naturally occurring sugars plus added sugars. On the updated label, sugars added during manufacturing, such as refined sugar, will appear on the label as "added sugars." The American Heart Association recommends that men limit added sugar intake to 36 grams per day, women 25 grams. Naturally occurring sugars, like fructose in fruit and lactose in milk, are part of a well-balanced meal plan and do not count as added sugars.

| Nutrition Facts | | |
|---|---|---|
| 8 servings per container | | |
| **Serving size** | **2/3 cup (55g)** | **1** |
| **Amount per serving** | | |
| **Calories** | **230** | **2** |
| | | % Daily Value* |
| **3** **Total Fat** 8g | | 10% |
| Saturated Fat 1g | | 5% |
| Trans Fat 0g | | |
| **Cholesterol** 0mg | | 0% |
| **4** **Sodium** 160mg | | 7% |
| **5** **Total Carbohydrate** 37g | | 13% |
| Dietary Fiber 4g **6** | | 14% |
| Total Sugars 12g | | |
| **7** Includes 10g Added Sugars | | 20% |
| **Protein** 3g | | |
| Vitamin D 2mcg | | 10% |
| Calcium 260mg | | 20% |
| Iron 8mg | | 45% |
| Potassium 235mg | | 6% |
| * The % Daily Value (DV) tells you how much a nutrient in a serving of food contributes to a daily diet. 2,000 calories a day is used for general nutrition advice. | | |

# claim cons

Don't let these food claims on labels trick you.

**ALL NATURAL** The U. S. Food and Drug Administration (FDA) hasn't defined "all natural" yet. This claim doesn't mean nutritious, diabetes-friendly, or really anything. It's best to ignore it and read the ingredients and Nutrition Facts panel carefully.

**MADE WITH WHOLE GRAINS** The words "made with" are your clue that the product may actually contain very little whole grains. Choose a product that clearly states "100% whole grain." Or look to see if a whole grain is the first ingredient.

**MADE WITH REAL FRUIT** There's no FDA regulation of this term. To use it, products don't have to contain a minimum amount of fruit. Check the label—or head to the produce department to buy the real deal.

**NO SUGAR ADDED** Products can make this claim if there were no sugars added during processing. This doesn't mean sugar-free (or carb-free!). It may contain naturally occurring sugars, such as lactose.

**NO HIGH-FRUCTOSE CORN SYRUP** (HFCS) When HFCS is removed from a product, it's often replaced with another sweetener, such as sugar, honey, and/or agave syrup. You should keep all added sugars to a minimum.

# eat the rainbow

## A spectrum of colors in your meal leads to a variety of health benefits.

OK, you can't taste color. But the color of your food is one sign of nutritional power.

Although it's essential to get at least five servings of fruit and vegetables per day, it's also important to diversify what you're eating. Researchers have found that nutrients and powerful phytochemicals vary by color. Thus, eating many different colors of produce allows you to harness maximum benefits—an ability we shouldn't take for granted. Some phytochemicals are even thought to reduce insulin resistance.

"Only humans and birds have color vision," says David Heber, director of UCLA's Center for Human Nutrition. He believes the ability to see color probably evolved as a way for us to better see—and eat—colorful fruits and veggies.

But eating all the colors of the rainbow each day can seem like a daunting task—especially if you're not eating as many fruits and vegetables as you should. If you're starting to feel overwhelmed, know there are easy ways to work in extra servings of healthful foods. "Include at least one fruit for breakfast every day—sliced into your cereal, blended into a smoothie, or as a whole piece in the car on the way to your job," suggests Sharon Palmer, RDN, author of *Plant-Powered for Life*. "At dinner, double or triple up on veggies—that little serving of green beans on the side of your plate isn't enough!"

Let's get familiar with the bounty of benefits from each food color.

> **"Go vegetable heavy. Reverse the psychology of your plate by making meat the side dish and vegetables the main course."**
> —*Bobby Flay*

# color it nutritious

Filling your plate with a full spectrum of colors is an easy way to make sure you're getting all of the nutrients your body needs.

| | | |
|---|---|---|
| **RED** | Many foods, like strawberries and cherries, get their red color from anthocyanins, antioxidants that can help prevent chronic diseases like cancer and heart disease. Cooked and processed tomato products like tomato sauce and juice are the best sources of lycopene, a powerful antioxidant known for heart health and bone health as well as its cancer-fighting properties. | red apple, beet, red cabbage, cherries, red grapes, red sweet pepper, red-skin potato, radishes, raspberries, rhubarb, strawberries, tomato, watermelon |
| **ORANGE AND YELLOW** | It's common knowledge that carrots promote healthy eyes and that oranges are loaded with vitamin C. Did you know that 1 cup mashed sweet potato contains 1,033% of the recommended daily value of vitamin A from beta-carotene? Plus, these bright fruits and vegetables may help your body fight off disease and promote healthy, pain-free joints. | yellow apple, apricot, butternut squash, cantaloupe, carrot, corn, lemon, mango, nectarine, orange, peach, pear, yellow sweet pepper, pumpkin, rutabaga, sweet potato |
| **GREEN** | Green vegetables tend to be high in vitamins A and C, folate, and plenty of other nutrients. A cup of chopped kale has 684% of the recommended daily need of vitamin K, which helps blood clot and may contribute to bone health. | green apple, artichoke, asparagus, avocado, green beans, broccoli, Brussels sprouts, cucumber, green grapes, honeydew melon, kale, kiwifruit, lettuce, lime, green onions, peas, green sweet pepper, spinach, zucchini |
| **BLUE AND PURPLE** | Purple is mighty. This royal shade comes from anthocyanins—disease-fighting antioxidants. Purple potatoes, for example, have antioxidant levels equal to kale and spinach. The pigment produces many red, blue, and violet foods, depending on which type of anthocyanin is present. | blackberries, blueberries, eggplant, fig, purple grapes, plums, prunes, purple potato |
| **WHITE AND BROWN** | Don't rule out white foods! White and brown vegetables offer a diverse range of health benefits, including nutrients in several different, necessary categories. Cauliflower contains high levels of sulforaphane, which might help fight certain kinds of cancer. Garlic is packed with a variety of compounds studied for their anticancer properties. Parsnips are loaded with fiber—3 grams in only ½ cup. | cauliflower, dates, garlic, onion, mushrooms, parsnip, potato, turnip |

# just try it

Give these nutritional powerhouse foods a fresh look or try them for the first time.

This once-dreaded side gets a tasty overhaul as a crunchy and nutritious flatbread topper.

## brussels sprouts

If you avoided them as a kid, it's time to give Brussels sprouts another try. It's all in how they're prepared. Get them crisp and caramelized by roasting or sautéing. If they turn Army green, they're overcooked—and you're in for a plate of bitter and mush. For no-fuss nutrition, try them raw. Just ½ cup contains two-thirds of your daily value of vitamin C and 4 grams carb.

### Brussels Spouts and Goat Cheese Flatbread

Bake **1 Flatout Artisan Thin Pizza Crust Rustic White** at 425°F 5 minutes or until crisp. Spread with **1 oz. soft goat cheese (chèvre)**. Top with ½ cup thinly sliced fresh Brussels sprouts, 3 Tbsp. snipped dried apricots, and 2 Tbsp. toasted chopped walnuts. If desired, bake 3 to 5 minutes more. Top with **½ tsp. each honey and lime zest**.

SERVES **2** (½ flatbread each) **CAL** 255, **FAT** 13 g (5 g sat. fat), **CHOL** 13 mg, **SODIUM** 333 mg, **CARB** 34 g (4 g fiber, 11 g sugars), **PRO** 10 g

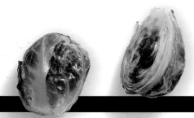

# beets

Colorful beets are exactly what health experts are talking about when they say to "eat the rainbow" for heart-healthy and cancer-fighting benefits. Buy beets with smooth skin and fresh stems. To store, remove stems and place in a plastic bag in the fridge up to three weeks.

Beets are sweet, but they can taste a little earthy. If that turns off your taste buds, we have you covered with this recipe: Tangy Greek yogurt, garlic, and lemon bring the best of beet flavor into focus. For optimal results, roast beets to maximize their natural sweetness. Save time by cutting them into chunks and boiling until tender, about 25 minutes, or just buy precooked beets.

## Beet Hummus

In a food processor combine **1 lb. cubed cooked beets; 15 oz. canned reduced-sodium chickpeas, rinsed and drained; 3 Tbsp. each tahini and lemon juice; 2 cloves garlic, minced;** and **¼ tsp. salt.** With processor running, add **3 Tbsp. canola oil.** To serve, swirl in **2 Tbsp. plain fat-free Greek yogurt.**

**SERVES 10** (¼ cup each) **CAL** 131, **FAT** 7 g (1 g sat. fat), **CHOL** 0 mg, **SODIUM** 250 mg, **CARB** 15 g (4 g fiber, 4 g sugars), **PRO** 4 g

Add a pop of color to your grocery cart with beets. They star in this flavor-packed dip that makes it easy to reach your five daily servings of fruit and vegetables.

# turnips

The humble turnip seems an unlikely candidate for a resurgence, but the lavender-skin root vegetable is getting a second look. It's versatile (bake, boil, roast, or mash), high in vitamin C, and has just 4 grams of carb per ½ cup. Peeling is optional, too—just give turnips a good scrub if you plan to eat the skin.

This quick and easy one-pan recipe will reacquaint you with the turnip. Pair this dish with pork, chicken, or steak for a hearty meal.

## Honey Butter Turnips

Heat a 15×10-inch baking pan in a 400°F oven 5 minutes. Spread **1 lb. turnips, peeled and cut into 1¼-inch pieces**, in hot pan. Drizzle with **3 Tbsp. honey** and **2 Tbsp. unsalted butter, melted**, and sprinkle with **¼ tsp. salt**. Roast 35 minutes or until turnips are tender, stirring once. Transfer to a serving dish. Sprinkle with **⅛ tsp. black pepper** and **snipped fresh thyme**.

SERVES 5 (½ cup each) **CAL** 105, **FAT** 5 g (3 g sat. fat), **CHOL** 12 mg, **SODIUM** 178 mg, **CARB** 16 g (2 g fiber, 14 g sugars), **PRO** 1 g

Don't toss those greens! Cook them as a side. Boil the greens 20–25 minutes, drain, then season with a little salt and lemon juice.

**Most Americans eat too much saturated fat. Replace it with healthy monounsaturated fat found in creamy avocados.**

# avocados

Avocados contain monounsaturated fat, which reduces cholesterol levels when it replaces some of the saturated fat in a diet. But the calories add up quickly: ½ cup avocado slices equals 117 calories. Still, its fiber content—5 grams per ½ cup—slows digestion, so you'll feel full longer. Toss it into salads and salsas or mash for guacamole (just add lime juice to prevent browning).

## Avocado and Pesto Stuffed Tomatoes

**Step One** Cut a thin slice from the tops of **30 cherry tomatoes**. (If necessary, cut a thin slice from the bottom of each tomato so it stands upright.) Using a small spoon or a melon baller, carefully hollow out tomatoes. Invert tomatoes on a baking sheet lined with paper towels. Let stand 30 minutes to drain.

**Step Two** For filling, in a food processor combine **½ of a medium avocado, peeled and cut up; 2 oz. cream cheese, softened; 2 Tbsp. basil pesto;** and **1 tsp. lemon juice**. Cover and process until smooth. If desired, line a serving platter with **fresh basil leaves**. Spoon filling into tomatoes and place on platter. If desired, sprinkle with **cracked black pepper**. Serve immediately or loosely cover with plastic wrap and chill up to 4 hours.

**SERVES 15** (2 stuffed tomatoes each) **CAL** 36, **FAT** 2 g (2 g sat. fat), **CHOL** 4 mg, **SODIUM** 32 mg, **CARB** 2 g (0 g fiber, 2 g sugars), **PRO** 0 g

# cooking school

You don't have to be an expert chef to cook well. Build your recipe arsenal with simple, delicious go-to recipes.

## Garlic and Herb Roast Pork and Vegetables

**40g**
**CARB**

**SERVES** 4
**HANDS ON** 30 min.
**TOTAL** 1 hr. 15 min.

- 4 5- to 6-oz. baking potatoes
- 2 Tbsp. canola oil
- ¾ tsp. salt
- 1 2½- to 2¾-lb. boneless pork top loin roast (single loin), trimmed of fat
- 2 tsp. salt-free garlic and herb seasoning, such as Mrs. Dash Nonstick cooking spray
- 6 medium carrots, peeled, quartered lengthwise, and cut into 2-inch pieces
- 8 oz. Brussels sprouts, trimmed and halved (if large)
- 1 large onion, cut into 1-inch wedges
- ½ tsp. black pepper
  Snipped fresh chives (optional)

**1.** Arrange oven racks in top third and bottom third of oven. Preheat oven to 425°F. Prick potatoes with a fork. Brush with 1 Tbsp. of the oil and sprinkle with ¼ tsp. of the salt. Wrap each potato in foil.
**2.** Sprinkle meat with garlic and herb seasoning. Coat a 10-inch oven-going skillet with cooking spray; heat over medium-high. Add meat and cook 4 minutes or until browned on

both sides. Transfer skillet to top oven rack. Place potatoes on rack next to skillet. Roast 25 minutes.

**3.** Meanwhile, line a 15×10-inch baking pan with foil; coat with cooking spray. In a large bowl combine carrots, Brussels sprouts, and onion. Drizzle with remaining 1 Tbsp. oil and sprinkle with pepper and remaining ½ tsp. salt; toss to coat. Spread vegetables in prepared pan. Transfer pan to bottom oven rack. Roast 25 to 30 minutes or until meat registers 145°F, potatoes are fork-tender, and roasted vegetables are tender and browned.

**4.** Transfer meat to a cutting board. Let stand 5 minutes before slicing. Serve half of the meat with potatoes and roasted vegetables, drizzling with pan juices and, if desired, topping with chives. Reserve remaining meat for another use.

**To Store** Place remaining meat in an airtight container and store in refrigerator up to 3 days or freeze up to 3 months.

**PER SERVING** *(4 oz. meat + 1 potato + 1 cup vegetables each)* **CAL** 422, **FAT** 13 g (2 g sat. fat), **CHOL** 89 mg, **SODIUM** 593 mg, **CARB** 40 g (9 g fiber, 9 g sugars), **PRO** 37 g

**Change It Up** Instead of potatoes, truse cubed butternut squash, parsnip pieces, or cauliflower florets. Instead of carrots, try green beans, fresh mushrooms, or apple slices.

## Prepare the Roast

**1.** Trim any fat from the surface of the pork loin. After starting the cut, lift and pull the fat taut, cutting between the fat and the meat.

**2.** Get a good sear on the pork to ensure deep flavor. Use a hot pan (really hot!). It can be stainless steel or nonstick, but it has to be oven-going.

### cook once, eat all week

This recipe uses a larger roast than you will eat in one meal. Use the leftovers to create easy dinners later in the week.

**1. Soup's On** Toss cubed pork into hot chicken or vegetable broth along with ramen, bok choy, and a sprinkle of green onion.

**2. Easy Italian** Serve sliced pork with creamy polenta topped with tomato sauce and Parmesan cheese shavings.

**3. Taco Night** Use 6-inch corn tortillas and top with pork, shredded cabbage, sriracha, plain Greek yogurt, cilantro, and a squeeze of lime.

**Boneless pork top loin roast—aka single loin—is an economical and lean option for healthful cooking. Pork labeled as natural doesn't contain any injected salt solution.**

**Is it done?**
Check for doneness in the thickest part of the breast (165°F) and thigh (175°F).

# Roasted Chicken with Root Vegetables

**26g**
CARB

**SERVES** 8
**HANDS ON** 55 min.
**TOTAL** 2 hr. 20 min.

1   5-lb. whole chicken, neck and giblets removed and excess fat trimmed
1   or 2 lemons
2   Tbsp. snipped fresh thyme or 2 tsp. dried thyme, crushed
1   Tbsp. light butter with canola oil
2   tsp. snipped fresh rosemary or ½ tsp. dried rosemary, crushed
4   cloves garlic, minced
1¼  tsp. kosher salt
½   tsp. freshly ground black pepper
    Nonstick cooking spray
4   medium red potatoes, cut into 1-inch wedges
6   large carrots, cut into thirds and thick pieces halved lengthwise
1   medium red onion, cut into 1-inch wedges
1   Tbsp. olive oil
1   Tbsp. snipped fresh thyme
1   tsp. snipped fresh rosemary
6   sprigs fresh thyme
1   sprig fresh rosemary, cut into 1-inch pieces

**1.** Wipe chicken cavity with paper towels. Let chicken stand at room temperature 30 minutes.
**2.** Place one oven rack in center of oven. Place a second oven rack in bottom third of oven. Preheat oven to 450°F. Line a roasting pan with foil and place a rack in prepared pan. Remove zest and squeeze juice from one of the lemons; set juice aside.
**3.** In a small bowl combine lemon zest and the next four ingredients

(through garlic). Slip your fingers under breast and leg skin to create pockets. Rub herb mixture over meat in pockets and inside body cavity. Sprinkle chicken and cavity with 1 tsp. of the kosher salt and ¼ tsp. of the pepper. Truss chicken. Insert a thermometer into center of one of the inside thigh muscles.

**4.** Place chicken, breast side up, on rack in prepared pan. Place pan on middle oven rack. Roast 55 minutes.

**5.** Meanwhile, line a 15×10-inch baking pan with foil and coat with cooking spray. In a large bowl combine the next six ingredients (though rosemary) and remaining ¼ tsp. salt and pepper. Spread vegetables in prepared pan. Top with thyme and rosemary sprigs.

**6.** After the chicken has roasted 55 minutes, place vegetables on bottom oven rack. Roast 25 to 35 minutes or until chicken is done (tip, *opposite*). Remove from oven. Roast vegetables 10 to 15 minutes more or until tender and golden.

**7.** Cover chicken with foil and let stand 15 minutes. If desired, remove zest from remaining lemon. To serve, remove and discard skin from chicken. Carve chicken and drizzle with reserved lemon juice and pan juices. Serve with vegetables and top with lemon zest and additional fresh thyme and rosemary.

**PER SERVING** *(3 oz. chicken + 1 cup vegetables each)* **CAL** 296, **FAT** 7 g (2 g sat. fat), **CHOL** 96 mg, **SODIUM** 333 mg, **CARB** 26 g (4 g fiber, 5 g sugars), **PRO** 32 g

## Truss the Chicken

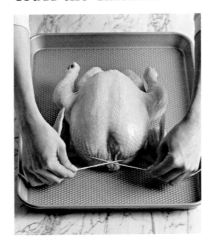

**1.** Start with 5 feet of 100%-cotton kitchen string. With the chicken on its back, slide string under its middle. Pull ends of string over the wings and cross them around the top of the breast, tightening skin.

**2.** Bring the ends of the string above the wings, running them along the side of the breast. Cross ends of the string, pulling tightly up and under the crown of the bird.

**3.** Bring the ends of the string under the legs, then loop over the tops of the legs. Cross and tighten. The thighs will pop outward.

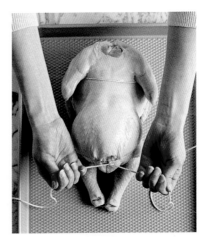

**4.** Flip the bird over and tie the strings in a knot around the tail. Snip off the ends. Cook the chicken breast side up.

# cooking school

Homemade salad dressings are lower in calories and fat than store-bought and far cheaper. You'll save big on carbs and sodium, too. If you know how to make a basic vinaigrette, the possibilities are endless.

### Mix It Up
To make any of the vinaigrettes creamy, just add ¼ cup plain Greek yogurt. These will last up to 7 days in the fridge.

## Basic Vinaigrette

- ¼ cup oil
- ¼ cup acid
   Something sweet
   Something with a kick
   Something aromatic
- ¼ tsp. salt
- ⅛ tsp. black pepper

For the first five ingredients, see Flavor Wheel *(opposite)*. Combine the ingredients in a screw-top jar. Cover and shake well.

## Try these combos:

### Citrus-Lime Vinaigrette

- ¼ cup canola oil
- ¼ cup lime juice
- ¼ cup orange juice
- 2 tsp. minced fresh jalapeño pepper (tip, *p. 250*)
- ¼ cup snipped fresh cilantro
- ¼ tsp. salt
- ⅛ tsp. black pepper

**PER SERVING** *(2 Tbsp. each)* **CAL** 66, **FAT** 7 g (1 g sat. fat), **CHOL** 0 mg, **SODIUM** 73 mg, **CARB** 2 g (0 g fiber, 1 g sugars), **PRO** 0 g

**Perfect Pair** Balance the sweet citrus notes with peppery arugula.

### Honey-Mustard Vinaigrette

- ¼ cup canola oil
- ¼ cup lemon juice
- 2 Tbsp. honey

- 2 tsp. stone-ground mustard
- 1 tsp. snipped fresh thyme
- ¼ tsp. salt
- ⅛ tsp. black pepper

**PER SERVING** *(2 Tbsp. each)* **CAL** 124, **FAT** 11 g (1 g sat. fat), **CHOL** 0 mg, **SODIUM** 143 mg, **CARB** 8 g (0 g fiber, 7 g sugars), **PRO** 0 g

**Perfect Pair** Baby kale stands up to this mustardy dressing. It's great with pork, too.

## Asian Vinaigrette

- ¼ cup toasted sesame oil
- ¼ cup rice vinegar
- 1 Tbsp. sugar or sugar sub equivalent
- 2 tsp. minced fresh ginger
- ¼ cup sliced green onions
- ¼ tsp. salt
- ⅛ tsp. black pepper

**PER SERVING** *(2 Tbsp. each)* **CAL** 95, **FAT** 9 g (1 g sat. fat), **CHOL** 0 mg, **SODIUM** 98 mg, **CARB** 3 g (0 g fiber, 3 g sugars), **PRO** 0 g

**Perfect Pair** Serve this vinaigrette over rice noodles, chicken, or shrimp.

## Apple-Balsamic Vinaigrette

- ¼ cup olive oil
- ¼ cup white balsamic vinegar or balsamic vinegar
- ¼ cup apple cider
- ¼ cup finely chopped shallots
- 2 tsp. Dijon-style mustard
- ¼ tsp. salt
- ⅛ tsp. black pepper

**PER SERVING** *(2 Tbsp. each)* **CAL** 82, **FAT** 7 g (1 g sat. fat), **CHOL** 0 mg, **SODIUM** 103 mg, **CARB** 5 g (0 g fiber, 5 g sugars), **PRO** 0 g

**Perfect Pair** Toss delicate greens, such as spring mix, with this subtly sweet dressing.

Citrus-Lime Vinaigrette

Honey-Mustard Vinaigrette

Asian Vinaigrette

Apple-Balsamic Vinaigrette

KICK

AROMATIC

ACID

SWEET

SALT & PEPPER

jalapeño

green onion

rice wine vinegar

apple cider

balsamic vinegar

thyme

OIL
- olive oil
- canola oil
- toasted sesame oil

ginger

sugar

lime juice

orange juice

shallot

red pepper flakes

lemon juice

honey

cilantro

stone-ground mustard

Dijon-style mustard

salt

black pepper

## Flavor Wheel

Use this wheel to create variations from the Basic Vinaigrette *(opposite)*. Have fun and experiment, with just one rule: Use 1 part oil to 1 part acid. Start with ¼ tsp. of an ingredient, then taste before adding more.

**Keep added sugars and sodium in check with this do-it-yourself quick bread.**

## Whole Wheat Quick Bread

**15g CARB**

| | |
|---|---|
| SERVES | 16 |
| HANDS ON | 15 min. |
| TOTAL | 2 hr. |

Nonstick cooking spray
2 cups white whole wheat flour
½ cup ground flaxseeds or flaxseed meal
2 tsp. baking powder
½ tsp. baking soda
¼ tsp. salt
1 egg, lightly beaten
1½ cups buttermilk
¼ cup vegetable oil
2 Tbsp. sugar*

**1.** Preheat oven to 350°F. Lightly coat a 9×5-inch loaf pan with cooking spray.
**2.** In a large bowl stir together the next five ingredients (through salt). Make a well in center of flour mixture.
**3.** In a medium bowl combine the remaining ingredients. Add all at once to flour mixture. Stir just until moistened (batter should be lumpy). Spread batter in the prepared pan.
**4.** Bake 45 to 50 minutes or until a toothpick comes out clean. Cool in pan 10 minutes. Remove bread from pan; cool on a wire rack.

**PER SERVING** *(1 slice each)* **CAL** 120, **FAT** 5 g (1 g sat. fat), **CHOL** 13 mg, **SODIUM** 166 mg, **CARB** 15 g (2 g fiber, 3 g sugars), **PRO** 4 g

**\*Sugar Sub** Choose Splenda Sugar Blend. Follow package directions to use 2 Tbsp. equivalent.
**PER SERVING WITH SUB:** Same as above, except **CAL** 118, **CARB** 14 g (2 g sugars)

## Make the Batter

**1.** Stir together the dry ingredients in a large bowl. Make a well in the center of the dry ingredients to make it easy to quickly stir in the wet ingredients.

**2.** Add the wet ingredients all at once to the dry ingredients. Stir it just until the dry ingredients are moistened. The batter will be lumpy. If you overstir, the bread may be tough or have holes in it.

### Try It
Sprinkle the top of the dough with flaxseeds before baking to add healthy fats and fiber.

### Skip the Butter
Spread bread with healthy toppers:

**1.** Mash together peas and avocado; spread onto bread. Sprinkle with fresh mint.

**2.** Smear bread with reduced-fat cream cheese (neufchatel); sprinkle with fresh dill and lemon zest.

**3.** Top bread with hummus and fresh cucumber slices. Sprinkle with a pinch of crushed red pepper flakes.

**4.** Spread bread with part-skim ricotta cheese. Top with diced fresh tomato and a sprinkle of freshly cracked black pepper.

# 5-day meal plans

These meal plans provide fewer than 1,600 calories per day and are ideal when trying to lose weight. You may need more than this, so consult with your health care provider.

## Week 1

DRINKING 8-OZ. LOW-FAT MILK AT DINNER HELPS YOU REACH YOUR DAILY CALCIUM NEEDS. FACTOR IN 110 CAL. AND 13 G CARB.

### Day 1
1,536 CAL., 163 G CARB.

**BREAKFAST**
1 cup oatmeal (prepared with water) + 1 Tbsp. almond butter + 1 cup strawberries + 2 tsp. chia seeds

**SNACK**
1 small pear + 1 low-fat cheese stick

**LUNCH**
Country-Style Wedge Salad with Turkey, *p. 125* + 1 slice whole wheat bread topped with 2 tsp. light buttery spread + ¾ cup low-fat milk

**SNACK**
Harissa Deviled Egg, *p. 234*

**DINNER**
Bulgogi Beef and Vegetable Bowls, *p. 109* + 1 cup low-fat milk

### Day 2
1,491 CAL., 174 G CARB.

**BREAKFAST**
Fruity Coconut Smoothie Bowls with Toasted Oats, *p. 104* + 1 hard-cooked egg

**SNACK**
¼ cup toasted walnuts + 2 Tbsp. dried cranberries

**LUNCH**
Beef Goulash Soup, *p. 141* + ¾ cup grapes + ¾ cup low-fat milk

**SNACK**
2 Tbsp. hummus + 1 cup fresh vegetables

**DINNER**
Jerk-Marinated Chicken with Caribbean Rice, *p. 211* + ½ cup steamed green beans + 1 orange + 1 cup low-fat milk

### Day 3
1,520 CAL., 189 G CARB.

**BREAKFAST**
Confetti Hash Browns and Eggs, *p. 95*

**SNACK**
1 medium apple + 1 Tbsp. peanut butter

**LUNCH**
Chicken Broccoli Salad with Buttermilk Dressing, *p. 125* + 1 cup low-fat milk

**SNACK**
1 carton light fat-free yogurt + 2 Tbsp. toasted walnuts + 2 tsp. chia seeds

**DINNER**
Cheeseburger Shepherd's Pie, *p. 172* + 1 small banana + 1 cup low-fat milk

## Day 4

1,484 CAL., 195 G CARB.

### BREAKFAST
2 slices toasted whole wheat bread + 2 Tbsp. almond butter + ½ cup blueberries + sprinkle of ground cinnamon

### SNACK
1 hard-cooked egg + ½ cup carrot sticks

### LUNCH
Vegetarian Chili, *p. 145* + 1 cup low-fat milk

### SNACK
Toasted Carrot Chips, *p. 232*

### DINNER
Chicken and Chickpea Buddha Bowls, *p. 113* + 1 small pear + 1 cup low-fat milk

**SIP WATER THROUGHOUT THE DAY.**
AIM FOR 64 OZ. DAILY. CHECK AT LUNCHTIME TO MAKE SURE YOU'RE HALFWAY THERE.

## Day 5

1,457 CAL., 174 G CARB.

### BREAKFAST
Mushroom and Asparagus Omelets, *p. 92* + Refrigerator Pumpkin Muffins, *p. 101*

### SNACK
½ cup celery sticks + 1 Tbsp. peanut butter + 2 Tbsp. raisins

### LUNCH
Hearty Italian Zoup, *p. 149* + 1 cup fresh pineapple

### SNACK
Turkey Roll-Up with Chili-Lime Cream, *p. 237*

### DINNER
Shrimp and Rice Bowls, *p. 117* + 1 cup fresh blueberries + 1 cup low-fat milk

Peanut Cluster Butterscotch Bites, *p. 245*

### SWEET TREAT
AS CALORIE AND CARB GOALS ALLOW, CHOOSE A DESSERT TO SATISFY CRAVINGS.

# Week 2

AT
BREAKFAST
ENJOY
COFFEE WITH
2 TSP.
LOW-FAT MILK
AND A
DASH OF
CINNAMON
FOR JUST
5 CALORIES
AND 1 CARB.

## Day 1
1,513 CAL., 196 G CARB.

### BREAKFAST
Cherry-Orange-Kissed Meusli with Peaches, *p. 104*

### SNACK
¾ cup grapes + ¼ cup roasted pistachio nuts

### LUNCH
Sandwich (2 slices whole wheat bread + 1 Tbsp. light mayo + 2 oz. lower-sodium deli turkey + ⅓ cup spinach + 2 tomato slices) + ½ cup sweet pepper strips + 1 cup low-fat milk

### SNACK
Sweet Ricotta and Strawberry Parfaits, *p. 243*

### DINNER
Mango-Lime Fish Tacos, *p. 204* + 1 cup fresh pineapple

## Day 2
1,471 CAL., 191 G CARB.

### BREAKFAST
2 frozen whole grain waffles, toasted + 3 Tbsp. light cream cheese + ¾ cup sliced strawberries + ¼ cup chopped toasted walnuts

### SNACK
1 medium apple + 1 low-fat cheese stick

### LUNCH
Falafel and Vegetable Pitas, *p. 188* + 1 cup low-fat milk

### SNACK
Crunchy Puffed Cherry Granola, *p. 235* + 1 carton light fat-free yogurt

### DINNER
Teriyaki Pork Skillet Casserole, *p. 180* + 1 cup low-fat milk

## Day 3
1,471 CAL., 189 G CARB.

### BREAKFAST
Savory Breakfast Bread Pudding, *p. 90* + ⅔ cup raspberries + 1 cup low-fat milk

### SNACK
¼ cup hummus + 1 cup vegetable dippers + 6 baked whole grain crackers

### LUNCH
Shrimp and Edamame Salad with Ginger Dressing, *p. 132* + ¾ cup grapes

### SNACK
1 medium pear + 1 Tbsp. roasted pistachio nuts

### DINNER
Spicy Beef Sloppy Joes, *p. 170* + ⅔ cup steamed broccoli tossed with 1 tsp. olive oil + 1 cup low-fat milk

# Day 4

1,472 CAL., 189 G CARB.

## BREAKFAST
Mexican-Style Ham and Egg
Breakfast Sandwiches, *p. 96*
+ ½ grapefruit

## SNACK
½ cup celery sticks + 1 Tbsp.
peanut butter + 3 Tbsp. raisins

## LUNCH
Korean Ahi Poke Bowl, *p. 118*
+ 1 medium pear

## SNACK
2 Tbsp. hummus + 1 cup
vegetable dippers

## DINNER
Loaded Barbecue Sweet
Potatoes, *p. 181* + 1 cup
low-fat milk

**SIP WATER
THROUGHOUT
THE DAY.**
INFUSE FLAVOR
INTO WATER BY
ADDING SLICES OF
FRESH FRUIT
AND/OR FRESH
HERB SPRIGS.

# Day 5

1,457 CAL., 174 G CARB.

## BREAKFAST
Quick Skillet Granola with Fruit
and Yogurt, *p. 102*

## SNACK
1 medium pear + 1 Tbsp.
roasted pistachio nuts

## LUNCH
Burrito Bowls, *p. 114* + 1 cup
low-fat milk

## SNACK
Sesame-Almond Bites, *p. 238*

## DINNER
Oven-Fried Drumsticks and
Thighs, *p. 178* + 1 3-oz. baked
potato topped with 2 tsp. light
buttery spread + ⅔ cup
steamed green beans + 1 cup
low-fat milk

Frozen Yogurt Bark,
*p. 241*

**SWEET TREAT**
AS CALORIE AND
CARB GOALS ALLOW,
CHOOSE A DESSERT
TO SATISFY CRAVINGS.

let's eat

# good morning

Be sure to eat breakfast every day. It helps you power up and stay balanced through your morning activities.

## Quinoa Cake Benedict with Roasted Tomatoes

**27g** CARB | **SERVES** 4
**HANDS ON** 20 min.
**TOTAL** 50 min.

- 3 egg whites, lightly beaten
- ½ cup soft whole wheat bread crumbs
- ¼ cup finely shredded Asiago cheese
- 2 Tbsp. chopped shallot
- ⅛ tsp. salt
- 1¾ cups cooked quinoa
- 4 tsp. olive oil
- 2 cups grape tomatoes
- 1 medium shallot, thinly sliced
- ¼ tsp. salt
- ¼ tsp. black pepper
- 2 cups baby arugula or baby kale
- 2 tsp. champagne vinegar or white wine vinegar
- 1 recipe Poached Eggs

**1.** Preheat oven to 400°F. In a bowl combine the first five ingredients (through ⅛ tsp. salt). Stir in quinoa. Let stand 20 minutes. Form mixture into four 3½-inch-diameter cakes. In a 10-inch nonstick skillet heat 2 tsp. of the oil over medium. Carefully add cakes. Cook patties about 5 minutes per side or until golden, turning carefully once.
**2.** Meanwhile, in a foil-lined shallow baking pan combine the tomatoes and shallot. Drizzle with the remaining 2 tsp. olive oil; stir to coat. Sprinkle with salt and pepper. Roast 12 to 15 minutes or until skins start to burst, gently stirring once. Remove from oven. Cool 5 minutes. Add arugula and sprinkle with vinegar; toss to combine.
**3.** To serve, arrange quinoa cakes on plates. Top with Poached Eggs and tomato mixture.

**Poached Eggs** In a 10-inch skillet combine **4 cups water** and **1 Tbsp. vinegar**. Bring to boiling; reduce heat to simmering (bubbles should begin to break the surface of the water). Break an **egg** into a cup and slip egg into the simmering water. Repeat with **three more eggs**, allowing each egg an equal amount of space in the skillet. Simmer eggs, uncovered, 3 to 5 minutes or until the whites are completely set and yolks begin to thicken but are not hard. Using a slotted spoon, remove eggs from skillet. Season with **salt** and **black pepper**.

**Tip** For cooked quinoa, in a medium saucepan combine **1 cup water** and **½ cup uncooked quinoa**, rinsed and drained. Bring to boiling; reduce heat. Cover and simmer about 15 minutes or until quinoa is tender. Drain if necessary. Cool.

**PER SERVING** *(1 cake + 1 egg + ⅔ cup tomato mixture each)* **CAL** 302, **FAT** 14 g (4 g sat. fat), **CHOL** 193 mg, **SODIUM** 520 mg, **CARB** 27 g (4 g fiber, 5 g sugars), **PRO** 16 g

# Sweet Potato Egg Bake

**12g**
**CARB**

**SERVES** 9
**HANDS ON** 20 min.
**TOTAL** 1 hr. 20 min.

Nonstick cooking spray
6 slices lower-sodium, less-fat bacon
2 cups sliced fresh cremini or
button mushrooms
1 cup sliced leek (white part only)
1 Tbsp. olive oil
2 cups torn fresh spinach
3 cups coarsely shredded, peeled
sweet potato
2 Tbsp. all-purpose flour
¾ cup shredded reduced-fat Swiss cheese
(3 oz.) or 3 slices reduced-fat Swiss
cheese, thinly sliced into shreds
4 eggs
4 egg whites
1¼ cups fat-free milk
¼ tsp. salt
¼ tsp. black pepper

**1.** Preheat oven to 350°F. Coat a 2-qt. square baking dish with cooking spray. In a 12-inch nonstick skillet cook bacon over medium until crisp. Drain on paper towels. Crumble bacon.
**2.** Wipe out skillet. In the same skillet cook mushrooms and leek in hot oil over medium about 6 minutes or until tender, stirring occasionally. Stir in spinach. Cook 2 minutes more or until wilted.
**3.** In a bowl toss together sweet potato and flour to coat. Arrange in prepared baking dish. Sprinkle with bacon, cooked vegetables, and cheese.
**4.** In a bowl whisk together the remaining ingredients. Pour over layers in dish. Bake, uncovered, 45 to 50 minutes or until a knife inserted near the center comes out clean.

**PER SERVING** *(¾ cup each)* **CAL** 153,
**FAT** 7 g (2 g sat. fat), **CHOL** 92 mg, **SODIUM** 221 mg,
**CARB** 12 g (1 g fiber, 4 g sugars), **PRO** 12 g

## Savory Breakfast Bread Pudding

**11g**
CARB

**SERVES** 6
**HANDS ON** 30 min.
**TOTAL** 1 hr. 15 min.

12 oz. artisan-style multigrain bread, cut into ½-inch cubes (5 cups)
  Nonstick cooking spray
3 tsp. canola oil
1 cup chopped fresh cremini mushrooms
½ cup finely chopped red sweet pepper
½ cup thinly sliced leek
3 egg yolks
1 cup fat-free milk
⅓ cup reduced-sodium chicken or vegetable broth
1 tsp. snipped fresh dill or ½ tsp. dried dill
¼ tsp. black pepper
1 cup shredded Gruyère or Swiss cheese (4 oz.)
4 egg whites
½ cup sliced shallots
¾ cup halved grape tomatoes
¾ cup bite-size strips red sweet pepper

**1.** Preheat oven to 300°F. In a 15×10-inch baking pan spread bread cubes in a single layer. Bake 10 to 15 minutes or until dried, stirring once or twice. Remove pan from oven. Increase oven temperature to 375°F. Lightly coat six 8-oz. ramekins or custard cups with cooking spray.
**2.** In a 10-inch nonstick skillet heat 2 tsp. of the oil over medium. Add mushrooms, the ½ cup sweet pepper, and leek; cook and stir about 4 minutes or until tender.
**3.** In a large bowl lightly beat egg yolks. Whisk in milk, broth, dill, and

black pepper. Add bread cubes, mushroom mixture, and cheese; toss to combine. In a second bowl beat egg whites with a mixer on high until soft peaks form (tips curl). Gently fold egg whites into bread mixture. Spoon bread mixture into prepared ramekins. Arrange ramekins in the baking pan used to dry bread cubes.

**4.** Bake about 20 minutes or until puffed, golden, and a knife inserted in the center comes out clean.

**5.** Meanwhile, wipe out skillet. Add the shallots and remaining 1 tsp. oil. Cook over medium-high about 3 minutes or until golden, stirring occasionally. Add tomatoes and the ¾ cup pepper; cook about 4 minutes or until softened, gently stirring occasionally.

**6.** Spoon tomato mixture over puddings and sprinkle with additional snipped fresh dill.

**PER SERVING** *(1 individual bread pudding + ¼ cup topper each)* **CAL** 192, **FAT** 11 g (5 g sat. fat), **CHOL** 114 mg, **SODIUM** 244 mg, **CARB** 11 g (2 g fiber, 6 g sugars), **PRO** 13 g

# Chicken Sausage Omelets with Spinach

**5g** **CARB**

**SERVES** 2
**HANDS ON** 20 min.
**TOTAL** 30 min.

Nonstick cooking spray
2   cups chopped fresh spinach
½   of a 7-oz. pkg. (5 links) frozen fully cooked chicken and maple breakfast sausage links, thawed and chopped
3   eggs, lightly beaten

2   Tbsp. water
¼   cup shredded part-skim mozzarella cheese (1 oz.)
2   green onions (green tops only), thinly sliced
½   cup grape tomatoes, quartered (optional)
¼   cup fresh basil leaves, thinly sliced

**1.** Coat a 10-inch nonstick skillet with flared sides with cooking spray; heat over medium. Add spinach and sausage; cook and stir until spinach is wilted and sausage is heated; remove from skillet.

**2.** In a bowl whisk together eggs and the water. Add egg mixture to skillet; reduce heat to medium-low. Immediately begin stirring the eggs gently but continuously with a wooden spoon until mixture resembles small pieces of cooked egg surrounded by liquid egg. Stop stirring. Cook 30 to 60 seconds more or until egg is set and shiny.

**3.** Spoon spinach and sausage mixture over half of the omelet. Sprinkle with cheese and green onions. Fold the opposite side of omelet over sausage mixture. Cook 30 to 60 seconds more or until filling is heated and cheese is melted. Transfer omelet to a plate. Cut in half; transfer half of the omelet to a second plate. Top with tomatoes (if using) and basil.

**PER SERVING** *(½ of an omelet each)* **CAL** 252, **FAT** 16 g (6 g sat. fat), **CHOL** 326 mg, **SODIUM** 521 mg, **CARB** 5 g (1 g fiber, 2 g sugars), **PRO** 21 g

# Mushroom and Asparagus Omelets

**7g**
**CARB**

**SERVES** 4
**TOTAL** 30 min.

- 4 eggs, lightly beaten, or 1 cup refrigerated or frozen egg product, thawed
- 6 egg whites, lightly beaten, or 1 cup refrigerated or frozen egg product, thawed
- ¼ cup water
- 1 to 2 Tbsp. finely snipped fresh Italian parsley or dill
  Dash salt
  Dash black pepper
- 2 Tbsp. olive oil
- 1½ cups sliced fresh button or cremini mushrooms
- 8 oz. fresh asparagus spears, trimmed and cut into 1-inch pieces
- ½ cup chopped red sweet pepper
- ½ cup sliced green onions
- 1 clove garlic, minced
- ¾ cup shredded reduced-fat Italian-blend cheeses (3 oz.)

**1.** In a large bowl combine the first six ingredients (through black pepper).
**2.** In a 10-inch nonstick skillet heat 2 tsp. of the oil over medium-high. Add the next five ingredients (through garlic). Cook 5 to 8 minutes or until mushrooms begin to brown and asparagus is just tender, stirring frequently. Remove vegetables from skillet; cover and keep warm.
**3.** Heat an 8-inch nonstick skillet with flared sides over medium-high. Add 1 tsp. of the oil, swirling to coat bottom of skillet. Add one-fourth of the egg mixture (about ½ cup); reduce heat to medium. Immediately stir egg mixture gently but continuously until mixture resembles small pieces of cooked egg surrounded by liquid egg. Stop stirring. Cook 30 to 60 seconds more or until egg mixture is set.
**4.** Spoon one-fourth of the vegetables onto half of the omelet. Sprinkle with one-fourth of the cheese. Lift and fold the unfilled half of the omelet over filling. Gently slide omelet out of skillet onto a warm plate. Cover and keep warm. Repeat with the remaining oil, egg mixture, vegetables, and cheese to make three more omelets.

**PER SERVING** *(1 omelet each)* **CAL** 247, **FAT** 15 g (5 g sat. fat), **CHOL** 197 mg, **SODIUM** 362 mg, **CARB** 7 g (2 g fiber, 3 g sugars), **PRO** 21 g

# 🍲 Crustless Spinach and Mushroom Quiche

**11g**
**CARB**

**SERVES** 8
**HANDS ON** 20 min.
**SLOW COOK** 5 hr.

  Nonstick cooking spray
- 1 10-oz. pkg. frozen chopped spinach, thawed and well drained
- 4 slices turkey bacon
- 1 Tbsp. olive oil
- 2 cups coarsely chopped fresh portobello mushrooms
- ½ cup chopped orange sweet pepper

1   cup shredded Swiss cheese
    (4 oz.)
8   eggs, lightly beaten, or 2 cups
    refrigerated or frozen egg
    product, thawed
2   cups reduced-fat milk
1   Tbsp. snipped fresh chives or
    1 tsp. dried chives
¼   tsp. salt
¼   tsp. black pepper
½   cup low-fat biscuit mix
    Salsa (optional)

**1.** Line a 3½- or 4-qt. slow cooker with a disposable slow cooker liner. Lightly coat liner with cooking spray. Press spinach with paper towels to remove as much liquid as possible.
**2.** In a 10-inch skillet cook bacon until crisp. Drain and chop bacon. Discard drippings. In the same skillet heat oil over medium. Add mushrooms and sweet pepper; cook until tender. Stir in spinach and cheese.
**3.** In a bowl combine eggs, milk, chives, salt, and black pepper. Stir into spinach mixture in skillet. Gently fold in biscuit mix. Pour mixture into the prepared cooker. Sprinkle with bacon.
**4.** Cover and cook on low 5 to 6 hours or high 2 to 3 hours or until a knife inserted into center comes out clean. Turn off cooker. If possible, remove crockery liner from cooker. Let stand 15 to 30 minutes.
**5.** Carefully lift disposable liner from cooker and transfer quiche to a cutting board. Peel back liner and cut quiche into eight slices. If desired, serve with salsa.

**PER SERVING** (1 slice each) **CAL** 243, **FAT** 15 g (6 g sat. fat), **CHOL** 237 mg, **SODIUM** 455 mg, **CARB** 11 g (1 g fiber, 5 g sugars), **PRO** 17 g

# Confetti Hash Browns and Eggs

**33g**
**CARB**

**SERVES** 4
**TOTAL** 30 min.

- 2 tsp. olive oil
- 1 cup chopped onion
- 2 cups chopped red, orange, green, and/or yellow sweet peppers
- 1 cup finely chopped broccoli
- 2½ cups frozen diced hash brown potatoes, thawed
- 1 tsp. snipped fresh thyme
- 1 tsp. Worcestershire sauce
- ½ tsp. salt
- ¼ tsp. black pepper
  Dash hot pepper sauce
- 4 eggs

**1.** In a 10-inch nonstick skillet heat oil over medium. Add onion; cook 2 minutes. Add sweet peppers and broccoli; cook about 4 minutes or until vegetables are crisp-tender, stirring occasionally. Stir in the next six ingredients (through hot pepper sauce). Cook, covered, over medium about 12 minutes or just until potatoes are tender and golden, stirring occasionally.

**2.** Using a large spoon, make four indentations in potato mixture. Break an egg into each indentation. Cook, covered, 4 to 5 minutes more or until whites are completely set.

**PER SERVING** ( ¾ cup hash browns + 1 egg each) **CAL** 240, **FAT** 8 g (2 g sat. fat), **CHOL** 186 mg, **SODIUM** 417 mg, **CARB** 33 g (4 g fiber, 4 g sugars), **PRO** 11 g

GOOD FOR YOU
Hash browns don't need cheese to be loaded. These are packed with a rainbow of veggies.

# Mexican-Style Ham and Egg Breakfast Sandwiches

**35g** | **SERVES** 2
CARB | **TOTAL** 20 min.

- ½  of a medium avocado, peeled
- 2  Tbsp. thinly sliced green onion tops
- 1  Tbsp. lime juice
- 1  clove garlic, minced
- 2  whole grain English muffins, split and toasted
- ¾  cup fresh baby spinach
- 2  oz. thin-sliced lower-sodium honey ham
   Nonstick cooking spray
- 2  eggs
- 2  Tbsp. fresh pico de gallo, salsa, or salsa verde

**1.** Place avocado in a medium bowl. Add green onion, lime juice, and garlic; mash with a fork or potato masher. Spread mixture onto cut sides of English muffins. Top bottom halves with spinach and ham.

**2.** Coat a 10-inch nonstick skillet with cooking spray; heat over medium. Break eggs into skillet, keeping them separate. Reduce heat to low; cook 3 to 4 minutes or until whites are completely set and yolks start to thicken.

**3.** Turn eggs and cook 30 seconds more for over-easy or 1 minute more for over-hard. Top sandwiches with eggs and pico de gallo. Replace muffin tops.

**TIP** To save leftover avocado half, wrap tightly with plastic wrap, then with foil. Store in refrigerator up to 24 hours. Using a spoon, scrape a thin layer off the top of avocado flesh before serving.

**PER SERVING** *(1 sandwich each)* **CAL** 315, **FAT** 12 g (3 g sat. fat), **CHOL** 201 mg, **SODIUM** 578 mg, **CARB** 35 g (5 g fiber, 4 g sugars), **PRO** 16 g

# Baked Breakfast Taquitos

**39g**
**CARB**

**SERVES** 4
**HANDS ON** 25 min.
**TOTAL** 40 min.

Nonstick cooking spray
2 cups chopped fresh cremini mushrooms
¾ cup chopped red sweet pepper
⅓ cup chopped onion
2 cups chopped kale leaves
4 eggs, lightly beaten
4 egg whites, lightly beaten
½ cup shredded Monterey Jack cheese with jalapeños (2 oz.)
1 4-oz. can diced green chiles, undrained
8 6-inch whole wheat flour tortillas
¼ cup fresh salsa
Toppers: light sour cream, snipped fresh cilantro, sliced green onions, and/or chopped black olives (optional)

**1.** Preheat oven to 425°F. Line a baking sheet with parchment paper. Coat a 10-inch nonstick skillet with cooking spray. Heat skillet over medium. Add mushrooms, sweet pepper, and onion; cook about 4 minutes or until tender, stirring occasionally. Add kale; cook and stir about 1 minute or until wilted. Remove from skillet.

**2.** Add eggs to hot skillet. Cook over medium, without stirring, until mixture begins to set on the bottom and around edges. With a spatula or large spoon, lift and fold the partially cooked egg mixture so uncooked portion flows underneath. Continue cooking 2 to 3 minutes or until egg mixture is cooked through but still glossy and moist. Return vegetable mixture to skillet with cheese and chiles; stir gently to combine.

**3.** Fill each tortilla with about ⅓ cup egg mixture; roll up as tightly as possible. Arrange taquitos, seam sides down, on the prepared baking sheet, leaving space between each. Coat taquitos evenly with cooking spray.

**4.** Bake about 15 minutes or until evenly browned and crispy. Serve with salsa and, if desired, toppers.

**PER SERVING** *(2 taquitos each)* **CAL** 360,
**FAT** 14 g (6 g sat. fat), **CHOL** 199 mg, **SODIUM** 786 mg,
**CARB** 39 g (7 g fiber, 7 g sugars), **PRO** 23 g

TRY THIS
Save a little time by stirring in baby kale or spinach for the chopped kale.

## Strawberries and Cream Pancakes

**22g**
**CARB**

SERVES 12

TOTAL 25 min.

- 1 large orange
- 3 cups coarsely chopped fresh strawberries
- 1 cup whole wheat pastry flour
- ½ cup all-purpose flour
- ¼ cup oat flour or oat bran
- 2 Tbsp. chia seeds or flaxseeds
- 1 Tbsp. sugar*
- 1 Tbsp. baking powder
- ¼ tsp. salt
- 1½ cups fat-free milk
- ¼ cup refrigerated or frozen egg product, thawed, or 1 egg, lightly beaten
- 2 Tbsp. canola oil
- ¾ cup whipped Greek cream cheese, softened

**1.** Remove 1 Tbsp. zest and squeeze 6 Tbsp. juice from orange. In a bowl combine strawberries, orange zest, and ¼ cup of the orange juice. Cover and let stand 20 to 30 minutes to blend flavors, stirring occasionally.
**2.** In a large bowl stir together the next seven ingredients (through salt). In another bowl use a fork to combine milk, egg, and oil. Add egg mixture to flour mixture. Stir just until moistened (batter should be slightly lumpy).
**3.** For each pancake, pour 2 Tbsp. batter onto a hot, lightly greased griddle or heavy skillet. Spread batter to an even layer if necessary. Cook over medium 1 to 2 minutes per side or until pancakes are golden brown; turn over when surfaces are bubbly

and edges are slightly dry. Keep pancakes warm in a 200°F oven while making the rest.

**4.** To serve, in a bowl combine cream cheese and 1 to 2 Tbsp. of the remaining orange juice; spread evenly over pancakes. Top with strawberries.

**PER SERVING** *(2 pancakes + 1 Tbsp. cream cheese mixture + ¼ cup strawberries each)* **CAL** 158, **FAT** 5 g (1 g sat. fat), **CHOL** 8 mg, **SODIUM** 242 mg, **CARB** 22 g (3 g fiber, 7 g sugars), **PRO** 6 g

**\*Sugar Sub**  We do not recommend a sugar sub for this recipe.

---

# Refrigerator Pumpkin Muffins

**17g**
**CARB**

**SERVES**  24
**HANDS ON**  15 min.
**TOTAL**  35 min.

1½  cups whole wheat flour
1  cup all-purpose flour
½  cup packed brown sugar*
½  cup chopped walnuts, toasted (tip, *p. 102*)
4  tsp. baking powder
1  Tbsp. pumpkin pie spice
¾  tsp. baking soda
½  tsp. salt
1  15-oz. can pumpkin
1½  cups buttermilk
½  cup refrigerated or frozen egg product, thawed
¼  cup butter, melted
2  tsp. lemon zest
    Nonstick cooking spray

**1.** In a large bowl stir together the first eight ingredients (through salt). Make a well in the center of the flour mixture. In another bowl combine the next five ingredients (through lemon zest). Add egg mixture to flour mixture. Stir just until moistened. Place plastic wrap over the surface of the batter. Cover tightly; refrigerate up to 3 days (or bake immediately).

**2.** To bake, coat desired number of 2½-inch muffin cups with cooking spray. Preheat oven to 400°F. Spoon about ¼ cup of the batter into each prepared muffin cup. Bake 15 to 18 minutes or until a toothpick comes out clean.

**3.** Cool in cups 5 minutes. Remove from cups. Cool completely on a wire rack.

**PER SERVING** *(1 muffin each)*  **CAL** 113, **FAT** 4 g (2 g sat. fat), **CHOL** 6 mg, **SODIUM** 215 mg, **CARB** 17 g (2 g fiber, 6 g sugars), **PRO** 3 g

**\*Sugar Sub**  Choose Splenda Brown Sugar Blend. Follow package directions to use ½ cup equivalent.
**PER SERVING WITH SUB** Same as above, except **CAL** 106, **SODIUM** 213 mg, **CARB** 15 g (3 g sugars)

# Quick Skillet Granola with Fruit and Yogurt

**41g**
**CARB**

| SERVES 4 |
| --- |
| **TOTAL** 20 min. |

⅔ cup regular rolled oats
⅓ cup slivered almonds
2 Tbsp. flaxseeds
2 Tbsp. light butter
1 Tbsp. honey
½ tsp. ground cinnamon
2 medium bananas, peeled and sliced crosswise
1 cup fresh strawberries, hulled and quartered
2 5.3- to 6-oz. cartons fruit-flavor light Greek yogurt

**1.** Heat a 10-inch nonstick skillet over medium. Add oats and almonds. Cook 3 to 5 minutes or until mixture is lightly browned, stirring frequently. (Reduce heat to medium-low if mixture browns too quickly.) Stir in flaxseeds, butter, honey, and cinnamon. Cook and stir 1 to 2 minutes more or until most of the liquid is absorbed and the almonds and oats are golden brown.

**2.** Divide bananas and strawberries among dishes. Sprinkle with granola. Spoon yogurt over top.

**PER SERVING** (⅓ cup granola + ⅔ cup fruit + ⅓ cup yogurt each) **CAL** 281, **FAT** 10 g (2 g sat. fat), **CHOL** 10 mg, **SODIUM** 84 mg, **CARB** 41 g (9 g fiber, 18 g sugars), **PRO** 11 g

## go nuts

Nuts are an easy way to add healthy fats and fiber to recipes. Because they contain high amounts of oil, they can turn rancid fairly quickly. Store them in resealable plastic freezer bags or containers in the freezer up to 8 months. To toast whole nuts or large pieces, spread in a shallow baking pan lined with parchment paper. Bake in a 350°F oven 5 to 10 minutes or until golden, shaking pan once or twice. For hazelnuts, rub the warm nuts in a dry dish towel until the skins come loose.

# Cherry-Orange-Kissed Muesli with Peaches

**29g**
**CARB**

**SERVES** 12
**HANDS ON** 30 min.
**TOTAL** 12 hr. 30 min.

- 2¼ cups water
- ½ cup steel-cut oats
- ½ cup bulgur
- 2 oranges
- 2 5.3- to 6-oz. cartons plain fat-free Greek yogurt
- 1¼ cups fat-free milk
- ½ cup dried tart cherries
- ¼ cup ground flaxseeds
- 3 Tbsp. honey
- ½ tsp. ground ginger
- ½ tsp. ground cardamom (optional)
- ¼ tsp. salt
- 4 cups thinly sliced peaches
- ¾ cup sliced almonds, toasted (tip, *p. 102*)
  Halved orange sections (optional)

**1.** In a large saucepan combine the water, oats, and bulgur. Bring to boiling; reduce heat. Simmer 8 minutes (grains will not be tender). Transfer to a large bowl; cool 10 minutes.

**2.** Meanwhile, remove ½ tsp. zest and squeeze ½ cup juice from oranges. Wrap zest in plastic wrap; chill. Stir orange juice and the next eight ingredients (through salt) into cereal. Cover and chill at least 12 hours or up to 3 days.

**3.** To serve, transfer cereal to a large saucepan. Cook over low until heated through, stirring occasionally. (Or let stand at room temperature 15 minutes before serving.) Stir in orange zest. Top servings with peaches, almonds, and, if desired, halved orange sections.

**PER SERVING** (*½ cup cereal + ⅓ cup toppers each*) **CAL** 180, **FAT** 5 g (0 g sat. fat), **CHOL** 2 mg, **SODIUM** 73 mg, **CARB** 29 g (4 g fiber, 16 g sugars), **PRO** 8 g

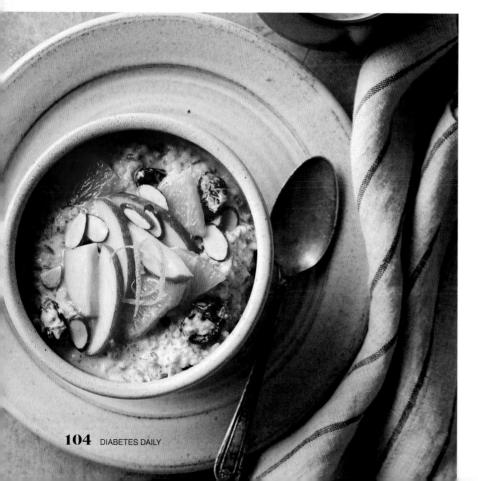

# Fruity Coconut Smoothie Bowls with Toasted Oats

**33g**
**CARB**

**SERVES** 4
**TOTAL** 20 min.

- ⅓ cup regular rolled oats
- ⅓ cup unsweetened coconut flakes
- 1½ cups refrigerated unsweetened coconut milk beverage
- 1 cup unsweetened frozen mango chunks
- 1 cup unsweetened frozen raspberries
- 1 cup unsweetened frozen blueberries
- ½ cup chopped, peeled, and seeded fresh mango
- ½ cup fresh raspberries
- ½ cup fresh blueberries
- ½ cup slivered almonds, toasted (tip, *p. 102*)

**1.** Heat an 8-inch skillet over medium. Add oats and coconut. Cook, stirring frequently, 3 to 5 minutes or until oats and coconut are lightly toasted. Remove from heat.

**2.** Meanwhile, in a blender combine the next four ingredients (through frozen blueberries). Cover; blend until smooth, stopping and scraping sides as needed.

**3.** To serve, pour smoothie into shallow bowls. Top with the remaining ingredients and the toasted oats and coconut.

**Tip** Frozen fruit makes the smoothie thick. Buy fresh fruit, then freeze what you need in a single layer in a shallow baking pan. Store the frozen pieces in resealable freezer bags until ready to use.

**PER SERVING** *(1½ cups each)* **CAL** 252, **FAT** 13 g (5 g sat. fat), **CHOL** 0 mg, **SODIUM** 18 mg, **CARB** 33 g (8 g fiber, 18 g sugars), **PRO** 5 g

# Cherry-Berry Oatmeal Smoothies

**21g**
CARB

| | |
|---|---|
| **SERVES** | 3 |
| **HANDS ON** | 10 min. |
| **TOTAL** | 15 min. |

- ½ cup water
- ⅓ cup quick-cooking rolled oats
- ½ cup light almond milk or fat-free milk
- ¾ cup fresh or frozen unsweetened strawberries, partially thawed
- ½ cup fresh or frozen unsweetened pitted dark sweet cherries, partially thawed
- 1 to 2 Tbsp. almond butter
- 1 Tbsp. honey
- ½ cup small ice cubes

**1.** In a medium bowl combine the water and oats. Microwave 1 minute. Stir in ¼ cup of the milk. Microwave 30 to 50 seconds more or until oats are very tender. Cool 5 minutes.

**2.** In a blender combine oat mixture, the remaining ¼ cup milk, and the next four ingredients (through honey). Cover and blend until smooth, scraping container as needed. Add ice cubes; cover and blend until smooth. If desired, top each serving with additional fruit.

**PER SERVING** (¾ cup each) **CAL** 121, **FAT** 4 g (0 g sat. fat), **CHOL** 0 mg, **SODIUM** 41 mg, **CARB** 21 g (3 g fiber, 12 g sugars), **PRO** 3 g

# Apple-Cran-Oat Breakfast Cookies

**34g**
**CARB**

SERVES 20
HANDS ON 25 min.
TOTAL 45 min.

- 2½ cups regular rolled oats
- 1 cup almond meal
- ½ cup whole wheat flour
- ¼ cup nonfat dry milk powder
- 1 tsp. baking soda
- 1 tsp. ground cinnamon
- ¼ tsp. salt
- 1 orange
- 1 cup packed brown sugar*
- 2 eggs, lightly beaten
- 1 6-oz. carton plain fat-free Greek yogurt
- 1½ tsp. vanilla
- 1½ cups chopped apple (1 large)
- 1½ cups coarsely chopped fresh cranberries
- ⅔ cup powdered sugar*

**1.** Preheat oven to 350°F. Line two cookie sheets with parchment paper. In a large bowl combine the first seven ingredients (through salt).
**2.** Remove 2 tsp. zest and squeeze juice from orange; set juice aside. In another bowl combine brown sugar, eggs, yogurt, orange zest, and 1 tsp. of the vanilla; stir until well mixed. Stir egg mixture into oat mixture until evenly moistened. Fold in chopped apple and cranberries. Drop ¼-cup mounds of dough onto prepared cookie sheets. Pat each into a flattened circle (approximately ½ inch thick).
**3.** Bake about 15 minutes or until set and baked through. Cool on cookie sheets 5 minutes. Remove; cool on wire racks.

**4.** For icing, in a small bowl whisk together powdered sugar, 1 Tbsp. of the orange juice, and the remaining ½ tsp. vanilla. If needed, stir in enough additional orange juice, ½ tsp. at a time, to make drizzling consistency. Drizzle icing over cookies.

**Tip** Almond meal is ground whole almonds. It is different from almond flour because it is coarser and may be made with unblanched almonds.

PER SERVING *(1 cookie each)* **CAL** 201, **FAT** 5 g (1 g sat. fat), **CHOL** 19 mg, **SODIUM** 111 mg, **CARB** 34 g (4 g fiber, 17 g sugars), **PRO** 7 g

**\*Sugar Sub** We do not recommend using sugar subs for this recipe.

**To Store** Layer cookies between sheets of waxed paper in an airtight container; cover. Store in the refrigerator up to 3 days or freeze up to 3 months.

# bowls of goodness

Each dish holds a nutritious, well-rounded meal. And the colorful bowls make serving easy.

## Bulgogi Beef and Vegetable Bowls

**43g CARB**

**SERVES** 4
**HANDS ON** 35 min.
**TOTAL** 4 hr. 35 min.

- 1 lb. boneless beef sirloin steak, cut 1 inch thick
- ½ cup coarsely chopped onion
- ¼ cup honey
- ¼ cup water
- 2 Tbsp. reduced-sodium soy sauce
- 2 Tbsp. toasted sesame oil
- 1 Tbsp. finely chopped fresh ginger
- 4 cloves garlic, halved
  Nonstick cooking spray
- 1⅓ cups cooked brown rice
- 1 cup coarsely shredded carrots
- 1 cup finely shredded red cabbage
- ¾ cup cooked small broccoli florets
- ½ cup coarsely shredded cucumber
- ¼ cup snipped fresh cilantro or mint
- 1 to 2 tsp. sriracha sauce
- ½ cup kimchi (optional)

**1.** Trim fat from meat. Cut meat across the grain into very thin slices. Place meat in a resealable plastic bag set in a shallow dish. For marinade, in a blender or food processor combine onion, 2 Tbsp. each of the honey and water, the soy sauce, 1 Tbsp. of the sesame oil, the ginger, and garlic. Cover and blend or process until smooth. Pour marinade over meat. Seal bag; turn to coat meat. Marinate in the refrigerator 4 to 6 hours, turning bag occasionally.
**2.** Drain meat, discarding marinade. Coat an extra-large wok or 12-inch nonstick skillet with cooking spray; heat over medium-high. Working in batches, add meat; cook and stir 40 to 60 seconds or just until slightly pink in center.
**3.** To assemble, divide meat and the next five ingredients (through cucumber) among shallow bowls, keeping ingredients in separate piles. In a small bowl combine the remaining 2 Tbsp. each honey and water, the remaining 1 Tbsp. sesame oil, the cilantro, and sriracha sauce. Top servings with honey mixture and, if desired, kimchi and additional cilantro or mint.

**Tip** Partially freeze the meat for easier slicing.

**PER SERVING** *(1 bowl each)* **CAL** 397, **FAT** 13 g (3 g sat. fat), **CHOL** 77 mg, **SODIUM** 435 mg, **CARB** 43 g (3 g fiber, 23 g sugars), **PRO** 30 g

# Barbecued Pulled Pork Bowls

**47g**
**CARB**

| **SERVES** 4 |
| **TOTAL** 40 min. |

3 Tbsp. plain fat-free Greek yogurt
3 Tbsp. light mayonnaise
1 Tbsp. cider vinegar
¼ tsp. bottled hot pepper sauce
3 cups packaged shredded broccoli (broccoli slaw mix)
1 medium red sweet pepper, cut into bite-size strips
2 cups Slow Cooker Pulled Pork
1 cup no-salt-added pinto or red beans, rinsed and drained
2 cups frozen roasted corn, thawed and heated
¼ cup barbecue sauce
¼ cup thinly sliced red onion
12 dill pickle chips, chopped

**TRY THIS**
Roast plain fresh or frozen corn in a skillet coated with cooking spray over medium-high until slightly charred.

**1.** In a large bowl stir together the first four ingredients (through hot pepper sauce). Add shredded broccoli and sweet pepper; stir to coat.
**2.** In a medium saucepan combine Slow Cooker Pulled Pork and the beans. Heat over medium until heated through.
**3.** In shallow bowls arrange slaw, pork and bean mixture, and corn. Drizzle with barbecue sauce and top with red onion slivers and dill pickles.

**Slow Cooker Pulled Pork** Place one **4-lb. boneless pork shoulder roast, trimmed and cut into 2-inch chunks,** and **1 cup chopped onion** in a 4- to 5-qt. slow cooker. Stir in **one 8-oz. can no-salt-added tomato sauce; 6 cloves garlic, minced; 2 Tbsp. each packed brown sugar** and **balsamic or cider vinegar; 1 Tbsp. each chili powder and Worcestershire sauce; 1 tsp. dry mustard;** and **½ tsp. each salt and black pepper.** Cover and cook on low 10 to 11 hours or high 5 to 5½ hours. Remove meat from cooker, reserving liquid. Shred meat using two forks. Skim fat from liquid. Add enough liquid to meat to moisten. Place 2-cup portions of meat in airtight containers. Cover and refrigerate up to 3 days or freeze up to 3 months. Thaw in the refrigerator before using.

**PER SERVING** *(1 bowl each)* **CAL** 399, **FAT** 11 g (32 g sat. fat), **CHOL** 66 mg, **SODIUM** 578 mg, **CARB** 47 g (8 g fiber, 18 g sugars), **PRO** 28 g

## Chicken Meatball Noodle Bowl

**41g**
**CARB**

| SERVES | 4 |
| TOTAL | 30 min. |

4 oz. dried thin rice noodles or angel hair pasta
12 oz. ground chicken breast
2 Tbsp. flaxseed meal
2 Tbsp. snipped fresh cilantro
1 Tbsp. chia seed powder
1 Tbsp. grated fresh ginger or 1 tsp. ground ginger
½ tsp. salt
3 Tbsp. canola oil
1 medium red Fresno chile pepper, seeded and finely chopped (tip, *p. 250*) (optional)
⅓ cup rice vinegar
2 Tbsp. honey
1 Tbsp. lime juice
4 cups shredded romaine lettuce
1 cup finely shredded carrot
Lime wedges (optional)

**1.** Prepare noodles according to package directions; drain.
**2.** Meanwhile, in a bowl combine next six ingredients (through salt). Shape mixture into 16 meatballs (coat hands with nonstick cooking spray if necessary). In a 10-inch skillet heat 1 Tbsp. of the oil over medium. Add meatballs; cook about 10 minutes or until done (165°F), turning to brown evenly. Remove meatballs from skillet. Remove skillet from heat.
**3.** Add the remaining 2 Tbsp. oil and, if desired, the chopped chile pepper to the warm skillet. Stir in vinegar, honey, and lime juice.
**4.** Divide noodles, lettuce, and carrot among shallow bowls. Top

with meatballs; drizzle with vinegar mixture. If desired, top with additional cilantro and sliced chile pepper and serve with lime wedges.

**Tip** If you don't have chia seed powder but you have chia seeds, use a spice grinder. Grind 1½ tsp. chia seeds to yield 1 Tbsp. chia powder.

PER SERVING *(1 bowl each)* **CAL** 382, **FAT** 14 g (1 g sat. fat), **CHOL** 70 mg, **SODIUM** 450 mg, **CARB** 41 g (5 g fiber, 11 g sugars), **PRO** 27 g

---

# Chicken and Chickpea Buddha Bowls

**34g** CARB | **SERVES** 4
**HANDS ON** 35 min.
**TOTAL** 55 min.

2 cups ¾-inch cubes peeled butternut squash
2 medium shallots, peeled and cut into thin wedges
2 tsp. olive oil
½ tsp. salt
⅛ tsp. black pepper
1½ cups halved fresh green beans, trimmed if desired
1 Tbsp. lemon juice
2 cloves garlic, minced
4 cups torn fresh kale
1 cup chopped cooked chicken breast (6 oz.)
8 Tbsp. Sesame-Dijon Dressing
½ cup purchased crunchy Bombay spice or falafel-flavor chickpeas

**1.** Preheat oven to 425°F. In a 13×9-inch baking pan combine squash, shallots, oil, ¼ tsp. of the salt, and the pepper; toss to coat. Spread in single layer. Roast 20 to 25 minutes or until squash is tender, stirring twice.
**2.** Meanwhile, in a medium saucepan cook beans, covered, in a small amount of boiling water 6 to 8 minutes or until just tender; drain. Rinse with cold water; drain well.
**3.** In a bowl combine lemon juice, garlic, and the remaining ¼ tsp. salt. Add kale. Toss and rub kale leaves gently with your fingers until kale is well coated and leaves start to look wilted and glossy.
**4.** Divide kale, squash mixture, beans, and chicken among four bowls. Drizzle with Sesame-Dijon Dressing and top with chickpeas.

**Sesame-Dijon Dressing** In a bowl whisk together ½ cup tahini (sesame seed paste), ½ cup water, 3 Tbsp. each lemon juice and honey, 2 Tbsp. olive oil, 1 Tbsp. Dijon-style mustard, and ¼ tsp. salt. Transfer unused dressing to an airtight container; cover and chill up to 3 days.

**Tip** For a cold salad meal, prepare as directed through Step 2. Place squash mixture and beans in separate airtight containers; cover and chill up to 24 hours. Prepare Sesame-Dijon Dressing as directed; place in an airtight container. Chill up to 24 hours. Continue as directed.

PER SERVING *(1 bowl each)* **CAL** 321, **FAT** 14 g (2 g sat. fat), **CHOL** 30 mg, **SODIUM** 530 mg, **CARB** 34 g (6 g fiber, 11 g sugars), **PRO** 20 g

# Burrito Bowls

**31g**
**CARB**

**SERVES** 6
**HANDS ON** 35 min.
**TOTAL** 1 hr.

- 4 cups cauliflower florets
- 3 Tbsp. canola oil
- ½ tsp. salt
- 1 lb. lean boneless pork loin or skinless, boneless chicken breast halves, cut into thin bite-size strips
- 1 Tbsp. reduced-sodium taco seasoning mix
  Nonstick cooking spray
- 1 medium poblano pepper, cut into thin bite-size strips (tip, *p. 250*)
- 2 cups frozen whole kernel corn, thawed
- 1 cup canned reduced-sodium black beans, rinsed and drained
- 1 lime
- 1 medium avocado, halved, seeded, and peeled
- 5 cups shredded romaine lettuce
- 1 cup refrigerated pico de gallo
- ¼ cup shredded reduced-fat Mexican-style four-cheese blend (1 oz.)
  Lime wedges and/or snipped fresh cilantro (optional)

**1.** Preheat oven to 425°F. Place cauliflower in a food processor. Cover and pulse several times until cauliflower is evenly chopped into rice-size pieces. (If necessary, process cauliflower in batches.) Transfer cauliflower to a foil-lined 15×10-inch baking pan. Drizzle with 1 Tbsp. of the oil and sprinkle with ¼ tsp. of the salt; toss to coat. Spread cauliflower in an even layer in the pan. Roast, uncovered, 25 minutes or until lightly charred, stirring once.

**2.** Meanwhile, in a bowl toss together pork strips, 2 tsp. of the taco seasoning, and the remaining ¼ tsp. salt. Coat a 12-inch nonstick skillet with cooking spray; heat over medium-high. Cook pork and poblano pepper in hot skillet 4 to 6 minutes or just until pork is slightly pink, stirring occasionally. Reduce heat to medium-low. Add corn and beans; cook 2 minutes or until heated through.

**3.** Remove ½ tsp. zest and squeeze 3 Tbsp. juice from lime. In a bowl mash together avocado and lime zest. In another bowl whisk together the remaining 2 Tbsp. oil, 1 tsp. taco seasoning, and the lime juice.

**4.** Divide lettuce among six bowls. Top with cauliflower and pork mixture. Spoon avocado mixture into centers of bowls. Top with pico de gallo and cheese. Drizzle with lime juice mixture. If desired, serve with lime wedges and/or cilantro.

**PER SERVING** *(1 bowl each)* **CAL** 334, **FAT** 15 g (2 g sat. fat), **CHOL** 45 mg, **SODIUM** 604 mg, **CARB** 31 g (7 g fiber, 6 g sugars), **PRO** 26 g

# Cuban Chicken and Black Bean Bowls

**40g**
**CARB**

**SERVES** 4
**HANDS ON** 30 min.
**TOTAL** 1 hr.

- 12 oz. skinless, boneless chicken thighs
- 2 tsp. lime zest
- ½ cup lime juice
- 2 tsp. salt-free fiesta lime or chipotle Southwest seasoning blend, such as Mrs. Dash
- 2 tsp. canola oil

¼ tsp. salt
1 15-oz. can reduced-sodium black beans, rinsed and drained
  Nonstick cooking spray
1⅓ cups cooked quinoa
1 recipe Mango Salsa
¼ cup snipped fresh cilantro
  Orange and/or lime wedges (optional)

**1.** Place chicken in a resealable plastic bag set in a shallow dish. For marinade, in a bowl whisk together the next five ingredients (through salt). Remove 2 Tbsp. marinade and add to beans; chill until needed. Add the remaining marinade to chicken; seal bag, turning to coat. Marinate chicken in the refrigerator 30 minutes to 1 hour, turning once halfway through.
**2.** Coat a 10-inch skillet with cooking spray. Heat skillet over medium-high. Drain chicken, discarding marinade. Cook chicken in hot skillet 12 to 15 minutes or until chicken is done (170°F), turning occasionally. Transfer chicken to a plate. Wipe skillet clean.
**3.** Cook beans in skillet over medium 3 to 4 minutes or until heated, stirring occasionally. Meanwhile, shred chicken using two forks.
**4.** Arrange quinoa, chicken, and beans in four bowls. Top with Mango Salsa and cilantro. If desired, serve with orange and/or lime wedges.

**Mango Salsa** In a bowl combine **1 cup chopped fresh peeled mango, ½ cup chopped red sweet pepper, 3 Tbsp. each snipped fresh cilantro and finely chopped red onion**, and **1 Tbsp. lime juice**.

**PER SERVING** *(1 bowl each)* **CAL** 319, **FAT** 7 g (1 g sat. fat), **CHOL** 80 mg, **SODIUM** 338 mg, **CARB** 40 g (8 g fiber, 8 g sugars), **PRO** 25 g

# Shrimp and Rice Bowls

**38g** **CARB**

**SERVES** 4
**HANDS ON** 30 min.
**TOTAL** 50 min.

- 1¼ cups water
- ¼ tsp. salt
- ⅔ cup uncooked long grain brown rice
- 12 oz. frozen large shrimp in shells, thawed
- ½ tsp. ground coriander
- ¼ tsp. ground ginger
- ¼ tsp. black pepper
- ⅛ tsp. ground nutmeg
- 1 Tbsp. canola oil
- 4 cups coarsely shredded napa cabbage
- ½ cup slivered onion
- ½ cup fresh or frozen edamame
- 1 recipe Peanut Sauce
  Lime wedges, chopped peanuts, and/or crushed red pepper (optional)

**1.** In a small saucepan bring the water and salt to boiling. Stir in rice; reduce heat. Simmer, covered, about 40 minutes or until rice is tender and water is absorbed. Remove from heat. Let stand, covered, 5 minutes.

**2.** Meanwhile, peel and devein shrimp. Rinse shrimp; pat dry. In a bowl sprinkle shrimp with coriander, ginger, pepper, and nutmeg; toss to coat.

**3.** In an extra-large wok or 12-inch nonstick skillet heat oil over medium-high. Add shrimp; cook and stir 3 to 4 minutes or until opaque. Remove shrimp; keep warm. Add cabbage and onion to wok. Cook 3 to 5 minutes or until crisp-tender, stirring frequently.

**4.** Divide cabbage mixture among bowls. Top with rice, edamame, and shrimp. Drizzle with warm Peanut Sauce and, if desired, garnish with lime wedges, chopped peanuts, and/or crushed red pepper.

**Peanut Sauce** In a small saucepan combine ¼ **cup creamy peanut butter, 3 Tbsp. water, 1 Tbsp. honey, 2 tsp. reduced-sodium soy sauce, and ⅛ to ¼ tsp. crushed red pepper**. Cook and stir over medium-low 2 to 3 minutes or until heated. Cool slightly. If needed, stir in additional water to reach desired consistency. Serve warm.

**Tip** If using frozen edamame, add it to the simmering rice the last 5 minutes.

**PER SERVING** *(1 bowl each)* **CAL** 365, **FAT** 14 g
(2 g sat. fat), **CHOL** 119 mg, **SODIUM** 404 mg, **CARB** 38 g
(4 g fiber, 9 g sugars), **PRO** 24 g

# Korean Ahi Poke Bowl

**29g**
CARB

**SERVES** 4
**HANDS ON** 15 min.
**TOTAL** 55 min.

- ½ cup thin carrot strips
- 2 Tbsp. cider vinegar
- ¼ tsp. kosher salt
- 2 Tbsp. reduced-sodium soy sauce
- 2 Tbsp. toasted sesame oil
- 1 to 2 Tbsp. gochujang (Korean hot chile paste)
- 1 lb. sashimi-grade fresh ahi tuna, cut into ½-inch pieces
- 1 cup ½-inch pieces seedless cucumber
- ½ cup thinly sliced green onions
- ¼ cup chopped white onion
- 1 Tbsp. dried hijiki seaweed, soaked according to package directions and drained (optional)
- 1½ cups water
- 1 cup uncooked short grain brown rice
- 1 cup kimchi
- 1 Tbsp. sesame seeds, toasted

**1.** For pickled carrots, in a small bowl combine carrot strips, vinegar, and salt. In a medium bowl combine soy sauce, sesame oil, and gochujang. Add tuna, cucumber, ¼ cup of the green onions, the white onion, and, if desired, seaweed; stir gently to coat. If desired, cover and marinate in refrigerator 30 minutes or up to 2 hours.

**2.** Meanwhile, in a medium saucepan bring the water to boiling. Stir in rice; reduce heat. Simmer, covered, 30 minutes or until rice is tender and water is absorbed. Let stand, covered, 10 minutes.

**3.** Divide rice among bowls. Drain pickled carrots. Top rice with pickled carrots, tuna mixture, remaining ¼ cup green onions, the kimchi, and sesame seeds.

**PER SERVING** *(1 bowl each)* **CAL** 323, **FAT** 9 g (1 g sat. fat), **CHOL** 44 mg, **SODIUM** 827 mg, **CARB** 29 g (4 g fiber, 7 g sugars), **PRO** 31 g

# salad meals

Eat your greens! Adding main-dish salads to your meal plan each week makes it easy to get what you need.

## Chicken, Spinach, and Pasta Salad

**39g** CARB

SERVES 4
TOTAL 30 min.

- 2 cups dried cavatappi or penne pasta (6 oz.)
  Nonstick cooking spray
- 8 oz. skinless, boneless chicken breast halves, cut into 1-inch pieces
- 1 cup sliced fresh mushrooms
- ¼ cup chopped onion
- 1 clove garlic, minced
- 3 Tbsp. olive oil
- 3 Tbsp. balsamic vinegar
- 3 Tbsp. snipped fresh basil or 2 tsp. dried basil, crushed
- ¼ tsp. salt
- ⅛ tsp. black pepper
- 1 6-oz. pkg. fresh baby spinach or spinach
- 1 cup seeded and chopped roma tomatoes
- ½ cup shredded Parmesan cheese (2 oz.)

**1.** Cook pasta according to package directions; drain. Rinse with cold water; drain again. Meanwhile, coat a 10-inch nonstick skillet with cooking spray; heat over medium. Add chicken, mushrooms, onion, and garlic; cook 8 to 10 minutes or until chicken is no longer pink and vegetables are tender, stirring occasionally. Cool slightly.

**2.** In an extra-large bowl combine cooked pasta and chicken mixture. For vinaigrette, in a screw-top jar combine oil, vinegar, basil, salt, and pepper. Cover and shake well.

**3.** Pour vinaigrette over pasta mixture; toss to coat. Add spinach, tomatoes, and Parmesan cheese; toss to combine.

**PER SERVING** (2½ cups each) **CAL** 398, **FAT** 15 g (4 g sat. fat), **CHOL** 49 mg, **SODIUM** 383 mg, **CARB** 39 g (3 g fiber, 5 g sugars), **PRO** 25 g

# Lemon-Lime Chicken, Kale, and Mango Salad

**22g**
CARB

**SERVES** 4
**HANDS ON** 20 min.
**TOTAL** 30 min.

**TRY THIS**
If you can't find
5-oz. breast halves,
buy two larger halves
and cut them in half
horizontally for
four portions.

- 1   lemon
- 4   5-oz. skinless, boneless chicken breast halves
- 3   Tbsp. lime juice
- ¼   tsp. kosher salt
- ¼   tsp. crushed red pepper
- ¼   tsp. black pepper
- 4   cups coarsely chopped fresh kale leaves
- 1½   tsp. canola oil
- 1   ripe mango
- 1   tsp. minced fresh ginger
- ¼   tsp. kosher salt
- ⅛   tsp. black pepper
- 1   cup fresh blueberries
- ¼   cup hazelnuts, toasted (tip, *p. 102*) and coarsely chopped

**1.** Remove ½ tsp. zest and squeeze 6 Tbsp. juice from lemon. Place chicken in a resealable plastic bag set in a shallow dish. For marinade, in a bowl combine 3 Tbsp. of the lemon juice, the lime juice, ¼ tsp. salt, the crushed red pepper, and the ¼ tsp. black pepper. Pour marinade over chicken. Seal bag; turn to coat chicken. Marinate in the refrigerator 15 minutes.

**2.** Meanwhile, place kale in an extra-large bowl. Drizzle with oil. Using clean hands, massage oil into kale until leaves are lightly wilted and glossy.

**3.** Halve, seed, peel, and chop mango, reserving the juice. For dressing, in a bowl combine the reserved mango juice, lemon zest, the remaining 3 Tbsp. lemon juice, the ginger, ¼ tsp. salt, and the ⅛ tsp. black pepper.

**4.** Drain chicken, discarding marinade. Heat a grill pan over medium-high. Add chicken. Cook 8 to 10 minutes or until done (165°F), turning once. If chicken browns too quickly, reduce heat to medium. Slice chicken.

**5.** Add mango, blueberries, and hazelnuts to kale in bowl. Drizzle with dressing; toss gently to coat. Top kale mixture with sliced chicken.

**PER SERVING** *(1 chicken breast half + 1½ cups kale mixture each)* **CAL** 311, **FAT** 11 g (1 g sat. fat), **CHOL** 91 mg, **SODIUM** 355 mg, **CARB** 22 g (4 g fiber, 13 g sugars), **PRO** 35 g

# Country-Style Wedge Salad with Turkey

**8g** CARB | **SERVES** 4
**TOTAL** 25 min.

- 1 large head Bibb or butterhead lettuce, quartered
- 1 recipe Buttermilk-Avocado Dressing
- 2 cups shredded cooked turkey breast
- 1 cup halved grape or cherry tomatoes
- 2 hard-cooked eggs, chopped
- 4 slices lower-sodium, less-fat bacon, crisp-cooked and crumbled
- ¼ cup finely chopped red onion
  Cracked black pepper

**1.** Arrange one lettuce quarter on each plate. Drizzle half of the dressing over wedges. Top with turkey, tomatoes, and eggs. Drizzle with the remaining dressing. Sprinkle with bacon, onion, and pepper.

**Buttermilk-Avocado Dressing** In a blender combine ¾ cup buttermilk; half of an avocado, peeled and seeded; 1 Tbsp. snipped fresh Italian parsley; ¼ tsp. each onion powder, salt, dry mustard, and black pepper; and 1 clove garlic, minced. Cover and blend until smooth.

**PER SERVING** (1 wedge salad + ¼ cup dressing each) **CAL** 228, **FAT** 9 g (2 g sat. fat), **CHOL** 149 mg, **SODIUM** 381 mg, **CARB** 8 g (2 g fiber, 5 g sugars), **PRO** 29 g

# Chicken-Broccoli Salad with Buttermilk Dressing

**29g** CARB | **SERVES** 4
**HANDS ON** 20 min.
**TOTAL** 2 hr. 20 min.

- 3 cups packaged shredded broccoli slaw mix
- 2 cups coarsely chopped cooked chicken breast
- ½ cup dried cherries
- ⅓ cup thinly sliced celery
- ¼ cup finely chopped red onion
- ⅓ cup buttermilk
- ⅓ cup light mayonnaise
- 1 Tbsp. honey
- 1 Tbsp. cider vinegar
- 1 tsp. dry mustard
- ½ tsp. salt
- ⅛ tsp. black pepper
- 4 cups fresh baby spinach

**1.** In a large bowl combine the first five ingredients (through onion). In a small bowl whisk together the next seven ingredients (through pepper). Pour buttermilk mixture over broccoli mixture; toss gently to combine. Cover and chill at least 2 hours or up to 24 hours before serving.
**2.** Just before serving, add baby spinach and toss gently to combine.

**PER SERVING** (2 cups each) **CAL** 278, **FAT** 7 g (2 g sat. fat), **CHOL** 64 mg, **SODIUM** 585 mg, **CARB** 29 g (4 g fiber, 19 g sugars), **PRO** 26 g

GOOD FOR YOU
Using homemade salad dressing is a wholesome way to eat—you avoid additives like preservatives, colorings, and added sugars.

# Massaged Kale and Pork Salad

**47g**
**CARB**

**SERVES** 4
**TOTAL** 25 min.

6 cups torn fresh kale leaves
1 recipe Honey-Grapefruit Vinaigrette
1 15-oz. can cannellini (white kidney) beans, rinsed and drained
1 grapefruit, peeled and sectioned
1 avocado, peeled, seeded, and chopped
½ cup sliced radishes
1 1-lb. natural pork tenderloin, trimmed and cut crosswise into ¼-inch-thick slices
¼ tsp. salt
¼ tsp. black pepper
   Nonstick cooking spray

**1.** Place kale in a large bowl. Drizzle with Honey-Grapefruit Vinaigrette. Using clean hands, massage kale 3 to 4 minutes or until leaves are lightly wilted and glossy. Add the next four ingredients (through radishes); toss to combine.
**2.** Season pork with salt and pepper. Coat a 10-inch nonstick skillet with cooking spray. Heat over medium. Add pork and cook 3 to 4 minutes or until no longer pink, turning once. Serve over kale salad.

**Honey-Grapefruit Vinaigrette** In a screw-top jar combine ¼ **cup grapefruit juice**, 3 **Tbsp. honey**, 2 **Tbsp. olive oil**, 1 **Tbsp. snipped fresh mint**, and ¼ **tsp. each salt and black pepper**. Cover and shake well.

**Tip** To section grapefruit, use a paring knife to cut off a thin slice from both ends of grapefruit. Place a flat end on a cutting board and cut away the peel and white part of the rind, working from top to bottom. Holding grapefruit over a bowl, cut into center between one section and membrane. Cut along the other side of the section next to the membrane to free the section. If desired, use juice in bowl to make Honey-Grapefruit Vinaigrette.

**PER SERVING** (1½ cups each) **CAL** 456, **FAT** 16 g (3 g sat. fat), **CHOL** 74 mg, **SODIUM** 624 mg, **CARB** 47 g (12 g fiber, 21 g sugars), **PRO** 35 g

TRY THIS
Rubbing kale between your fingers helps break it down a little, making it softer in texture and more flavorful.

# Roasted Steak and Tomato Salad

**16g**
**CARB**

| | |
|---|---|
| **SERVES** 4 | |
| **HANDS ON** 20 min. | |
| **TOTAL** 40 min. | |

- 2 8-oz. beef shoulder petite tenders or two 8-oz. beef tenderloin steaks, trimmed
- 1 tsp. cracked black pepper
- ¼ tsp. kosher salt
- 6 small tomatoes, halved, or 3 tomatoes, quartered
- 2 tsp. olive oil
- ¼ cup finely shredded Parmesan cheese
- ½ tsp. dried oregano, crushed
- 8 cups torn romaine lettuce
- 1 14-oz. can artichoke hearts, drained and quartered
- ⅓ cup red onion slivers
- 3 Tbsp. balsamic vinegar
- 1 Tbsp. olive oil

**1.** Preheat oven to 400°F. Sprinkle meat with pepper and salt, pressing gently to adhere. Let stand at room temperature 20 minutes.

**2.** Arrange tomato halves, cut sides down, on half of a large rimmed baking sheet. In a 10-inch skillet heat the 2 tsp. oil over medium-high. Add meat; cook about 8 minutes or until well browned on all sides. Transfer meat to other side of baking sheet.

**3.** Roast 8 to 10 minutes for medium (145°F). Remove meat from oven. Cover with foil and let stand. Move oven rack for broiling.

**4.** Turn oven to broil. Turn tomatoes cut sides up. Combine Parmesan and oregano; sprinkle over tomatoes. Broil 4 to 5 inches from heat about 2 minutes or until cheese is melted and golden.

**5.** In a bowl combine lettuce, artichoke hearts, and onion. Drizzle with vinegar and the 1 Tbsp. oil; toss to coat. Arrange on plates. Slice steak and arrange over lettuce with tomato halves.

**Tip** Beef shoulder petite tenders are lean and flavorful cuts that are a better value than beef tenderloin. They can be hard to find, so ask for them at the meat counter

**PER SERVING** (2 cups salad + 3 oz. beef + 3 tomato pieces each) **CAL** 299, **FAT** 14 g (4 g sat. fat), **CHOL** 69 mg, **SODIUM** 416 mg, **CARB** 16 g (5 g fiber, 8 g sugars), **PRO** 29 g

# Fresh Taco Salad

**29g** | **SERVES** 6
**CARB** | **TOTAL** 30 min.

- 4 cups mixed salad greens
- 1 15-oz. can black beans, rinsed and drained
- 2 ears corn, husks and silks removed and kernels cut off the cobs
- ¾ cup matchstick-size pieces peeled jicama
- ½ cup chopped tomato
- 1 medium avocado, halved, seeded, peeled, and sliced
- 1 fresh jalapeño chile pepper, stemmed, seeded, and thinly sliced (tip, *p. 250*)
- 2 cups multigrain tortilla chips with flaxseeds
- ½ cup refrigerated fresh salsa
- ½ cup crumbled queso fresco (2 oz.)
- 1 recipe Cilantro Ranch Dressing

**1.** Line a large platter with salad greens. In a medium bowl combine the next four ingredients (through tomato). Spoon over greens. Arrange avocado and chile pepper slices over top. Top with chips, salsa, and cheese. Drizzle with Cilantro Ranch Dressing.

**Cilantro Ranch Dressing** In a bowl whisk together ⅓ cup light sour cream; ¼ cup buttermilk; 2 Tbsp. snipped fresh cilantro; 1 Tbsp. each snipped fresh chives and lime juice; 2 cloves garlic, minced; and 1 tsp. chili powder.

**PER SERVING** *(2¼ cups each)* **CAL** 214, **FAT** 9 g (3 g sat. fat), **CHOL** 11 mg, **SODIUM** 447 mg, **CARB** 29 g (8 g fiber, 4 g sugars), **PRO** 10 g

TRY THIS
If fresh corn isn't in season, use 1 cup frozen whole kernel corn, thawed.

# Shrimp and Edamame Salad with Ginger Dressing

**25g** CARB | **SERVES** 4
**TOTAL** 45 min.

- 6 oz. fresh or frozen peeled, cooked medium shrimp, halved lengthwise
- ½ cup frozen edamame
- 1 cup dried radiatore or rotini pasta (2 oz.)
- 3 cups shredded napa cabbage
- 2 cups shredded romaine lettuce
- 1 cup halved fresh strawberries
- ¾ cup packaged fresh julienned carrots
- ¾ cup fresh snow pea pods, trimmed, strings removed, and halved
- 1 small yellow sweet pepper, cut into thin bite-size strips
- ¼ cup thinly sliced green onions
- 3 Tbsp. rice vinegar or cider vinegar
- 2 Tbsp. reduced-sodium soy sauce
- 1 Tbsp. canola oil
- 4 cloves garlic, minced
- 2 tsp. grated fresh ginger
- 1 tsp. toasted sesame oil
- ⅛ tsp. crushed red pepper

1. Thaw shrimp, if frozen. Cook edamame according to package directions; drain. Cook pasta according to package directions; drain. Rinse with cold water; drain again.
2. In an extra-large bowl combine edamame, shrimp, pasta, and the next seven ingredients (through green onions). Toss to combine.
3. For dressing, in a screw-top jar combine the remaining ingredients. Cover and shake well. Drizzle dressing over salad. Toss gently to coat.

**PER SERVING** (2 cups each) **CAL** 224, **FAT** 6 g (1 g sat. fat), **CHOL** 80 mg, **SODIUM** 351 mg, **CARB** 25 g (5 g fiber, 8 g sugars), **PRO** 17 g

GOOD FOR YOU
Get your pasta fix by using noodles as an accent in this veggie-loaded salad rather than as its foundation.

# 🍲 Warm Eggplant and Kale Panzanella

**34g** CARB | **SERVES** 6
**HANDS ON** 25 min.
**SLOW COOK** 4 hr. 15 min.

- 4 cups chopped eggplant
- 1 14.5-oz. can diced fire-roasted tomatoes with garlic, undrained
- ¾ cup coarsely chopped yellow sweet pepper
- 1 medium red onion, halved and cut into thin wedges
- 4 cups coarsely chopped fresh kale leaves
- 3 Tbsp. red wine vinegar
- 2 Tbsp. olive oil
- 1 tsp. Dijon-style mustard
- ½ tsp. black pepper
- 1 clove garlic, minced

½ cup fresh basil leaves, cut into strips

4 cups cubed whole wheat or multigrain baguette-style French bread, toasted

½ cup finely shredded Parmesan cheese (2 oz.)

**1.** In a 3½- or 4-qt. slow cooker combine the first four ingredients (through red onion). Cover and cook on low 4 hours or on high 2 hours.

**2.** If slow cooker is on low, turn to high. Stir in kale. Cover and cook 15 minutes more.

**3.** Meanwhile, for dressing, in a small bowl whisk together the next five ingredients (through garlic).

**4.** Using a slotted spoon, transfer vegetable mixture to a large bowl. Add dressing and basil; toss gently to coat. Add toasted bread cubes; toss gently to combine. Transfer salad to a serving platter. Sprinkle with cheese. Serve immediately.

**Tip** To toast bread cubes, spread them in a 15×10-inch baking pan. Bake in a 350°F oven 10 minutes or until golden, stirring once.

**PER SERVING** *(1⅔ cups each)* **CAL** 243, **FAT** 9 g (2 g sat. fat), **CHOL** 5 mg, **SODIUM** 421 mg, **CARB** 34 g (7 g fiber, 8 g sugars), **PRO** 9 g

# soups & stews

Mealtime is easy with these satisfying, veggie-filled, nutrient-loaded bowls. Grab your spoon!

## Spring Chicken-Veggie Stew

**18g**
**CARB**

| | |
|---|---|
| **SERVES** | 6 |
| **HANDS ON** | 30 min. |
| **TOTAL** | 1 hr. 5 min. |

- 4 large bone-in chicken thighs (about 1¼ lb. total), skinned
- 2 tsp. salt-free garlic-and-herb seasoning blend
- 1 Tbsp. olive oil
- 2 medium shallots, thinly sliced
- 6 cups unsalted chicken broth or stock
- 3 medium parsnips, peeled and cut into ½-inch chunks
- 8 oz. new potatoes (2-inch diameter), scrubbed and quartered
- 3 cloves garlic, minced
- ¾ tsp. salt
- 1 cup 1-inch pieces trimmed fresh green beans
- ½ cup fresh or frozen peas
- 2 cups fresh stemmed arugula, torn escarole, or baby spinach
- 2 Tbsp. lemon juice
  Shaved Parmesan cheese and/or cracked black pepper (optional)

**1.** Sprinkle chicken evenly with seasoning blend and rub in with your fingers. In a large saucepan heat oil over medium. Add seasoned chicken and shallots. Cook 6 to 8 minutes or until chicken is well browned on both sides, turning chicken once and stirring shallots occasionally.

**2.** Add broth, parsnips, potatoes, garlic, and salt. Bring to boiling; reduce heat. Simmer, covered, 12 to 15 minutes or until chicken is done (175°F) and parsnips and potatoes are just tender. Transfer chicken to a cutting board; let cool slightly. Using a slotted spoon, remove about one-third of the vegetables from the pan. Remove chicken from bones; discard bones. Shred chicken using two forks.

**3.** Transfer soup from pan to a blender or food processor. Cover; blend or process until smooth. Return soup to pan. Stir in green beans and fresh peas (if using). Bring to boiling; reduce heat. Simmer, covered, 4 to 6 minutes or until beans and peas are crisp-tender. Stir in shredded chicken, reserved parsnips and potatoes, and the frozen peas (if using). Heat through. Remove from heat. Stir in arugula and lemon juice. If desired, top each serving with Parmesan cheese and/or pepper.

**Tip** If you have an immersion blender, use it to blend the soup in the pan rather transferring to a blender or food processor.

**PER SERVING** (1¾ cups each) **CAL** 162, **FAT** 4 g (1 g sat. fat), **CHOL** 33 mg, **SODIUM** 378 mg, **CARB** 18 g (4 g fiber, 4 g sugars), **PRO** 13 g

# Chicken Pot Pie Stew

**30g** CARB

**SERVES** 6
**HANDS ON** 25 min.
**TOTAL** 55 min.

**TRY THIS**
Substitute dried herbs for fresh. Use ½ tsp. thyme and ¼ tsp. oregano. Crush them lightly and add with the broth.

- 4 tsp. canola oil
- 1 lb. skinless, boneless chicken thighs, cut into ¾-inch pieces
- 1 cup chopped celery
- 1 cup chopped carrots
- ½ cup chopped onion
- 2 cloves garlic, minced
- 2½ cups reduced-sodium chicken broth
- 2 cups fresh mushrooms, sliced
- 1 cup fresh sweet corn kernels or frozen whole kernel corn, thawed
- ½ cup frozen peas, thawed
- 1 12-oz. can evaporated fat-free milk
- ¼ cup all-purpose flour
- 1 tsp. snipped fresh thyme
- ½ tsp. snipped fresh oregano
- ¼ tsp. salt
- ¼ tsp. black pepper
- 1 recipe Piecrust Leaves (use about ¼ of the recipe)

**1.** In a 4- to 5-qt. nonstick Dutch oven heat 2 tsp. of the oil over medium. Add chicken. Cook and stir 4 to 5 minutes or until chicken pieces are browned on all sides. Transfer chicken to a bowl.

**2.** In the same Dutch oven heat the remaining 2 tsp. oil over medium heat. Add celery, carrots, onion, and garlic. Cook and stir 8 to 10 minutes or until vegetables are just tender.

**3.** Add chicken broth to pot; bring to boiling. Add chicken, mushrooms, corn, and peas. Return to boiling; reduce heat. Simmer, uncovered, about 8 minutes or until chicken is done and vegetables are just tender.

**4.** In a small bowl whisk together evaporated milk and flour. Add flour mixture to soup mixture. Cook and stir until mixture thickens and bubbles. Cook and stir 2 minutes more to thicken soup mixture. Stir in fresh thyme, fresh oregano, salt, and pepper. Top each serving with about three Piecrust Leaves.

**Piecrust Leaves** Preheat oven to 400°F. Let half of a 15-oz. pkg. rolled refrigerated unbaked piecrust (1 crust) stand according to package directions. Unroll piecrust onto a lightly floured surface. In a bowl whisk together **1 Tbsp. refrigerated or frozen egg product, thawed,** and **¼ tsp. water.** Lightly brush mixture over piecrust. Sprinkle piecrust with **1 tsp. chopped fresh thyme leaves.** Using a 1- to 1¼-inch floured cutter, cut piecrust into leaves or desired shapes. Place piecrust shapes on a baking sheet. Bake 6 to 8 minutes or until golden brown. Cool completely on baking sheet. To store, place extra leaves in an airtight container and freeze up to 1 month. Use as soup or salad toppers. Makes about 70 leaves.

**PER SERVING** *(1⅛ cups stew + about 3 Piecrust Leaves each)* **CAL** 295, **FAT** 9 g (2 g sat. fat), **CHOL** 72 mg, **SODIUM** 557 mg, **CARB** 30 g (3 g fiber, 12 g sugars), **PRO** 24 g

Pho (pronounced fuh), a Vietnamese staple, is all about the broth. Long simmering in a slow cooker develops its rich, complex flavor.

## 🍲 Chicken Pho

**27g**
**CARB**

**SERVES** 6
**HANDS ON** 25 min.
**SLOW COOK** 7 hr. 10 min.

- 6 oz. fresh shiitake mushrooms
- 1 3-inch piece fresh ginger, peeled and sliced
- 1 Tbsp. coriander seeds
- 4 whole cloves
- 2 lb. bone-in chicken thighs, skin removed
- 4 cups water
- 1 32-oz. carton unsalted chicken stock
- 1 large onion, sliced
- 1 oz. dried porcini mushrooms, rinsed, drained, and broken
- 1 Tbsp. packed brown sugar*
- 5 cloves garlic, sliced
- 1 tsp. salt
- 4 oz. dried rice noodles, soaked Julienned carrots, slivered red onion, thinly sliced fresh jalapeño chile peppers (tip, *p. 250*), fresh cilantro, Thai basil, mint leaves, sriracha sauce, and/or lime wedges (optional)

**1.** Remove and reserve stems from shiitake mushrooms. Thinly slice caps and chill until needed. Place shiitake stems, ginger, coriander seeds, and cloves on a double-thick 8-inch square of 100%-cotton cheesecloth. Bring up corners; tie closed with 100%-cotton kitchen string.
**2.** In a 5- to 6-qt. slow cooker combine spice bag and the next eight ingredients (through salt). Cover and cook on low 7 to 8 hours or high 3½ to 4 hours. Remove and discard spice bag.

**3.** Remove chicken from cooker. Remove meat from bones; discard bones. Coarsely shred chicken using two forks; cover and keep warm. Stir the reserved shiitake caps and the noodles into broth mixture. Cover and cook 10 minutes more.

**4.** Ladle noodle mixture into shallow bowls. Add shredded chicken and desired toppers.

**Tip** To soak rice noodles, in a large bowl combine noodles and enough boiling water to cover. Let stand 3 to 7 minutes or until noodles are tender but still firm (al dente), stirring occasionally.

**PER SERVING** *(1¾ cups each)* **CAL** 246, **FAT** 4 g (1 g sat. fat), **CHOL** 85 mg, **SODIUM** 623 mg, **CARB** 27 g (3 g fiber, 7 g sugars), **PRO** 24 g

**\*Sugar Sub** Choose Splenda Brown Sugar Blend. Follow package directions to use 1 Tbsp. equivalent.
**PER SERVING WITH SUB** Same as above, except **CAL** 243, **CARB** 26 g (5 g sugars)

---

## 🥘 Chipotle BBQ Beef Meatball Chili

**36g**
**CARB**

SERVES 8
HANDS ON 30 min.
SLOW COOK 6 hr.

- 2  14.5-oz. cans no-salt-added fire-roasted diced tomatoes
- 1  15-oz. can hominy, rinsed and drained
- 1  15-oz. can no-salt-added red beans or kidney beans, rinsed and drained
- 1½  cups water
- 1  6-oz. can no-salt-added tomato paste
- 1  cup frozen sweet corn kernels
- ½  cup chopped red or green sweet pepper
- ½  cup finely chopped red onion
- ¼  cup barbecue sauce
- 1  Tbsp. chili powder
- ½  tsp. salt
- 1  recipe BBQ Meatballs Chopped fresh cilantro

**1.** In a 4- to 6-qt. slow cooker combine the first 11 ingredients (through salt). Stir until well combined. Add partially cooked BBQ Meatballs. Stir gently to combine.

**2.** Cover and cook on low 6 to 7 hours or high 3 to 3½ hours. Top each serving with cilantro.

**BBQ Meatballs** Preheat broiler. Line a 15×10-inch baking pan with foil.

In a large bowl lightly beat **1 egg.** Whisk in **1 Tbsp. barbecue sauce, 1½ tsp. coarse-ground mustard,** and **¼ tsp. ground chipotle pepper or chili powder.** Stir in **½ cup finely chopped red onion** and **⅓ cup cornmeal.** Add **1½ lb. 90% lean ground beef;** mix well. Shape meat mixture into 1-inch balls. Place meatballs 1 inch apart in the prepared pan. Broil meatballs (in batches if necessary) 6 inches from heat about 7 minutes or until lightly browned (meatballs will not be cooked through).

**PER SERVING** *(1½ cups each)* **CAL** 327, **FAT** 9 g (3 g sat. fat), **CHOL** 78 mg, **SODIUM** 503 mg, **CARB** 36 g (8 g fiber, 11 g sugars), **PRO** 24 g

### GOOD FOR YOU
Canned foods, such as tomatoes and beans, are convenient but generally high in sodium. Low-sodium products help you stay in control of the sodium content in meals.

# Spicy Chicken-Coconut Noodle Soup

**16g** **CARB**

**SERVES** 6
**HANDS ON** 20 min.
**TOTAL** 40 min.

1 cup stemmed shiitake mushrooms or button mushrooms, thinly sliced
1 red sweet pepper, cut into thin bite-size strips (1 cup)
1 medium shallot, thinly sliced
4 tsp. toasted sesame oil

2 6- to 8-oz. skinless, boneless chicken breast halves
6 cups unsalted chicken broth or stock
1 stalk celery, thinly sliced (½ cup)
3 Tbsp. reduced-sodium soy sauce
½ tsp. crushed red pepper
2 cups dried wide egg noodles
2 medium carrots, thinly sliced
1 cup canned unsweetened light coconut milk
½ cup chopped fresh cilantro
¼ cup unsweetened large flaked coconut, toasted (optional)
Sriracha sauce (optional)

**1.** In a 4-qt. saucepan cook mushrooms, sweet pepper, and shallot in 2 tsp. of the oil over medium 5 to 7 minutes or until vegetables are tender, stirring occasionally. Remove vegetables from saucepan.

**2.** Add the remaining 2 tsp. oil to the saucepan. Add chicken. Cook over medium 6 to 8 minutes or until browned, turning once. Add the next four ingredients (through crushed red pepper). Bring to boiling; reduce heat. Simmer, covered, 5 minutes. Stir in egg noodles and carrots. Return to boiling; reduce heat. Simmer, covered, 5 to 7 minutes more or until noodles are tender and chicken is no longer pink, stirring occasionally.

**3.** Transfer chicken to a cutting board. Cut chicken into cubes or shred chicken using two forks. Return chicken to soup. Stir in mushroom mixture and coconut milk. Cook and stir over medium 1 to 2 minutes or just until heated. Stir in half of the cilantro.

**4.** Sprinkle individual servings with remaining cilantro and, if desired, toasted coconut. If desired, serve with sriracha.

**Tip** Be sure to use the coconut milk that comes in a can in the Asian section of the supermarket. Refrigerated coconut beverage will not produce as creamy a soup.

**PER SERVING** (1½ cups each) **CAL** 221, **FAT** 8 g (3 g sat. fat), **CHOL** 52 mg, **SODIUM** 433 mg, **CARB** 16 g (2 g fiber, 4 g sugars), **PRO** 20 g

# Beef Goulash Soup

**16g CARB**

**SERVES** 4
**HANDS ON** 30 min.
**TOTAL** 50 min.

- 6 oz. boneless beef top sirloin steak
- 1 tsp. olive oil
- ½ cup chopped onion
- 2 cups water
- 1 14.5-oz. can beef broth
- 1 14.5-oz. can no-salt-added diced tomatoes, undrained
- ½ cup thinly sliced carrot
- 1 tsp. unsweetened cocoa powder
- 1 clove garlic, minced
- 1 cup thinly sliced cabbage
- ½ cup dried wide noodles (1 oz.)
- 2 tsp. paprika
- ¼ cup light sour cream
  Snipped fresh parsley (optional)

**1.** Trim fat from meat. Cut meat into ½-inch cubes. In a large saucepan cook and stir meat in hot oil over medium-high about 6 minutes or until browned. Add onion; cook and stir 3 minutes more or until onion softens.

**2.** Stir in the the next six ingredients (through garlic). Bring to boiling; reduce heat. Simmer, uncovered, about 15 minutes or until meat is tender.

**3.** Stir in the cabbage, noodles, and paprika. Simmer, uncovered, 5 to 7 minutes more or until noodles are tender but still firm. Remove from heat. Top each serving with some of the sour cream. If desired, sprinkle with parsley and additional paprika.

**PER SERVING** *(1½ cups each)* **CAL** 188, **FAT** 7 g (3 g sat. fat), **CHOL** 36 mg, **SODIUM** 397 mg, **CARB** 16 g (3 g fiber, 6 g sugars), **PRO** 14 g

# French Lentil and Salmon Soup

**35g** **CARB**

| | |
|---|---|
| **SERVES** 6 | |
| **HANDS ON** 20 min. | |
| **TOTAL** 50 min. | |

- 12 oz. fresh or frozen skinless salmon
- 1 medium fennel bulb
- 6 cups unsalted vegetable broth or stock
- 4 medium carrots, cut into 1-inch pieces
- 1 cup dried French green lentils, rinsed and drained
- 4 cloves garlic, minced
- 1 bay leaf
- ¼ tsp. salt
- ¼ tsp. black pepper
- 2 Tbsp. snipped fresh dill or 1½ tsp. dried dill
- 3 cups spinach
- 3 Tbsp. lemon juice
- ¼ cup light sour cream (optional)

**1.** Thaw fish, if frozen. Coarsely snip 2 Tbsp. of the fennel fronds. Set aside for garnish. Cut off and discard upper stalks of fennel bulb. Remove any wilted outer layers; cut off and discard a thin slice from base of fennel. Halve, core, and chop remaining fennel.

**2.** In a large saucepan combine chopped fennel and the next seven ingredients (through pepper). Bring to boiling; reduce heat. Simmer, covered, about 25 minutes or until lentils are just tender, stirring occasionally.

**3.** Meanwhile, rinse salmon with cold water; pat dry with paper towels. Cut salmon into 1-inch pieces. Add salmon and dried dill weed (if using) to soup when lentils are tender. Return to boiling; reduce heat. Simmer, uncovered, 4 to 5 minutes or just until fish flakes easily. Remove from heat. Remove and discard bay leaf.

**4.** Add fresh dill (if using), spinach, and lemon juice to soup. If desired, top each serving with sour cream. Top with reserved fennel fronds and additional pepper.

**Tip** French lentils are small, round, and dark. They cook faster and hold their shape better than their brown or yellow cousins, which shouldn't be used as substitutes. Look for them in the health food and bulk food sections of your supermarket.

**PER SERVING** *(1⅔ cups each)* **CAL** 254, **FAT** 4 g (1 g sat. fat), **CHOL** 31 mg, **SODIUM** 387 mg, **CARB** 35 g (6 g fiber, 8 g sugars), **PRO** 20 g

**DID YOU KNOW?** You can also use 2 cups purchased or leftover cooked brown rice. Reheat before using.

# Vegetarian Chili

**42g**
**CARB**

| SERVES | 6 |
| --- | --- |
| **HANDS ON** | 25 min. |
| **TOTAL** | 40 min. |

- 1  Tbsp. canola oil
- 2  medium sweet potatoes, peeled and cut into 1-inch pieces
- 1  medium red sweet pepper, seeded and cut into ½-inch pieces
- ½  cup coarsely chopped onion
- 1  fresh jalapeño chile pepper, chopped (tip, *p. 250*)
- 1  clove garlic, minced
- 1  Tbsp. chili powder
- 1  tsp. ground cumin
- ¼  tsp. cayenne pepper
- 3  cups vegetable broth
- 1  15-oz. can reduced-sodium black beans, rinsed and drained
- 1  14.5-oz. can no-salt-added diced tomatoes, undrained
- 1  cup frozen whole kernel corn
- ¼  cup snipped fresh cilantro
- ¼  cup lime juice
- 6  Tbsp. light sour cream

**1.** In a 4- to 5-qt. Dutch oven heat oil over medium-high. Add the next five ingredients (through garlic). Cook and stir 4 minutes. Stir in chili powder, cumin, and cayenne pepper; cook and stir 1 minute more.
**2.** Add broth, beans, tomatoes, and corn. Bring to boiling; reduce heat. Simmer, uncovered, about 15 minutes or until sweet potatoes are tender, stirring occasionally.
**3.** Stir in cilantro and lime juice. Top individual servings with sour cream.

**Tip** Jump-start supper by preparing this soup as directed through Step 2. Place cooled soup in an airtight container; cover. Refrigerate up to 2 days. Reheat and continue with Step 3.

**PER SERVING** *(1⅓ cups each)* **CAL** 229, **FAT** 4 g (1 g sat. fat), **CHOL** 4 mg, **SODIUM** 639 mg, **CARB** 42 g (8 g fiber, 10 g sugars), **PRO** 7 g

---

# Pumpkin Soup with Lentils

**30g**
**CARB**

| SERVES | 4 |
| --- | --- |
| **HANDS ON** | 15 min. |
| **TOTAL** | 40 min. |

- 1  small sweet onion, cut into wedges
- 1  yellow sweet pepper, seeded and sliced
- ½  cup dried yellow lentils or lentils, rinsed and well drained
- 1  Tbsp. olive oil
- 1  26-oz. carton chicken stock
- 1  15-oz. can pumpkin
- 2  tsp. grated fresh ginger
- 1  tsp. curry powder
- 1  tsp. ground cumin
- ¼  tsp. salt
- ¼  tsp. black pepper
   Freshly grated nutmeg (optional)
   Snipped fresh Italian parsley (optional)

**1.** In a 4- to 5-qt. Dutch oven cook onion, sweet pepper, and lentils in hot oil over medium-high 2 minutes. Whisk in the next five ingredients (through cumin). Bring to boiling; reduce heat. Simmer, covered, about 25 minutes or until lentils are tender, stirring occasionally. Stir in salt and black pepper.
**2.** If desired, top each serving with grated nutmeg and parsley.

**PER SERVING** *(1½ cups each)* **CAL** 190, **FAT** 4 g (1 g sat. fat), **CHOL** 0 mg, **SODIUM** 255 mg, **CARB** 30 g (7 g fiber, 7 g sugars), **PRO** 11g

## GOOD FOR YOU

Pumpkin is not just for pie. It is rich in vitamin A and contains high levels of potassium, which plays a key role in regulating blood pressure and can reduce the risk of stroke when consumed regularly.

## Charred Sweet Peppers Potato Chowder

**30g** **SERVES** 4
**CARB** **HANDS ON** 20 min.
**TOTAL** 40 min.

TRY THIS

Instead of bacon, sprinkle soup with a little shredded white or sharp cheddar cheese.

Nonstick cooking spray
3 cups chopped red sweet peppers
2 cups chopped yellow onions
1 large russet potato (10 oz.), peeled and chopped
½ cup vegetable broth
2 cups milk
⅛ tsp. cayenne pepper (optional)
1 Tbsp. butter
¼ cup chopped fresh parsley
¼ tsp. salt
¼ tsp. black pepper
¼ cup plain Greek yogurt (optional)
Crumbled lower-fat, less-sodium bacon (optional)

**1.** Coat a 4-qt. Dutch oven with cooking spray. Heat pan over medium-high. Add the peppers; coat with cooking spray. Cook, uncovered, about 15 minutes or until charred, stirring frequently.

**2.** Add onions; cook 5 to 6 minutes more or until soft and golden brown, stirring occasionally. Stir in potato and broth. Bring to boiling; reduce heat. Simmer, covered, about 12 minutes or until potatoes is very tender.

**3.** Coarsely mash vegetables with a potato masher. Add the milk and, if desired, cayenne pepper. Heat through.

**4.** Remove from heat; stir in butter, parsley, salt, and black pepper. If desired, top servings with yogurt, bacon, and additional parsley.

**PER SERVING** (1¼ cups each) **CAL** 255,
**FAT** 11 g (6 g sat. fat), **CHOL** 32 mg, **SODIUM** 284 mg,
**CARB** 30 g (5 g fiber, 15 g sugars), **PRO** 11 g

# Hearty Italian Zoup

**18g**
**CARB**

**SERVES** 6

**TOTAL** 35 min.

1  medium zucchini, trimmed
1  Tbsp. olive oil
8  oz. uncooked turkey Italian sausage links,
   casings removed
½  cup chopped onion
1  cup coarsely shredded carrots
2  cloves garlic, minced
2  14.5-oz. cans reduced-sodium
   chicken broth
1  14.5-oz. can no-salt-added diced
   tomatoes, undrained
4  cups torn escarole or fresh baby spinach
1  15-oz. can no-salt-added cannellini (white
   kidney) beans, rinsed and drained
1  Tbsp. snipped fresh marjoram or oregano
¼  tsp. black pepper
1  Tbsp. red wine vinegar (optional)
¼  tsp. salt
   Finely shredded Asiago cheese (optional)

**1.** Using a spiralizer, cut zucchini into spaghetti-size noodles. If desired, cut into shorter lengths.

**2.** In a 4- to 6-qt. Dutch oven heat oil over medium. Add the next four ingredients (through garlic); cook 5 to 8 minutes or until sausage is browned and vegetables are tender, stirring occasionally. Add broth and tomatoes. Bring to boiling. Stir in zucchini noodles and the next four ingredients (through pepper). Return to boiling; reduce heat. Simmer, uncovered, about 4 minutes or just until zucchini noodles are tender and escarole is wilted.

**3.** Stir in vinegar (if desired) and salt. If desired, top servings with Asiago cheese.

**Tip** If you don't have a spiralizer, cut zucchini into thin 2-inch strips.

**PER SERVING** (1½ cups each) **CAL** 182,
**FAT** 6 g (1 g sat. fat), **CHOL** 28 mg, **SODIUM** 577 mg,
**CARB** 18 g (6 g fiber, 6 g sugars), **PRO** 15 g

# veggie-packed meals

Move over, meat! These veggie-centered recipes make vegetables the stars of your dinner plate.

## Sweet Potato and Chicken in Browned Butter

**17g** CARB

**SERVES** 5
**HANDS ON** 25 min.
**TOTAL** 30 min.

- 2 medium sweet potatoes (about 1 lb. total), peeled
- ¼ cup butter
- 1 to 2 Tbsp. snipped fresh sage or rosemary
- 4 cups fresh baby spinach
- ¾ cup thinly sliced tart green apple
- ¼ tsp. salt
- 2 cups cooked chicken breast strips
- ½ to ⅔ cup reduced-sodium chicken broth
- 2 Tbsp. finely shredded Parmesan cheese
- 1 Tbsp. coarsely chopped walnuts, toasted (optional)

**1.** In a large saucepan cook sweet potatoes in enough boiling water to cover 5 minutes. Remove from pan, reserving cooking water. Cool potatoes until they are easy to handle. Using a spiral vegetable slicer fitted with the large blade, cut potatoes into long strands (you should have about 4 cups lightly packed strands). Return cooking water to boiling. Add sweet potato strands; cook 2 minutes. Drain.

**2.** Meanwhile, in a 12-inch skillet cook butter and sage over medium-low about 15 minutes or until butter turns golden brown. Add spinach, apple, and salt; cook and stir over medium heat 1 minute. Gently stir in sweet potato, chicken, and enough of the broth to moisten; heat. Sprinkle with Parmesan cheese and, if desired, walnuts.

**PER SERVING** *(1¼ cups each)* **CAL** 260, **FAT** 12 g (7 g sat. fat), **CHOL** 73 mg, **SODIUM** 389 mg, **CARB** 17 g (3 g fiber, 5 g sugars), **PRO** 21 g

# Zoodles with Tomato Sauce and Sausage

**20g** **SERVES** 6
**CARB** **HANDS ON** 30 min.
**TOTAL** 1 hr. 45 min.

4 lb. tomatoes, cored, halved, and seeded
1 red sweet pepper, halved and seeded
2 Tbsp. olive oil
1 cup chopped sweet onion
4 cloves garlic, minced
1 Tbsp. white balsamic vinegar
¼ tsp. salt
¾ tsp. black pepper
½ cup chopped fresh basil, Italian parsley, and/or oregano
Nonstick cooking spray
3 3-oz. links fully cooked chicken sausage, bias-sliced
24 cups zucchini or yellow summer squash noodles (about 6 squash)

**1.** Preheat broiler. Lightly brush tomatoes and sweet pepper with 1 Tbsp. of the oil. Arrange half of the tomatoes and the pepper, cut sides down, in a 15×10-inch baking pan. Broil 5 to 6 inches from heat 8 to 10 minutes or until charred. Remove from pan; wrap pepper in foil. Repeat with the remaining tomatoes. Let tomatoes and pepper stand 20 minutes or until cool enough to handle. Peel off and discard skins. Chop tomatoes and pepper.
**2.** In a large saucepan heat the remaining 1 Tbsp. oil over medium. Add onion and garlic; cook 5 to 7 minutes or until onion is tender, stirring occasionally. Add tomatoes, sweet pepper, vinegar, salt, and ¼ tsp. of the black pepper. Bring to boiling; reduce heat. Simmer, uncovered, 20 to 30 minutes or until tomatoes have broken down and mixture is slightly thick, stirring occasionally. Cool slightly. Blend with an immersion blender until smooth. Return to saucepan; heat through. Stir in herbs. Transfer half of the sauce to a freezer container, let cool, and freeze up to 3 months.
**3.** Meanwhile, coat a 12-inch nonstick skillet with cooking spray. Heat over medium. Add sausage; cook about 5 minutes or until golden, turning once. Stir into warm sauce.
**4.** To cook zoodles, coat the 12-inch skillet with cooking spray. Heat over medium-high. Add half of the zoodles; cook and toss with tongs 2 to 3 minutes or until tender. Sprinkle with ¼ tsp. of the black pepper. Repeat with remaining zoodles and black pepper. Serve sauce over hot zoodles.

**Tip** Use a spiralizer to cut zucchini into noodles or look for them already prepared in the produce aisle of your supermarket. You really do want 24 cups of zoodles because you will have half as much after cooking.

**To Use Frozen Sauce** Thaw sauce overnight in refrigerator. Reheat in a medium saucepan over medium-low until heated through. Use as desired.

**PER SERVING** *(½ cup sauce + 2 cups zoodles each)* **CAL** 175, **FAT** 7 g (2 g sat. fat), **CHOL** 30 mg, **SODIUM** 313 mg, **CARB** 20 g (4 g fiber, 15 g sugars), **PRO** 11 g

# Delicata Squash with Pork Medallions

**19g**
**CARB**

**SERVES** 4

**TOTAL** 30 min.

- 12 oz. pork tenderloin, cut into ½-inch slices
- ¼ tsp. salt
- ½ tsp. black pepper
- 1 Tbsp. olive oil
- 3 slices lower-sodium, less-fat bacon
- 1 lb. delicata squash, seeds removed and cut into 1-inch pieces
- ¾ cup unsweetened apple juice
- ¼ cup water
- 2 shallots, thinly sliced
- 3 Tbsp. cider vinegar
- 1 tsp. snipped fresh thyme or ¼ tsp. dried thyme, crushed
- 6 cups fresh baby spinach

**1.** Sprinkle pork with salt and ¼ tsp. of the pepper. In a 10-inch nonstick skillet cook pork in hot oil over medium-high about 5 minutes or until browned but still slightly pink in center, turning once. Remove from skillet; keep warm.
**2.** In the same skillet cook bacon over medium until crisp. Drain bacon on paper towels; crumble bacon. Wipe out skillet. Add the next four ingredients (through shallots) to skillet. Bring to boiling; reduce heat. Cook, covered, 6 to 8 minutes or until squash is just tender.
**3.** Add vinegar, thyme, and the remaining ¼ tsp. pepper to skillet. Return pork and any accumulated juices to skillet; heat. Serve over spinach. Sprinkle with bacon.

**PER SERVING** *(1 cup pork mixture + 1½ cups spinach each)* **CAL** 226, **FAT** 6 g (1 g sat. fat), **CHOL** 58 mg, **SODIUM** 315 mg, **CARB** 19 g (4 g fiber, 5 g sugars), **PRO** 22 g

# Asparagus-Egg Sandwich

**34g**
**CARB**

**SERVES** 2

**TOTAL** 10 min.

- 4 slices whole wheat bread, toasted
- 1 tsp. Dijon-style mustard
- 1 avocado, seeded, peeled, and mashed
- 8 to 12 asparagus spears, steamed
- 1 hard-cooked egg, sliced
- ⅛ tsp. coarse sea salt
- ⅛ tsp. cracked black pepper

**1.** Spread two toast slices with mustard. Spread remaining two toast slices with mashed avocado. Top with asparagus and egg slices. Sprinkle with salt and pepper. Top with mustard-coated toast slices.

**PER SERVING** *(1 sandwich each)* **CAL** 317, **FAT** 15 g (3 g sat. fat), **CHOL** 93 mg, **SODIUM** 518 mg, **CARB** 34 g (10 g fiber, 5 g sugars), **PRO** 14 g

# 🍲 Beef-Vegetable Ragout

**19g**
**CARB**

**SERVES** 8
**HANDS ON** 30 min.
**SLOW COOK** 8 hr. 5 min..

- 1½ lb. boneless beef chuck roast
  Nonstick cooking spray
- 3 cups sliced fresh cremini or button mushrooms
- 1 cup chopped onion
- 4 cloves garlic, minced
- ½ tsp. salt
- ½ tsp. black pepper
- ¼ cup quick-cooking tapioca, crushed
- 2 14.5-oz. cans 50%-less-sodium beef broth
- ½ cup port or dry sherry (optional)
- 4 cups sugar snap pea pods, trimmed if desired
- 2 cups cherry tomatoes, halved
- 4 cups hot cooked multigrain noodles (optional)

**1.** Trim fat from meat. Cut meat into ¾-inch pieces. Lightly coat a 10-inch nonstick skillet with cooking spray; heat skillet over medium-high. Cook meat, half at a time, in hot skillet until browned.

**2.** In a 3½- or 4-qt. slow cooker combine the next five ingredients (through pepper). Sprinkle with tapioca. Add meat. Pour broth and, if desired, port over mixture in cooker.

**3.** Cover and cook on low 8 to 10 hours or high 4 to 5 hours. If slow cooker is on low, turn to high. Stir in sugar snap peas. Cover and cook about 5 minutes more or until peas are tender. Stir in cherry tomatoes. If desired, serve meat mixture over hot cooked noodles.

**PER SERVING** *(1 cup each)* **CAL** 208, **FAT** 4 g (1 g sat. fat), **CHOL** 50 mg, **SODIUM** 401 mg, **CARB** 19 g (4 g fiber, 3 g sugars), **PRO** 24 g

---

# Meatballs, Greens, and Orecchiette

**32g**
**CARB**

**SERVES** 6
**HANDS ON** 45 min.
**TOTAL** 1 hr.

- 1 recipe Veggie-Full Meatballs
- 1¾ cups dried orecchiette pasta
- 3 Tbsp. olive oil
- 1 8-oz. pkg. button or cremini mushrooms, sliced
- 1 cup sliced zucchini
- ¾ cup chopped red sweet pepper
- 3 cloves garlic, minced
- 8 cups chopped Swiss chard, beet greens, arugula, and/or spinach
- 2 Tbsp. balsamic vinegar
- ¼ cup chopped fresh basil and/or Italian parsley
- ⅛ tsp. salt
- ⅛ tsp. black pepper
  Grated Parmesan cheese (optional)

**1.** Prepare Veggie-Full Meatballs. Meanwhile, cook orecchiette according to package directions; drain, reserving some of the pasta water.

**2.** In a 12-inch skillet or wok heat 1 Tbsp. of the olive oil over medium-high. Add mushrooms, zucchini, and sweet pepper; cook and stir about 6 minutes or until vegetables are tender and any liquid has evaporated. Stir in garlic.

**3.** Add 1 Tbsp. of the oil to the skillet. Add Swiss chard, in batches, cooking and stirring until chard is wilted. Add the remaining 1 Tbsp. oil, the balsamic vinegar, and orecchiette. Toss to combine. Add enough pasta water to reach desired consistency. Stir in basil, salt, and black pepper. Stir in meatballs. If desired, top with Parmesan.

**Veggie-Full Meatballs** Preheat oven to 450°F. Line a 15×10-inch baking sheet with foil; coat **with nonstick cooking spray.** In a large bowl stir together **1 lightly beaten egg, ¼ cup unsweetened applesauce, ½ cup shredded zucchini, ¼ cup finely chopped onion,** and **½ tsp. each salt and dried Italian seasoning, crushed.** Stir in **½ cup soft whole wheat bread crumbs.** Add **1 lb. lean ground beef or ground turkey**; mix well. Shape meat mixture into 48 meatballs. Place in pan; bake about 15 minutes or until cooked through (160°F for beef or 165°F for turkey), turning once.

**Tip** Using applesauce and shredded zucchini in the meatballs keeps them moist even though they are made with lean ground beef.

**PER SERVING** *(8 meatballs + 1 cup pasta mixture each)* **CAL** 344, **FAT** 14 g (3 g sat. fat), **CHOL** 79 mg, **SODIUM** 476 mg, **CARB** 32 g (3 g fiber, 6 g sugars), **PRO** 23 g

# Zucchini Ribbons, Pasta, and Arugula

**38g** **SERVES** 4
**CARB** **TOTAL** 30 min.

6 oz. dried fettuccine pasta
2 medium zucchini or yellow summer squash, cut lengthwise into thin ribbons
¼ cup sliced pepperoncini peppers
2 Tbsp. olive oil
1 to 2 cloves garlic, minced
1 lemon
3 cups fresh arugula
1½ tsp. snipped fresh oregano
¼ cup chopped toasted almonds (tip, *p. 102*)

**1.** Cook pasta according to package directions. Place zucchini in a colander; drain pasta over zucchini. Immediately run cold water over pasta and zucchini to cool; drain well.
**2.** Place pasta and zucchini in a bowl. Add peppers, oil, and garlic. Remove 1 tsp. zest and 1 Tbsp. juice from lemon. Add lemon zest and juice, arugula, and oregano to pasta mixture; toss to combine. Top with almonds.

**PER SERVING** *(2 cups each)* **CAL** 274, **FAT** 11 g (1 g sat. fat), **CHOL** 0 mg, **SODIUM** 90 mg, **CARB** 38 g (4 g fiber, 5 g sugars), **PRO** 8 g

TRY THIS
Use a vegetable peeler to cut zucchini into ribbons. Peel from one end of the zucchini to the other.

# Plank-Smoked Portobellos

**15g** CARB

**SERVES** 4
**HANDS ON** 30 min.
**TOTAL** 1 hr. 30 min.

- 1 14×6-inch pecan or cedar grilling plank
- 5 medium portobello mushroom caps
- 1 Tbsp. olive oil
- ½ cup chopped onion
- 2 cloves garlic, minced
- 1 5-oz. pkg. fresh baby spinach
- ¾ cup coarse soft white bread crumbs (1 slice bread)
- ½ cup shredded sharp white cheddar cheese (2 oz.)
- 2 Tbsp. chopped pecans
- 1 Tbsp. snipped fresh sage
- 1 Tbsp. spicy brown mustard

**1.** Soak plank in enough water to cover at least 1 hour. Place a weight on plank so it stays submerged during soaking.
**2.** Meanwhile, remove any stems from four of the mushroom caps; chop stems. Chop the fifth mushroom cap. Scrape and discard gills from the remaining four mushroom caps.
**3.** For filling, in a 10-inch skillet heat oil over medium; add chopped mushroom and stems, onion, and garlic. Cook and stir about 5 minutes or until vegetables are tender. Stir in spinach; cook and stir about 2 minutes or until wilted. Remove from heat. Stir in the remaining ingredients.
**4.** Grill plank, uncovered, over medium 3 to 5 minutes or until plank begins to crackle and smoke. Meanwhile, grill mushroom caps, stemmed sides up, uncovered, over medium about 3 minutes or until grill marks appear. Place mushroom caps on plank, stemmed sides up. Spoon filling into caps. Cover and grill about 15 minutes or until mushrooms are browned and filling is heated.
**5.** Transfer plank with mushrooms to a platter. If desired, top with small fresh sage leaves.

**Tip** Make more room in the mushroom caps for the stuffing. Hold a mushroom cap in one hand. With gentle, light strokes, use a spoon to gently scrape out and discard the gills.

**PER SERVING** *(1 stuffed mushroom each)* **CAL** 186, **FAT** 11 g (4 g sat. fat), **CHOL** 15 mg, **SODIUM** 241 mg, **CARB** 15 g (3 g fiber, 4 g sugars), **PRO** 8 g

# 🍲 Ziti with Eggplant and Sausage

**38g** CARB

**SERVES** 6
**HANDS ON** 25 min.
**SLOW COOK** 6 hr. 40 min.

- 4 oz. bulk sweet Italian sausage
- 4 cups peeled and chopped eggplant
- 2 medium fennel bulbs, trimmed, cored, and thinly sliced
- 1 14.5-oz. can crushed fire-roasted tomatoes, undrained

½ cup water
¼ cup dry white wine
2 Tbsp. tomato paste
2 cloves garlic, minced
1 tsp. dried Italian seasoning, crushed
2 to 2⅔ cups dried ziti or penne pasta (6 to 8 oz.)
½ cup snipped fresh basil
1 cup shredded part-skim mozzarella cheese (4 oz.)

**1.** In a 10-inch skillet cook sausage over medium-high until browned. Drain off fat. In a 5- to 6-qt. slow cooker combine sausage and the next eight ingredients (through Italian seasoning). Cover and cook on low 6 to 7 hours or high 3 to 3½ hours.

**2.** If slow cooker is on low, turn to high. Stir in pasta and basil. Cover and cook 30 minutes more. Stir pasta mixture. Sprinkle with cheese. Cover and cook 10 minutes more. Let stand, uncovered, 10 minutes before serving. Sprinkle with additional snipped fresh basil.

**Tip** Skip 30 minutes of slow cooking by cooking the ziti according to package directions before stirring it into the eggplant mixture. Sprinkle with cheese and continue as directed.

**PER SERVING** *(1¼ cups each)* **CAL** 255, **FAT** 5 g (3 g sat. fat), **CHOL** 18 mg, **SODIUM** 479 mg, **CARB** 38 g (6 g fiber, 7 g sugars), **PRO** 14 g

# Polenta and Vegetable Torte

**23g**
**CARB**

**SERVES** 8
**HANDS ON** 30 min.
**TOTAL** 1 hr. 35 min.

¼ cup olive oil

3 cloves garlic, minced

2 16-oz. tubes refrigerated cooked polenta

¼ tsp. salt

¼ tsp. black pepper

1½ cups coarsely chopped red, green, and/or yellow sweet peppers

1 medium zucchini, cut diagonally into ¼-inch slices (1¼ cups)

1 medium yellow summer squash, cut diagonally into ¼-inch slices (1¼ cups)

1 cup sliced fresh mushrooms

2 cups shredded reduced-fat cheddar, Monterey Jack, or mozzarella cheese (8 oz.)

1 cup halved cherry, pear-shape, or grape tomatoes

⅓ cup lightly packed fresh basil leaves, coarsely torn

**1.** Preheat oven to 425°F. For garlic oil, in a small saucepan heat olive oil and garlic over medium about 4 minutes or until oil is fragrant and garlic is translucent but not brown. Remove from heat.

**2.** Line a 15×10-inch baking pan with foil. Cut each tube of polenta into 11 slices, making 22 slices total. Place polenta slices in the prepared baking pan. Brush with 1 Tbsp. of the garlic oil; sprinkle with salt and black pepper. Roast about 15 minutes or until polenta is heated and edges are lightly browned, turning once. Reduce oven temperature to 350°F.

**3.** In a 12-inch skillet heat the remaining garlic oil over medium-high. Add the next four ingredients (through mushrooms); cook about 6 minutes or until vegetables are crisp-tender, stirring occasionally.

**4.** In the bottom of a 9-inch springform pan place as many polenta slices that will fit in a single layer (about 11); there will be some gaps, but slices should be touching. Layer with ½ cup of the cheese, half of the vegetables, ½ cup of the cheese, remaining polenta, ½ cup of the cheese, remaining vegetables, the tomatoes, and the remaining ½ cup cheese.

**5.** Bake about 35 minutes or until heated through. Cool in pan on a wire rack at least 15 minutes. Using a small sharp knife, loosen edges of torte from sides of pan; remove sides of pan. Sprinkle torte with basil. Cut into eight wedges.

**PER SERVING** (1 wedge each) **CAL** 247, **FAT** 13 g (4 g sat. fat), **CHOL** 20 mg, **SODIUM** 607 mg, **CARB** 23 g (3 g fiber, 2 g sugars), **PRO** 11 g

# Cauliflower-Crust Pizza

**18g**
CARB

| | |
|---|---|
| **SERVES** | 4 |
| **HANDS ON** | 30 min. |
| **TOTAL** | 50 min. |

- 4 cups cauliflower florets
- 1 egg, lightly beaten
- ¼ cup shredded reduced-fat Italian-blend cheeses (1 oz.)
- ¼ cup grated Parmesan cheese
- ¼ cup panko bread crumbs
- ½ tsp. dried Italian seasoning, crushed
- ⅛ tsp. salt
- 2 cups sliced fresh mushrooms
- 1 cup yellow or green sweet pepper strips
- 1 small red onion, cut into thin wedges
- 1 tsp. olive oil
- ½ cup Fast Pizza Sauce
- 1 cup shredded Italian-blend cheeses (4 oz.)
  Snipped fresh basil, oregano, and/ or parsley

**1.** Place cauliflower in a food processor. Cover and pulse four to six times or until crumbly and mixture resembles the texture of couscous.

**2.** Place a pizza stone or baking sheet in the oven. Preheat oven to 425°F. Place cauliflower in a large bowl with 2 Tbsp. water. Cover with vented plastic wrap. Microwave 3 to 5 minutes or until tender, stirring once or twice. Cool. Transfer cauliflower to a 100%-cotton flour-sack towel. Wrap towel around cauliflower and squeeze until there is no more liquid (this step is critical).

**3.** In a bowl stir together cauliflower and the next six ingredients (through salt). On a piece of parchment paper pat cauliflower mixture into a 12-inch circle. Transfer crust on paper to the preheated pizza stone. Bake 12 to 15 minutes or until crisp and starting to brown.

**4.** Meanwhile, in a 10-inch skillet cook and stir mushrooms, sweet pepper, and onion in hot oil over medium 4 to 6 minutes or until crisp-tender. Remove from heat.

**5.** Spoon pizza sauce over baked crust, spreading evenly. Top with cooked vegetables. Sprinkle evenly with the 1 cup cheese. Bake about 5 minutes more or until heated and cheese is melted. If desired, sprinkle with snipped fresh herb. Cut into wedges to serve.

**Fast Pizza Sauce** In a small saucepan cook **½ cup chopped onion** and **2 cloves garlic, minced,** in **1 tsp. hot oil** over medium about 5 minutes or until onion is tender, stirring occasionally. Stir in **one 8-oz. can no-salt-added tomato sauce; ½ tsp. each dried oregano and basil, crushed;** and **¼ tsp. each salt and crushed red pepper.** Bring to boiling; reduce heat. Simmer, uncovered, about 5 minutes or until sauce reaches desired consistency.

**PER SERVING** *(2 wedges each)* **CAL** 245, **FAT** 12 g (6 g sat. fat), **CHOL** 75 mg, **SODIUM** 584 mg, **CARB** 18 g (5 g fiber, 7 g sugars), **PRO** 17 g

**TRY THIS**
For even faster prep, use canned pizza sauce. Be sure to use only ½ cup and choose the lowest-sodium option.

# Freestyle Wraps

Mix, match, and make these wraps your own.

**1.** Bibb lettuce + tempeh + jicama + salsa + green onions + cilantro
**2.** Red cabbage + white beans + cucumber + carrot + red onion + sriracha + mint
**3.** Kale + chicken + apple + avocado + mustard + parsley
**4.** Savoy cabbage + shrimp + radish + snap peas + chili sauce

## LEAVES

- Bibb lettuce, romaine lettuce, iceberg lettuce, or green leaf lettuce
- Napa cabbage, green cabbage, red cabbage, or savoy cabbage
- Tuscan kale
- Swiss chard

## PROTEIN

- Cooked shrimp
- Cooked chicken breast
- Cooked pork tenderloin
- Ground beef, pork, turkey, or chicken, browned and crumbled
- Canned beans, rinsed and drained
- Tofu, cubed
- Tempeh, crumbled and browned

## PRODUCE

- Sliced or chopped sweet pepper
- Sliced or cubed avocado
- Sliced cucumber
- Sliced or julienned carrots
- Sliced radishes
- Sliced or julienned jicama
- Halved or sliced snow or snap pea pods
- Chopped onion or sliced green onion
- Cored and sliced pears and/or apples

## TOPPERS

- Snipped fresh herbs (basil, cilantro, mint, parsley)
- Chopped nuts (pistachios, peanuts, walnuts, almonds)
- Lemon, orange, or lime zest
- Ground cumin, curry powder, chili powder
- Plain Greek yogurt
- Hoisin sauce, peanut sauce, Asian sweet chili sauce, or sriracha sauce
- Dijon-style mustard

Nutrition numbers will vary based on what you wrap—in general, go heavy on the freshness!

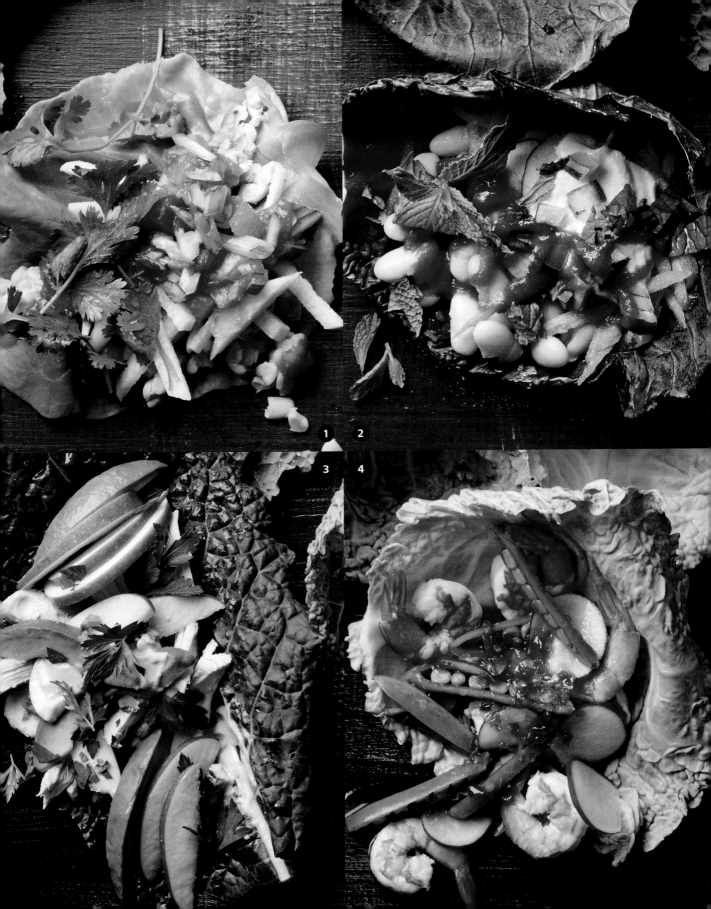

# classics made over

Keep enjoying the favorites that you grew up with. Share these updated and lightened versions with your family.

## 🍲 Classic Beef Stroganoff

**17g** **CARB**

**SERVES** 6
**HANDS ON** 30 min.
**SLOW COOK** 8 hr. 30 min.

- 1¼ lb. beef stew meat
- 2 tsp. vegetable oil
- 2½ cups sliced fresh mushrooms
- ½ cup sliced green onions or chopped onion
- 1 bay leaf
- 2 cloves garlic, minced
- ½ tsp. dried oregano, crushed
- ¼ tsp. salt
- ¼ tsp. dried thyme, crushed
- ¼ tsp. black pepper
- 1½ cups 50%-less-sodium beef broth
- ¼ cup dry sherry
- 1 8-oz. carton light sour cream
- ⅓ cup all-purpose flour
- ¼ cup water
- 12 cups sautéed zucchini noodles or hot cooked whole wheat pasta Snipped fresh parsley or basil (optional)

**1.** Cut up any large pieces of meat. In a 10-inch nonstick skillet cook half of the meat in hot oil over medium-high until browned. Using a slotted spoon, remove meat from skillet. Repeat with the remaining meat. Drain off fat.

**2.** In a 3½- or 4-qt. slow cooker combine the next eight ingredients (through pepper). Add meat. Pour broth and sherry over mixture in cooker.

**3.** Cover and cook on low 8 to 10 hours or high 4 to 5 hours. Remove and discard bay leaf.

**4.** If slow cooker is on low, turn to high. In a medium bowl stir together sour cream, flour, and the water until smooth. Gradually stir about 1 cup of the hot broth into sour cream mixture. Return sour cream mixture to cooker; stir to combine. Cover and cook about 30 minutes more or until thickened and bubbly. Serve over sautéed zucchini and, if desired, sprinkle with parsley.

**Tip** Use 24 cups zucchini noodles (about 6 medium zucchini). Coat a 12-inch skillet with nonstick cooking spray and heat over medium-high. Add half of the zucchini; cook and toss with tongs 2 to 3 minutes or until tender. Repeat.

**PER SERVING** *(⅔ cup beet mixture + 2 cups zucchini noodles each)* **CAL** 262, **FAT** 11 g (5 g sat. fat), **CHOL** 74 mg, **SODIUM** 324 mg, **CARB** 17 g (3 g fiber, 6 g sugars), **PRO** 27 g

# 🍲 Spicy Beef Sloppy Joes

**29g** CARB

**SERVES** 12
**HANDS ON** 20 min.
**SLOW COOK** 8 hr.

**TRY THIS**
Skip the buns. Spoon this saucy mixture into lettuce leaves for wraps, over baked sweet potatoes, or on a bed of greens.

2 lb. lean ground beef
2½ cups lower-sodium salsa
3 cups coarsely chopped fresh mushrooms (8 oz.)
1¼ cups shredded carrots
1¼ cups finely chopped red and/or green sweet peppers
½ of a 6-oz. can no-salt-added tomato paste
4 cloves garlic, minced
1 tsp. dried basil, crushed
¾ tsp. salt
½ tsp. dried oregano, crushed
¼ tsp. cayenne pepper
12 whole wheat hamburger buns, split and toasted

**1.** In a 12-inch skillet cook ground beef over medium until browned, stirring occasionally. Drain off fat. In a 5- to 6-qt. slow cooker combine meat and the next 10 ingredients (through cayenne pepper).
**2.** Cover and cook on low 8 to 10 hours or high 4 to 5 hours. Spoon ½ cup meat mixture onto each bun.

**Tip** Place any leftover meat mixture in a freezer container; seal. Freeze up to 3 months. Thaw overnight in refrigerator before using.

**PER SERVING** *(1 sandwich each)* **CAL** 278, **FAT** 8 g (3 g sat. fat), **CHOL** 48 mg, **SODIUM** 527 mg, **CARB** 29 g (4 g fiber, 8 g sugars), **PRO** 20 g

# Cheeseburger Shepherd's Pie

**30g**
CARB

**SERVES** 8
**HANDS ON** 25 min.
**TOTAL** 1 hr.

- 1¾ lb. russet potatoes, peeled and cut into 1½-inch pieces
- 2 cups cauliflower florets
- ½ cup light sour cream
- ¼ cup fat-free milk
- ¼ tsp. salt
- 1 cup shredded reduced-fat cheddar cheese (4 oz.)
- 1½ lb. extra-lean ground beef (95% lean)
- ¾ cup chopped red sweet pepper
- ½ cup chopped onion
- 2 cloves garlic, minced
- 1½ cups frozen whole kernel corn
- 1 15-oz. can no-salt-added tomato sauce
- ⅓ cup chopped dill pickles
- 3 Tbsp. yellow mustard
- 1 tsp. dried oregano, crushed
  Sliced green onions (optional)

**1.** Preheat oven to 350°F. In a large saucepan cook potatoes and cauliflower in enough boiling water to cover about 15 minutes or until tender; drain. Mash potatoes and cauliflower. Gradually add sour cream, milk, and salt, mashing until light and fluffy. Stir in ½ cup of the cheese.

**2.** Meanwhile, in a 10-inch skillet cook beef, sweet pepper, onion, and garlic over medium until browned. Drain off any fat. Stir in the next five ingredients (through oregano). Bring to boiling; reduce heat. Simmer, uncovered, 5 minutes to blend flavors.

**3.** Spoon beef mixture into a 3-qt. baking dish. Spoon mashed potato mixture in mounds over beef mixture. Sprinkle with remaining ½ cup cheese. Bake about 20 minutes or until heated. If desired, top with green onions.

**PER SERVING** *(1⅓ cups each)* **CAL** 294, **FAT** 9 g (5 g sat. fat), **CHOL** 67 mg, **SODIUM** 402 mg, **CARB** 30 g (5 g fiber, 6 g sugars), **PRO** 26 g

---

# Hot Beef Sandwiches

**34g**
**CARB**

**SERVES** 4
**HANDS ON** 30 min.
**TOTAL** 2 hr.

Nonstick cooking spray
1 lb. beef stew meat, trimmed of fat and cut into 1-inch cubes
1 14.5-oz. can unsalted beef broth
3 cloves garlic, minced
½ tsp. salt
¼ tsp. black pepper
2 cups 1-inch cubes peeled russet potatoes
2 cups small cauliflower florets
½ cup chopped carrot
¼ cup light sour cream
⅛ tsp. black pepper
¼ cup cold water
2 Tbsp. all-purpose flour
4 slices whole grain country-style bread, toasted
¼ cup sliced green onions

**1.** Coat a medium saucepan with cooking spray. Brown the stew meat, half at a time, over medium-high. Return all beef to pan. Add broth, two cloves of the garlic ¼ tsp. of the salt, and the ¼ tsp. pepper. Bring to boiling; reduce heat. Simmer, covered, about 1½ hours or until very tender.

**2.** Meanwhile, in a separate medium saucepan combine potatoes and the remaining one clove garlic. Add enough water to cover by 1 inch. Bring to boiling; reduce heat. Simmer, covered, 5 minutes. Add cauliflower and carrot. Return to boiling; reduce heat. Simmer, covered, about 10 minutes more or until vegetables are very tender. Drain well.

**3.** In a large bowl combine vegetable mixture, sour cream, the remaining ¼ tsp. salt, and the ⅛ tsp. pepper. Mash mixture until light and fluffy.

**4.** Using a slotted spoon, remove meat from pan. Shred beef using two forks. If desired, strain beef cooking liquid through a fine-mesh sieve. Measure 1 cup liquid; return to pan and discard remaining liquid. In a small bowl stir together the cold water and flour until smooth. Stir into cooking liquid in pan. Cook and stir over medium until thickened and bubbly; cook and stir 1 minute more. Return shredded meat to pan; stir to combine.

**5.** Serve vegetable mash over toasted bread. Top with beef mixture. Sprinkle with green onions.

**PER SERVING** *(1 open-face sandwich each)* **CAL** 335, **FAT** 8 g (3 g sat. fat), **CHOL** 77 mg, **SODIUM** 555 mg, **CARB** 34 g (5 g fiber, 4 g sugars), **PRO** 33 g

## Skillet Broccoli-Chicken Casserole

**32g CARB**

**SERVES** 4
**HANDS ON** 15 min.
**TOTAL** 30 min.

- 2 cups dried medium egg noodles (4 oz.)
- 3 cups broccoli florets
- 1 lb. skinless, boneless chicken breast halves, cut into 1-inch pieces
- ½ tsp. lemon-pepper seasoning
- ½ cup chopped onion
- 2 cloves garlic, minced
- 1 Tbsp. canola oil
- ⅓ cup light sour cream
- 2 Tbsp. all-purpose flour
- 1 tsp. Dijon-style mustard
- ¼ tsp. salt
- ¼ tsp. dried thyme, crushed
- ⅛ tsp. cayenne pepper (optional)
- 1 cup reduced-sodium chicken broth
- ½ cup shredded reduced-fat cheddar cheese (2 oz.)

**1.** In a large saucepan cook noodles according to package directions, adding broccoli the last 2 minutes. Drain.

**2.** Season chicken with lemon-pepper seasoning. In a 12-inch nonstick skillet cook chicken, onion, and garlic in hot oil over medium-high 6 to 8 minutes or until chicken is no longer pink, stirring occasionally. Meanwhile, in a bowl whisk together the next six ingredients (through cayenne if using). Whisk in broth. Stir into chicken mixture in skillet. Cook and stir 3 to 4 minutes or until thick and bubbly.

**3.** Add noodles and broccoli; toss to coat. Heat through. Remove from heat. Sprinkle with cheese; let stand 5 minutes before serving.

**PER SERVING** *(1½ cups each)* **CAL** 391, **FAT** 13 g (4 g sat. fat), **CHOL** 122 mg, **SODIUM** 493 mg, **CARB** 32 g (3 g fiber, 3 g sugars), **PRO** 37 g

## Pumpkin, Bean, and Chicken Enchiladas

**44g CARB**

**SERVES** 4
**HANDS ON** 35 min.
**TOTAL** 1 hr.

- Nonstick cooking spray
- 2 tsp. olive oil
- ½ cup chopped onion
- 1 fresh jalapeño chile pepper, seeded and finely chopped (tip, *p. 250*)
- 1 15-oz. can pumpkin
- 1½ to 1¾ cups water
- 1 tsp. chili powder
- ½ tsp. salt
- ½ tsp. ground cumin
- 1 cup canned no-salt-added red kidney beans, rinsed and drained
- 1½ cups shredded cooked chicken breast
- ½ cup shredded part-skim mozzarella cheese (2 oz.)
- 8 6-inch white corn tortillas, softened
  Pico de gallo or salsa (optional)
  Lime wedges (optional)

1. Preheat oven to 400°F. Lightly coat a 2-qt. rectangular baking dish with cooking spray. In a medium saucepan heat oil over medium-high. Add onion and jalapeño pepper; cook about 5 minutes or until onion is tender, stirring occasionally. Stir in pumpkin, 1½ cups of the water, the chili powder, salt, and cumin; heat through. If needed, stir in enough of the remaining ¼ cup water to reach desired consistency.

2. Place beans in a large bowl; mash slightly with a fork. Stir in half of the pumpkin mixture, the chicken, and ¼ cup of the cheese.

3. Spoon a generous ⅓ cup bean mixture onto each tortilla; roll up tortillas. Place, seam sides down, in the prepared baking dish. Pour remaining pumpkin mixture over enchiladas.

4. Bake, covered, 15 minutes. Sprinkle with the remaining ¼ cup cheese. Bake, uncovered, about 10 minutes more or until heated through. If desired, serve with pico de gallo and lime wedges.

**TIP** To soften tortillas, stack them between paper towels and microwave 30 to 40 seconds.

**PER SERVING** *(2 enchiladas each)* **CAL** 357, **FAT** 8 g (3 g sat. fat), **CHOL** 54 mg, **SODIUM** 465 mg, **CARB** 44 g (12 g fiber, 5 g sugars), **PRO** 28 g

# Stove-Top Chicken, Macaroni, and Cheese

**33g**
**CARB**

**SERVES** 5
**TOTAL** 35 min.

1½ cups dried multigrain or regular elbow macaroni (6 oz.)
 Nonstick cooking spray
12 oz. skinless, boneless chicken breast halves, cut into 1-inch pieces
¼ cup finely chopped onion
1 6.5-oz. pkg. light semisoft cheese with garlic and fines herbes
1⅔ cups fat-free milk
1 Tbsp. all-purpose flour
¾ cup shredded reduced-fat cheddar cheese (3 oz.)
2 cups fresh baby spinach
1 cup cherry tomatoes, quartered

**1.** Cook macaroni according to package directions; drain.
**2.** Meanwhile, coat a 10-inch nonstick skillet with cooking spray; heat skillet over medium-high. Add chicken and onion; cook 4 to 6 minutes or until chicken is no longer pink and onion is tender, stirring frequently. (If onion browns too quickly, reduce heat to medium.) Remove from heat. Stir in semisoft cheese until melted.
**3.** In a bowl whisk together milk and flour until smooth. Gradually stir milk mixture into chicken mixture. Cook and stir over medium until thickened and bubbly. Reduce heat to low. Gradually add cheddar cheese, stirring until melted. Add cooked macaroni; cook and stir 1 to 2 minutes or until heated through. Stir in spinach. Top with cherry tomatoes.

**PER SERVING** *(1⅓ cups each)* **CAL** 369, **FAT** 12 g (7 g sat. fat), **CHOL** 85 mg, **SODIUM** 393 mg, **CARB** 33 g (4 g fiber, 6 g sugars), **PRO** 33 g

TRY THIS
Add smoky flavor to this cheesy dish with grilled chicken breast and smoked provolone or cheddar.

## Taco-Penne Skillet

**42g** CARB

**SERVES** 4
**HANDS ON** 15 min.
**TOTAL** 40 min.

- 12 oz. ground turkey breast
- ¾ cup finely chopped red sweet pepper
- ½ cup finely chopped onion
- 1 medium fresh poblano pepper, seeded and chopped (tip, *p. 250*)
- 2 cloves garlic, minced
- 1 Tbsp. chili powder
- 1 tsp. ground cumin
- 1 tsp. dried oregano, crushed
- ⅛ tsp. salt
- 1 14.5-oz. can no-salt-added diced tomatoes, undrained
- 1 8-oz. can tomato sauce
- 1¼ cups dried mini penne pasta
- ¾ to 1 cup water
- ½ cup shredded reduced-fat Monterey Jack cheese with jalapeño peppers or cheddar cheese (2 oz.)
  Thinly sliced green onions and/or snipped fresh cilantro

**1.** In a 10-inch skillet cook the first nine ingredients (through salt) over medium until meat is no longer pink.
**2.** Stir in the next four ingredients (through water). Bring to boiling; reduce heat. Simmer, covered, about 20 minutes or until penne is tender, stirring occasionally.
**3.** Remove skillet from heat; sprinkle meat mixture with cheese. Cover and let stand about 5 minutes or until cheese is melted. Sprinkle with green onions and cilantro.

**Tip** To make it meatless, omit the turkey. Cook vegetables and spices in a 10-inch skillet coated with nonstick cooking spray over medium 5 minutes. Add one 15-oz. can reduced-sodium black beans or pinto beans, rinsed and drained, with the tomatoes.

**PER SERVING** (1½ cups each) **CAL** 324, **FAT** 4 g (2 g sat. fat), **CHOL** 60 mg, **SODIUM** 570 mg, **CARB** 42 g (6 g fiber, 9 g sugars), **PRO** 32 g

---

## Oven-Fried Drumsticks and Thighs

**17g** CARB

**SERVES** 6
**HANDS ON** 20 min.
**TOTAL** 1 hr. 5 min.

- 1 egg, lightly beaten
- 3 Tbsp. fat-free milk
- 1¼ cups crushed cornflakes or finely crushed rich round crackers (about 35)
- 1 tsp. dried thyme, crushed
- ½ tsp. paprika
- ¼ tsp. salt
- ⅛ tsp. black pepper
- 2 Tbsp. butter, melted
- 2½ to 3 lb. chicken drumsticks and/or thighs, skin removed
  Lemon wedges (optional)
  Fresh thyme (optional)

**1.** Preheat oven to 375°F. In a small bowl combine egg and milk. For coating, in a shallow dish combine the next five ingredients (through pepper); stir in melted butter. Dip chicken pieces, one at a time, into egg mixture; coat with crumb mixture.
**2.** In a greased 15×10-inch baking

pan, arrange chicken, bone sides down, so the pieces aren't touching. Sprinkle with any remaining crumb mixture to coat.

**3.** Bake, uncovered, 45 to 55 minutes or until chicken is done (180°F). Do not turn chicken pieces while baking. If desired, serve with lemon wedges and garnish with fresh thyme.

**PER SERVING** *(3 oz. chicken each)* **CAL** 265, **FAT** 9 g (4 g sat. fat), **CHOL** 157 mg, **SODIUM** 381 mg, **CARB** 17 g (1 g fiber, 2 g sugars), **PRO** 27 g

## Oven-Fried Parmesan Chicken

Prepare as directed, except omit thyme and salt and reduce crushed cornflakes to ½ cup. For coating, combine cornflakes; ½ cup grated Parmesan cheese; 1 tsp. dried oregano, crushed; the paprika; and pepper. Stir in melted butter. Continue as directed.

**PER SERVING** *(3 oz. chicken each)* **CAL** 253, **FAT** 11 g (5 g sat. fat), **CHOL** 162 mg, **SODIUM** 325 mg, **CARB** 8 g (1 g fiber, 1 g sugars), **PRO** 28 g

## Oven-Fried Chicken Breast Tenders

Prepare as directed, except substitute 1½ lb. chicken tenders for meaty chicken pieces, increase crushed cornflakes to 1¾ cups, and place tenders in a single layer in baking pan. Bake, uncovered, in a 400°F oven 10 to 12 minutes or until chicken is no longer pink. Do not turn tenders while baking.

**PER SERVING** *(4 tenders each)* **CAL** 252, **FAT** 8 g (3 g sat. fat), **CHOL** 124 mg, **SODIUM** 318 mg, **CARB** 17 g (1 g fiber, 2 g sugars), **PRO** 28 g

## Teriyaki Pork Skillet Casserole

**34g CARB**

**SERVES** 6
**HANDS ON** 25 min.
**TOTAL** 45 min.

- 1 cup reduced-sodium chicken broth
- ¼ cup reduced-sodium teriyaki sauce
- 2 Tbsp. cornstarch
- 2 tsp. grated fresh ginger
- ¼ tsp. crushed red pepper
  Nonstick cooking spray
- 1 lb. pork tenderloin, cut into 1-inch strips
- 1½ cups bias-sliced carrots (¼-inch slices)
- 2 cups broccoli florets
- 1 medium red onion, cut into thin wedges
- 2 Tbsp. chopped garlic
- 2 cups cooked brown rice
- 1 cup snow pea pods, halved
- ⅓ cup coarsely chopped unsalted cashews
- ¼ cup thinly sliced green onions
  Crushed red pepper (optional)

**1.** For sauce, in a medium bowl whisk together the first five ingredients (through crushed red pepper). Lightly coat a 12-inch skillet or extra-large wok with cooking spray; heat over medium-high. Add pork to skillet; cook until lightly browned, turning once. Remove from skillet. Add carrots; cook and stir 5 minutes. Add broccoli and onion; cook and stir 4 to 5 minutes more or until vegetables are just crisp-tender. Add garlic; cook and stir 30 seconds more. Stir in sauce; cook and stir 2 to 3 minutes or until sauce is thickened and bubbly. Stir in cooked rice and browned pork.

**2.** Reduce heat to medium. Simmer, covered, 10 to 15 minutes or until bubbly and pork is cooked through (145°F), stirring in pea pods during the last 2 minutes of cooking. Sprinkle with cashews, green onions, and, if desired, crushed red pepper.

**PER SERVING** *(1 cup each)* **CAL** 279, **FAT** 6 g (1 g sat. fat), **CHOL** 49 mg, **SODIUM** 384 mg, **CARB** 34 g (3 g fiber, 6 g sugars), **PRO** 22 g

# Loaded Barbecue Sweet Potatoes

**35g**
**CARB**

**SERVES** 4
**HANDS ON** 20 min.
**TOTAL** 1 hr. 20 min.

- 2  8- to 10-oz. sweet potatoes
- 12  oz. pork tenderloin or lean boneless pork
- 2  tsp. canola oil
- 1  small onion, halved and sliced
- 1  small fresh poblano chile pepper, seeded and cut into bite-size strips (tip, *p. 250*)
- ⅓  cup barbecue sauce
- ¼  cup light sour cream
- ¼  cup shredded reduced-fat cheddar cheese (1 oz.)
- ¼  cup sliced green onions
- 4  slices lower-sodium, less-fat bacon, crisp-cooked and crumbled

**1.** Preheat oven to 425°F. Scrub potatoes; pat dry. Prick potatoes with a fork. Wrap potatoes individually in foil and place in a 15×10-inch baking pan. Bake 50 to 60 minutes or until tender.

**2.** Meanwhile, cut pork into bite-size strips. In a 10-inch nonstick skillet heat oil over medium-high. Add pork; cook and stir about 4 minutes or until no pink remains. Remove meat from skillet. Add onion and poblano chile to skillet; cook and stir 4 to 6 minutes or until tender. Remove from heat. Return pork to skillet. Add barbecue sauce; toss to combine.

**3.** Cut baked sweet potatoes in half lengthwise. Top cut sides with pork mixture. Top with sour cream, cheese, green onions, and bacon.

**PER SERVING** *(1 loaded potato half each)* **CAL** 317, **FAT** 8 g (3 g sat. fat), **CHOL** 68 mg, **SODIUM** 461 mg, **CARB** 35 g (4 g fiber, 13 g sugars), **PRO** 24 g

GOOD
FOR YOU
This stuffed potato is loaded with tasty things that stay well within nutritional guidelines for a diabetes-smart meal. Be sure to eat the potato skin for all its benefits.

# Spicy Oven-Baked Fish and Sweet Potato Fries

**40g** CARB

**SERVES** 4
**HANDS ON** 20 min.
**TOTAL** 40 min.

- 1 lb. fresh or frozen whitefish fillets, about ½ inch thick
  Nonstick cooking spray
- 1 lb. sweet potatoes, cut into ¼- to ½-inch sticks
- 1 Tbsp. olive oil
- 2½ tsp. chili powder
- 1 tsp. Old Bay seasoning or seafood seasoning
- ½ tsp. salt
- ⅓ cup milk
- ⅓ cup all-purpose flour
- ⅓ cup fine dried bread crumbs
- 1 tsp. paprika
- ¼ tsp. black pepper
- 2 Tbsp. butter, melted
  Lemon wedges and/or fresh parsley (optional)

TRY THIS
Give this classic pub food a light sprinkling of malt vinegar instead of a squeeze of lemon.

**1.** Thaw fish, if frozen. Rinse fish; pat dry with paper towels. Cut fish into 3×2-inch pieces. Cover and chill until needed.

**2.** Preheat oven to 425°F. Line a large baking sheet with foil; lightly coat with cooking spray. For fries, pat potatoes dry with paper towels; place in a large bowl. Add olive oil, ½ tsp. of the chili powder, the Old Bay seasoning, and ¼ tsp. of the salt. Toss to coat. Arrange potatoes in a single layer on half of the prepared baking sheet. Bake 10 minutes.

**3.** Meanwhile, for fish, place milk in a shallow dish. Place flour in another shallow dish. In a third shallow dish combine bread crumbs, the remaining 2 tsp. chili powder, the paprika, the remaining ¼ tsp. salt, and the pepper. Stir in melted butter until combined.

**4.** Dip fish pieces in milk; coat with flour. Dip again in the milk, then in the bread crumb mixture. Remove baking sheet from oven. Carefully turn potatoes over. Place fish on the other half of the hot baking sheet; return to oven. Bake 10 to 15 minutes more or until potatoes are golden brown and fish flakes easily. If desired, serve fish with lemon wedges and/or fresh parsley.

**PER SERVING** *(2 pieces fish + 4 oz. fries each)* **CAL** 384, **FAT** 13 g (5 g sat. fat), **CHOL** 74 mg, **SODIUM** 575 mg, **CARB** 40 g (5 g fiber, 7 g sugars), **PRO** 28 g

# Creamy Tuna-Noodle Toss

**49g** **CARB** | **SERVES** 4
| **TOTAL** 30 min.

3 cups wide egg noodles (6 oz.)
1½ cups frozen peas
3 Tbsp. butter
1 small red onion, quartered and sliced
2 cloves garlic, minced
¼ tsp. black pepper
2 Tbsp. all-purpose flour
¼ tsp. salt
1¼ cups milk
1 5-oz. can solid white tuna, drained and broken into chunks
½ cup grated Parmesan cheese
1 to 2 Tbsp. milk (optional)
1 Tbsp. fresh lemon juice

**1.** Cook noodles according to package directions, adding peas the last 2 minutes of cooking. Drain and return to pan.
**2.** In a 10-inch skillet melt butter over medium. Add onion, garlic, and pepper; cook and stir about 3 minutes or until onion is just tender. Stir in flour and salt until blended. Add the 1¼ cups milk. Cook and stir until thickened and bubbly.
**3.** Add noodles and peas, tuna, and ¼ cup of the cheese to skillet; toss. Remove from heat. If desired, stir in additional milk, 1 Tbsp. at time, until desired consistency. Drizzle with lemon juice. Sprinkle with remaining cheese and additional pepper.

**PER SERVING** *(1½ cups each)* **CAL** 435, **FAT** 16 g (8 g sat. fat), **CHOL** 88 mg, **SODIUM** 632 mg, **CARB** 49 g (4 g fiber, 9 g sugars), **PRO** 23 g

# 🍲 Lentil- and Rice-Stuffed Peppers

**35g**
**CARB**

**SERVES** 8
**HANDS ON** 20 min.
**SLOW COOK** 3 hr.

- 3¼ cups water
- ¾ cup uncooked brown rice
- ½ tsp. salt
- ¾ cup dried brown lentils, rinsed and drained
- 1 14.5-oz. can diced tomatoes with garlic and onion, undrained
- 1 cup chopped carrots
- 1 cup chopped celery
- 1 Tbsp. packed brown sugar*
- 1 Tbsp. yellow mustard
- 1 Tbsp. cider vinegar
- 4 green and/or red sweet peppers
  Snipped fresh Italian parsley (optional)

**1.** In a large saucepan combine 3 cups of the water, the rice, and ¼ tsp. of the salt. Bring to boiling; reduce heat. Simmer, covered, 15 minutes. Stir in lentils. Cover and simmer 25 minutes more or until rice and lentils are tender. Drain off any liquid. Stir in the remaining ¼ tsp. salt and the next six ingredients (through vinegar).

**2.** Meanwhile, pour the remaining ¼ cup of the water into a 6-qt. oval slow cooker. Halve sweet peppers lengthwise; remove and discard seeds and membranes. Fill each pepper half with rice mixture and arrange in the prepared cooker, carefully stacking stuffed pepper halves on top of each other.

**3.** Cover and cook on low 3 to 3½ hours or until peppers are tender and filling is heated through. Using a large spoon, carefully remove peppers from cooker. If desired, sprinkle with parsley.

**PER SERVING** *(1 stuffed pepper each)* **CAL** 174, **FAT** 1 g (0 g sat. fat), **CHOL** 0 mg, **SODIUM** 343 mg, **CARB** 35 g (5 g fiber, 8 g sugars), **PRO** 7 g

***Sugar Sub** We do not recommend a sugar sub for this recipe.

# plant-based dinners

Getting your daily dose of protein from plants is easier than you think. Enjoy a variety of flavors and textures with recipes filled with soy, nuts, grains, and beans.

## Hoisin-Glazed Tofu and Green Beans

**33g CARB**

**SERVES** 4
**HANDS ON** 30 min.
**TOTAL** 40 min.

- 16 oz. extra-firm tofu, drained
- 3 Tbsp. water
- 2 Tbsp. hoisin sauce
- 1 Tbsp. soy sauce or tamari sauce
- 1 Tbsp. grated fresh ginger
- ¼ tsp. crushed red pepper (optional)
- 2 Tbsp. vegetable oil
- 3 cloves garlic, thinly sliced
- 8 oz. fresh green beans, trimmed and halved lengthwise
- 2 cups hot cooked rice noodles or rice
  Lime wedges

**1.** Cut tofu lengthwise into four 1-inch-thick slices. Lay tofu slices on a double layer of paper towels. Top with another double layer of paper towels. Weight down with a plate topped with cans to press excess water from tofu. Let stand 10 minutes. Cut the tofu into 1-inch cubes.

**2.** Meanwhile, stir together the next five ingredients (through crushed red pepper if using).

**3.** In a 12-inch skillet heat 1 Tbsp. of the oil over medium-high. Add tofu. Cook, without stirring, 4 to 5 minutes or until tofu begins to brown. Turn tofu and cook 4 to 5 minutes more or until tofu is golden brown on all sides, stirring occasionally.

**4.** Transfer tofu to a plate. Add remaining 1 Tbsp. oil to skillet. Add garlic; cook and stir 30 seconds. Add beans; cook and stir about 4 minutes or until barely tender. Return tofu to skillet. Add hoisin mixture, stirring to coat. Serve with rice noodles and lime wedges.

**Tip** If fresh green beans are not at their peak, substitute fresh snow pea pods, trimmed.

PER SERVING *(1 cup each)* **CAL** 295, **FAT** 13 g (2 g sat. fat), **CHOL** 0 mg, **SODIUM** 386 mg, **CARB** 33 g (3 g fiber, 5 g sugars), **PRO** 15 g

# Falafel and Vegetable Pitas

**43g**
CARB

**SERVES** 4
**HANDS ON** 25 min.
**TOTAL** 30 min.

GLOBAL
This Middle Eastern street food makes a light handheld lunch when stuffed in a pita. Opt for no bread and serve on salad.

1 lemon
1 15-oz. can reduced-sodium garbanzo beans (chickpeas), rinsed and drained
2 Tbsp. whole wheat flour
2 Tbsp. snipped fresh Italian parsley
3 cloves garlic, sliced
½ tsp. ground coriander
¼ tsp. salt
¼ tsp. black pepper
⅛ tsp. ground cumin
Olive oil nonstick cooking spray
2 whole grain pita bread rounds, halved
¾ cup fresh spinach or watercress
8 thin slices roma tomato
½ cup thinly sliced cucumber
1 recipe Yogurt Sauce

**1.** Remove 2 tsp. zest and squeeze 2 Tbsp. juice from lemon. For falafel, in a food processor combine the zest, juice, and the next eight ingredients (through cumin). Cover and process until finely chopped and mixture just holds together (there should be some visible pieces of garbanzo beans).
**2.** Using your hands, shape garbanzo bean mixture into four ½-inch-thick oval patties. Coat a 10-inch nonstick skillet with cooking spray; heat skillet over medium-high. Add patties and cook 4 to 6 minutes or until browned and heated through, turning once.
**3.** Open pita halves to make pockets. Fill pockets with spinach, tomato slices, and cucumber slices. Add falafel and top with Yogurt Sauce.

**Yogurt Sauce** In a bowl stir together ½ cup plain fat-free yogurt, 2 Tbsp. snipped fresh Italian parsley, and ⅛ tsp. each salt and black pepper.

**PER SERVING** *(1 sandwich each)* **CAL** 217, **FAT** 3 g (0 g sat. fat), **CHOL** 1 mg, **SODIUM** 582 mg, **CARB** 43 g (8 g fiber, 4 g sugars), **PRO** 11 g

# Tahini-Ginger Noodles & Veggies

**61g**
**CARB**

**SERVES** 4
**TOTAL** 20 min.

- ¼ cup tahini (sesame seed paste)
- ¼ cup lemon juice
- ¼ cup water
- 1 Tbsp. grated fresh ginger
- 1 Tbsp. agave syrup
- ¼ tsp. kosher salt
- 8 oz. dried linguine
- 3 cups broccoli florets
- 8 oz. sugar snap pea pods, halved
- 2 medium carrots, cut into ribbons with a vegetable peeler
- ¼ cup chopped peanuts or almonds
  Mint leaves (optional)

**1.** In a bowl stir together the first six ingredients (through kosher salt). In a large pot cook linguine in salted boiling water according to package directions. Drain; rinse under cold water. Return to pot.
**2.** Add broccoli, peas, carrots, and tahini mixture; toss to combine. Top with nuts and, if desired, mint leaves.

**PER SERVING** *(2½ cups each)* **CAL** 429, **FAT** 15 g (2 g sat. fat), **CHOL** 0 mg, **SODIUM** 242 mg, **CARB** 61 g (9 g fiber, 10 g sugars), **PRO** 17 g

TRY THIS
If you don't have agave syrup, use a mild-flavor honey in its place.

# Chickpea Alfredo with Spring Veggies

**49g**
CARB

**SERVES** 6
**TOTAL** 35 min.

- ⅓ cup unsalted raw cashews
  Boiling water
- 12 oz. dried whole grain or brown rice fettuccine
- 1 cup chopped fresh asparagus
- 2 cups lightly packed fresh spinach or arugula
- ½ cup frozen peas, slightly thawed
- 1¼ cups water
- ¼ cup garbanzo bean (chickpea) flour
- 1 Tbsp. lemon juice
- 2 tsp. olive oil
- 2 cloves garlic, minced
- ½ tsp. kosher salt
- ½ tsp. black pepper
- 2 Tbsp. snipped fresh basil and/or parsley (optional)
  Shaved Parmesan cheese (optional)

**1.** In a small bowl combine cashews and enough boiling water to cover. Let stand, covered, 20 minutes; drain. Rinse and drain again. Meanwhile, cook pasta according to package directions, adding asparagus the last 3 minutes and spinach and peas the last 1 minute of cooking; drain.

**2.** In a small saucepan whisk together the water and flour until smooth (mixture may be a bit foamy). Cook and stir over medium just until bubbly.

**3.** For sauce, in a blender combine soaked cashews, flour mixture, and next five ingredients (through pepper). Cover and pulse several times, then blend 5 minutes or until smooth. If desired, stir in basil and/or parsley.

**4.** Transfer pasta mixture to a serving dish. Drizzle with sauce; toss to coat. Sprinkle with additional pepper and, if desired, Parmesan cheese.

**PER SERVING** *(1 cup each)* **CAL** 290, **FAT** 7 g (1 g sat. fat), **CHOL** 0 mg, **SODIUM** 190 mg, **CARB** 49 g (8 g fiber, 4 g sugars), **PRO** 11 g

GOOD FOR YOU
This recipe is vegan and, if you choose the brown rice fettuccine option, gluten-free.

## Mediterranean Fried Quinoa

**41g**
**CARB**

**SERVES** 4
**TOTAL** 30 min.

- 2 cups reduced-sodium chicken broth
- 1 cup red quinoa
- 1 Tbsp. olive oil
- 3 cups ½-inch pieces eggplant
- ¾ cup coarsely chopped onion
- 2 cloves garlic, minced
- ¼ tsp. black pepper
- 1 cup grape tomatoes
- 4 cups fresh baby spinach
- ¼ cup pitted Kalamata olives, halved
- 1 Tbsp. snipped fresh oregano
- ¼ cup crumbled feta cheese (1 oz.)
  Lemon wedges

**1.** In a medium saucepan bring broth to boiling; add quinoa. Return to boiling; reduce heat. Simmer, covered, about 15 minutes or until liquid is absorbed. Remove from heat. Drain well; return quinoa to saucepan. Cook and stir over low to dry excess moisture from quinoa.
**2.** In a 12-inch skillet heat oil over medium-high. Add quinoa; cook and stir 2 to 4 minutes or until quinoa starts to brown. Add eggplant, onion, garlic, and pepper; cook and stir 3 minutes. Add tomatoes; cook and stir 2 minutes or until tomatoes start to burst. Remove from heat. Add spinach, olives, and oregano; toss. Sprinkle with feta cheese and serve with lemon wedges.

**PER SERVING** *(1½ cups each)* **CAL** 291,
**FAT** 10 g (2 g sat. fat), **CHOL** 8 mg,
**SODIUM** 593 mg, **CARB** 41 g (8 g fiber,
6 g sugars), **PRO** 11 g

## Asparagus and Greens with Farro

**43g**
**CARB**

**SERVES** 4
**HANDS ON** 10 min.
**TOTAL** 40 min.

- 3 cups water
- 1 cup uncooked farro
- 1 bunch thin asparagus, trimmed and cut into 2-inch pieces
- 3 Tbsp. lemon juice
- ½ cup whole almonds, toasted (tip, *p. 102*) and coarsely chopped
- 1 Tbsp. olive oil
- ½ tsp. kosher salt
- ¼ tsp. black pepper
- 3 cups baby spinach, baby kale, and/or baby mustard greens
- ⅓ cup shaved Parmesan cheese (1 oz.)

**1.** In a medium saucepan bring the water to boiling; add farro. Reduce heat. Simmer, covered, about 30 minutes or until just tender; drain. Meanwhile, place a steamer basket in a 10-inch skillet. Add water to just below basket. Bring water to boiling. Add asparagus to basket. Cover; steam about 3 minutes or until crisp-tender. Transfer to a large bowl.
**2.** Add farro to bowl with asparagus. While still warm, drizzle with lemon juice. Stir in almonds, olive oil, salt, and pepper. Add greens. Toss to combine. Top with Parmesan.

**Tip** Get this dish on the table in half the time. Place farro in a bowl and cover with water. Let soak in the refrigerator overnight. Drain and cook as directed, about 10 minutes.

**PER SERVING** *(2 cups each)* **CAL** 360,
**FAT** 15 g (2 g sat. fat), **CHOL** 5 mg,
**SODIUM** 447 mg, **CARB** 43 g (10 g fiber,
2 g sugars), **PRO** 15 g

# Toasted Walnut Tempeh Tacos

**37g**
**CARB**

**SERVES** 4
**TOTAL** 30 min.

Nonstick cooking spray
1 medium fresh poblano pepper, seeded and chopped (tip, *p. 250*)
½ cup chopped onion
1 8-oz. pkg. tempeh (fermented soybean cake), crumbled, or 2 cups frozen veggie (soy protein) crumbles
2 cloves garlic, minced
2 tsp. salt-free Mexican seasoning blend
¼ tsp. salt
¼ cup chopped walnuts, toasted (tip, *p. 102*)
½ cup chopped avocado
½ tsp. lime juice
⅛ tsp. salt
8 6-inch corn tortillas, warmed
1½ cups shredded romaine lettuce
1 cup refrigerated fresh salsa
¼ cup crumbled Cotija cheese or shredded reduced-fat Mexican-blend cheeses (1 oz.)
½ cup chopped fresh cilantro or cilantro leaves

**1.** Coat a 10-inch nonstick skillet with cooking spray. Heat skillet over medium. Add pepper and onion. Cook 3 to 5 minutes or until vegetables are crisp-tender, stirring occasionally. Add the next four ingredients (through the ¼ tsp. salt). Cook 6 to 8 minutes or until heated and tempeh is lightly browned, stirring occasionally. Remove from heat. Stir in walnuts.
**2.** Meanwhile, in a small bowl coarsely mash avocado with lime juice and the ⅛ tsp. salt.
**3.** Spread mashed avocado over tortillas, then top with lettuce. Spoon warm tempeh mixture over lettuce. Top with salsa, cheese, and cilantro.

**PER SERVING** *(2 tacos each)* **CAL** 380,
**FAT** 19 g (4 g sat. fat), **CHOL** 8 mg, **SODIUM** 545 mg,
**CARB** 37 g (6 g fiber, 5 g sugars), **PRO** 18 g

TRY THIS
Turn up the heat. Add some finely chopped fresh jalapeño chile pepper (tip, *p. 250*) to the mashed avocado.

# Mushroom-Lentil Shepherd's Pie

**51g**
**CARB**

| | |
|---|---|
| **SERVES** 6 | |
| **HANDS ON** 50 min. | |
| **TOTAL** 1 hr. 10 min. | |

- 2 cups vegetable broth
- ½ cup dried brown lentils, rinsed and drained
- ½ tsp. dried rosemary, crushed
- ½ tsp. dried thyme, crushed
- 2½ lb. round red potatoes, cut into 1-inch pieces
- 2 cloves garlic, peeled
- 5 Tbsp. butter
- ¾ tsp. salt
- 3 cups sliced fresh mushrooms
- 1 cup chopped onion
- 1½ cups frozen peas and carrots
- 4 tsp. reduced-sodium soy sauce
- 1 Tbsp. cornstarch
- 2 tsp. Worcestershire sauce

**1.** In a medium saucepan bring 1 cup of the broth to boiling. Stir in lentils, rosemary, and thyme. Simmer, covered, 30 to 40 minutes or until tender. Drain any excess liquid.

**2.** Meanwhile, preheat oven to 375°F. In a covered 4-qt. Dutch oven cook potatoes and garlic in enough boiling water to cover about 15 minutes or until potatoes are tender. Drain, reserving ½ cup of the cooking water. Coarsely mash potatoes. Mash in 3 Tbsp. of the butter and the salt. Stir in enough of the reserved cooking water to reach desired consistency.

**3.** In a 10-inch oven-going skillet heat 1 Tbsp. of the butter over medium. Add mushrooms and onion; cook 10 minutes, stirring occasionally. Stir in peas and carrots. In a small bowl combine the remaining 1 cup broth, the soy sauce, cornstarch, and Worcestershire sauce; stir into mushroom mixture. Cook and stir over medium-high until thickened and bubbly. Cook and stir 1 minute more. Stir in cooked lentils.

**4.** Top lentil mixture with mashed potatoes, spreading to edges. Dot with remaining 1 Tbsp. butter. Transfer skillet to oven. Bake about 20 minutes or until potatoes start to brown.

**PER SERVING** *(1½ cups each)* **CAL** 328, **FAT** 10 g (6 g sat. fat), **CHOL** 25 mg, **SODIUM** 849 mg, **CARB** 51 g (10 g fiber, 6 g sugars), **PRO** 11 g

TRY THIS
Use a mix of fresh mushrooms and swap frozen mixed vegetables for the peas and carrots.

# Sesame-Mushroom Oats with Charred Green Onions

**65g**
**CARB**

**SERVES** 1
**HANDS ON** 15 min.
**TOTAL** 45 min.

- 1 cup reduced-sodium chicken broth or water
- ½ cup steel-cut oats
- 2 tsp. toasted sesame oil
- 1 cup assorted fresh mushrooms, chopped or sliced
- 1 tsp. minced fresh ginger
- 2 green onions, cut into 1- to 2-inch pieces
- 1 tsp. reduced-sodium soy sauce
  Crushed red pepper

**1.** In a small saucepan bring broth to boiling. Stir in oats. Reduce heat to medium-low. Cook, uncovered, 25 to 30 minutes or until oats are tender and mixture is thickened and creamy, stirring occasionally.
**2.** Meanwhile, in an 8-inch skillet heat 1 tsp. of the oil over medium. Add mushrooms and ginger; cook and stir 3 to 4 minutes or until tender. Transfer to a bowl. Add remaining oil to skillet. Increase heat to medium-high. Add green onions; cook 1 to 2 minutes or until charred. Remove from heat.
**3.** Stir mushrooms into oats. Top with soy sauce, green onions, and crushed red pepper.

**PER SERVING** *(1⅔ cups each)* **CAL** 474, **FAT** 15 g (2 g sat. fat), **CHOL** 0 mg, **SODIUM** 748 mg, **CARB** 65 g (12 g fiber, 4 g sugars), **PRO** 21 g

# seafood favorites

Make the most of the fruits of the sea with fresh ingredients and quick cooking techniques.

## Fried Cauliflower Rice with Shrimp

**14g**
**CARB**

**SERVES** 4

**TOTAL** 30 min.

- 8 oz. fresh or frozen medium shrimp, peeled and deveined
- 1 1¾- to 2-lb. head cauliflower, cut into florets (5 cups)
- 1 tsp. toasted sesame oil
- 2 eggs, lightly beaten
- 1 Tbsp. olive oil
- 4 tsp. grated fresh ginger
- 4 cloves garlic, minced
- 2 cups coarsely chopped napa cabbage
- 1 cup coarsely shredded carrots
- ½ tsp. sea salt
- ½ tsp. crushed red pepper
- ⅓ cup sliced green onions
- 2 Tbsp. snipped fresh cilantro Lime wedges

**1.** Thaw shrimp, if frozen. Rinse shrimp; pat dry with paper towels. Working in batches, place cauliflower in a food processor; cover and pulse until pieces are rice size.

**2.** In an extra-large wok or 12-inch skillet heat sesame oil over medium. Add eggs; stir gently until set. Remove eggs; cool slightly. Cut eggs into strips.

**3.** In wok heat olive oil over medium-high. Add ginger and garlic; cook and stir 30 seconds. Add cabbage and carrots; cook and stir about 2 minutes or until vegetables start to soften. Add cauliflower; cook and stir about 4 minutes or until cauliflower starts to soften. Add shrimp, salt, and crushed red pepper; cook and stir about 2 minutes or until shrimp are opaque. Add cooked egg and green onions; cook and stir until heated through.

**4.** Sprinkle shrimp mixture with cilantro. Serve with lime wedges.

**Tip** Riced cauliflower is available in the produce and freezer sections of many grocery stores. Use 4 cups of prepared cauliflower rice in this recipe.

**PER SERVING** *(1½ cups each)* **CAL** 181, **FAT** 8 g (2 g sat. fat), **CHOL** 172 mg, **SODIUM** 434 mg, **CARB** 14 g (5 g fiber, 5 g sugars), **PRO** 17 g

# Quick Scallop and Noodle Toss

**9g**
**CARB**

**SERVES** 4
**TOTAL** 30 min.

12 fresh or frozen sea scallops (about 18 oz. total)
1 medium zucchini, trimmed
½ tsp. olive oil
2 Tbsp. orange juice
2 Tbsp. champagne or cider vinegar
1 Tbsp. toasted sesame oil
1 tsp. grated fresh ginger
½ tsp. lime zest
½ tsp. sea salt
1½ cups fresh baby spinach
1 cup chopped cucumber
⅔ cup thinly sliced radishes
¼ tsp. black pepper
1 Tbsp. olive oil
2 Tbsp. sesame seeds, toasted

**TRY THIS**
You can use fresh or frozen peeled and deveined shrimp for the scallops. Or use a combo of the two.

**1.** Thaw scallops, if frozen. Using a vegetable spiralizer, julienne cutter, or mandoline, cut zucchini into long, thin noodles. In a 10-inch skillet heat the ½ tsp. olive oil over medium-high. Add zucchini noodles. Cook and stir 1 minute or just until tender; cool.
**2.** Meanwhile, in a large bowl combine the next five ingredients (through lime zest) and ¼ tsp. of the salt. Stir in zucchini noodles, spinach, cucumber, and radishes.
**3.** Rinse scallops; pat dry with paper towels. Sprinkle with remaining ¼ tsp. salt and the pepper.
**4.** In the same skillet heat the 1 Tbsp. olive oil over medium-high. Add scallops; cook 3 to 5 minutes or until opaque, turning once. Serve zucchini noodle mixture with scallops and sprinkle with sesame seeds.

**Tip** To toast sesame seeds, spread seeds in a dry small skillet. Cook over medium until light brown, stirring often so they don't burn.

**PER SERVING** *(3 scallops + 1¼ cups noodle mixture each)* **CAL** 227, **FAT** 10 g (1 g sat. fat), **CHOL** 42 mg, **SODIUM** 527 mg, **CARB** 9 g (2 g fiber, 3 g sugars), **PRO** 24 g

## mindful seafood choices

Eating fish or shellfish once or twice a week is a healthful practice. It is a good idea to choose fish that are harvested in sustainable ways. Visit *seafoodwatch.org* for science-based information about the best fish choices and to download a handy consumer guide.

## Coastal Linguine

**39g**
**CARB**

| SERVES 6
| TOTAL 40 min.

- 12 oz. fresh or frozen tilapia fillets
- 8 oz. dried linguine
- ⅛ tsp. salt
- ⅛ tsp. black pepper
- 2 Tbsp. olive oil
- 1 cup finely chopped onion
- 1 8-oz. fennel bulb, trimmed, cored, and chopped (1 cup)
- 1 Tbsp. minced fresh garlic (6 cloves)
- 1 Tbsp. capers
- 1 tsp. dried Italian seasoning, crushed
- 1 14.5-oz. can diced tomatoes, undrained
- 1 8-oz. can tomato sauce
- 1 Tbsp. snipped fresh Italian parsley

**1.** Thaw fish, if frozen. Rinse fish; pat dry with paper towels.
**2.** Cook pasta according to package directions. Drain, reserving ¼ cup of the cooking water. Meanwhile, sprinkle fish with the salt and pepper. In a 12-inch skillet heat 1 Tbsp. of the oil over medium-high. Add fish. Cook about 6 minutes or until fish flakes easily. Remove fish from skillet.
**3.** Add the remaining 1 Tbsp. oil to skillet. Add onion and fennel. Cook and stir about 5 minutes or until tender. Stir in garlic, capers, and Italian seasoning; cook and stir 1 minute more. Stir in tomatoes, tomato sauce, and the reserved pasta water. Bring to boiling. Boil gently, uncovered, 8 minutes, stirring occasionally. Remove from heat. Stir

in the pasta and fish, stirring to break up fish slightly. Sprinkle with parsley.

**Tip** Fennel bulb has a mild licorice flavor that pairs well with seafood. Snip a few of its fronds and sprinkle over the top instead of parsley.

PER SERVING *(1⅓ cups each)* **CAL** 283, **FAT** 6 g (1 g sat. fat), **CHOL** 28 mg, **SODIUM** 458 mg, **CARB** 39 g (4 g fiber, 5 g sugars), **PRO** 18 g

# Cod with Eggplant Peperonata

**13g**
**CARB**

**SERVES** 4

**TOTAL** 45 min.

4   4-oz. fresh or frozen cod fillets
½   of a medium sweet onion, thinly sliced
1   Tbsp. olive oil
1   small eggplant (about 10 oz.), cut into 1-inch pieces (3 cups)
1   large yellow or red sweet pepper, seeded and thinly sliced
4   cloves garlic, minced
1   tsp. snipped fresh rosemary or ½ tsp. dried rosemary, crushed
½   tsp. salt
¼   tsp. black pepper
4   cups fresh spinach

**1.** Thaw fish, if frozen. Rinse fish; pat dry with paper towels.
**2.** For eggplant peperonata, in a 10-inch skillet cook onion in hot oil over medium 5 minutes, stirring occasionally. Add the next four ingredients (through rosemary) and ¼ tsp. of the salt. Cook 10 to

12 minutes more or until vegetables are very tender, stirring occasionally. Remove peperonata from skillet and keep warm.
**3.** Add about 1 inch of water to the same skillet. Place a steamer basket in the skillet; bring water to boiling. Sprinkle cod with the remaining ¼ tsp. salt and the black pepper.

Add fish to steamer basket. Cover and reduce heat to medium. Steam 6 to 8 minutes or just until fish flakes.
**4.** Top spinach with fish and eggplant peperonata.

PER SERVING *(1 fillet + 1 cup spinach + ½ cup peperonata each)* **CAL** 189, **FAT** 5 g (1 g sat. fat), **CHOL** 56 mg, **SODIUM** 396 mg, **CARB** 13 g (4 g fiber, 5 g sugars), **PRO** 23 g

## Parmesan-Crusted Cod with Garlicky Summer Squash

**8g** **CARB**

| | |
|---|---|
| **SERVES** | 4 |
| **HANDS ON** | 20 min. |
| **TOTAL** | 40 min. |

- 4 5- to 6-oz. fresh or frozen skinless cod fillets
- 4 small zucchini and/or yellow summer squash, cut into ¾-inch pieces
- 2 cloves garlic, minced
- ¼ cup olive oil
- ¼ tsp. salt
- ⅛ tsp. black pepper
- ¼ cup panko bread crumbs
- ¼ cup grated Parmesan cheese
- 2 Tbsp. snipped fresh parsley

**1.** Thaw fish, if frozen. Preheat oven to 350°F. In a 15×10-inch baking pan combine squash and garlic. Drizzle with 2 Tbsp. of the oil. Rinse fish; pat dry with paper towels. Place in pan with squash. Sprinkle fish and squash with ⅛ tsp. of the salt and the pepper.
**2.** In a bowl combine panko, cheese, parsley, and the remaining ⅛ tsp. salt. Drizzle with the remaining 2 Tbsp. oil; toss to coat. Sprinkle on top of fish; press lightly. Bake about 20 minutes or until fish flakes easily. If desired, sprinkle with additional parsley.

**Tip** Make cleanup easier by lining the baking pan with foil before adding the vegetables.

**PER SERVING** *(1 fillet + 1 cup zucchini each)* **CAL** 297, **FAT** 16 g (3 g sat. fat), **CHOL** 65 mg, **SODIUM** 409 mg, **CARB** 8 g (2 g fiber, 4 g sugars), **PRO** 29 g

## Mango-Lime Fish Tacos

**35g** **CARB**

| | |
|---|---|
| **SERVES** | 8 |
| **TOTAL** | 30 min. |

- 2 lb. fresh or frozen skinless tilapia, sole, or red snapper fillets
- ½ tsp. salt
- ½ tsp. garlic powder
- ¼ tsp. black pepper
- 2 limes, thinly sliced
- 2 tsp. canola oil
- ½ of a medium onion, halved and thinly sliced
- 1 tsp. cumin seeds
- 6 cups coarsely shredded red and/or green cabbage
- 16 6-inch white corn tortillas, warmed
- 2 cups peeled and chopped fresh mangoes
- 1½ cups crumbled Cotija cheese (6 oz.)
- ¾ cup light sour cream
  Radishes, cut into thin strips
  Lime wedges
  Sriracha sauce

1. Thaw fish, if frozen. Preheat oven to 425°F. Line an extra-large baking sheet with parchment paper.

2. Rinse fish; pat dry with paper towels. Arrange fish in a single layer on the prepared baking sheet. Sprinkle with ¼ tsp. of the salt, the garlic powder, and the pepper. Top with lime slices. Bake 5 to 8 minutes or until fish flakes easily.

3. Meanwhile, in a 10-inch nonstick skillet heat oil over medium. Add onion, cumin seeds, and the remaining ¼ tsp. salt. Cook and stir 30 seconds or until cumin is fragrant. Gradually add cabbage, tossing with tongs to combine with onion mixture. Cook 3 to 4 minutes or just until cabbage is softened.

4. Coarsely flake fish. Serve cabbage mixture in warm tortillas topped with fish, mangoes, cheese, sour cream, and radishes. Serve with lime wedges and sriracha sauce.

**Tip** For low-carb tacos, use large leaves of red cabbage in place of the tortillas.

**PER SERVING** *(2 tacos each)* **CAL** 373, **FAT** 13 g (6 g sat. fat), **CHOL** 84 mg, **SODIUM** 575 mg, **CARB** 35 g (6 g fiber, 11 g sugars), **PRO** 31 g

# Salmon in Parchment Paper

**13g** CARB

**SERVES** 4
**HANDS ON** 30 min.
**TOTAL** 55 min.

- 1 lb. fresh or frozen skinless salmon or halibut fillets, ¾ to 1 inch thick
- 4 cups fresh vegetables, such as sliced carrots, trimmed fresh green beans, sliced zucchini or yellow summer squash, sliced fresh mushrooms, and/or sliced red, yellow, and/or green sweet peppers
- ½ cup sliced green onions
- 1 Tbsp. snipped fresh oregano or 1 tsp. dried oregano, crushed
- 2 tsp. orange zest
- ¼ tsp. salt
- ¼ tsp. black pepper
- 4 cloves garlic, halved
- 4 tsp. olive oil
- 1 medium orange, halved and thinly sliced
- 4 sprigs fresh oregano (optional)

**1.** Preheat oven to 350°F. Thaw fish, if frozen. Rinse fish; pat dry with paper towels. If necessary, cut into four serving-size pieces. Tear off four 14-inch squares of parchment paper. In a large bowl combine the next seven ingredients (through garlic); toss gently.

**2.** Divide vegetable mixture among the four pieces of parchment, placing vegetables on one side of each parchment square. Place one fish piece on top of each vegetable portion. Drizzle 1 tsp. of the oil over each fish piece. Sprinkle lightly with additional black pepper; top with orange slices. Fold parchment over fish and vegetables; fold in the open sides several times to secure, curving the edge into a circular pattern. Place parchment packets in a single layer in a 15×10-inch baking pan.

**3.** Bake 25 to 30 minutes or until fish flakes easily. Cut an X in the top of a parchment packet to check doneness; open carefully (steam will escape). If desired, garnish with fresh oregano sprigs.

**Tip** If using carrots and/or green beans, precook them. In a covered medium saucepan cook the carrots and/or green beans in a small amount of boiling water 2 minutes; drain.

**PER SERVING** *(1 packet each)* **CAL** 262, **FAT** 12 g (2 g sat. fat), **CHOL** 62 mg, **SODIUM** 359 mg, **CARB** 13 g (4 g fiber, 8 g sugars), **PRO** 25 g

TRY THIS
Use foil to make packets if you don't have parchment. Use care when opening to avoid the steam.

# Lemon-Herb Roasted Salmon Sheet-Pan Dinner

**13g**
**CARB**

**SERVES** 4
**HANDS ON** 20 min.
**TOTAL** 35 min.

- 1 1-lb. fresh or frozen skinless salmon fillet
- 2 Tbsp. olive oil
- 1½ tsp. dried oregano, crushed
- ¼ tsp. salt
- ⅛ tsp. black pepper
- 2 cups grape or cherry tomatoes, halved
- 2 cups broccoli florets
- 2 cloves garlic, minced
- 1 lemon
- 2 Tbsp. snipped fresh basil
- 1 Tbsp. snipped fresh parsley
- 1 Tbsp. honey

**1.** Thaw salmon, if frozen. Preheat oven to 400°F. Line a 15×10-inch baking pan with parchment paper. Rinse fish; pat dry with paper towels. Place salmon in prepared pan. Drizzle with 1 Tbsp. of the oil and sprinkle with ¾ tsp. of the oregano, the salt, and pepper.
**2.** In a bowl combine tomatoes, broccoli, garlic, and the remaining 1 Tbsp. oil and ¾ tsp. oregano. Sprinkle lightly with additional salt and pepper; toss to coat. Place in pan with salmon. Roast 15 to 18 minutes or just until salmon flakes.

**3.** Meanwhile, remove 1 tsp. zest and squeeze 3 Tbsp. juice from lemon. In a small bowl combine lemon zest and juice and the remaining ingredients. Spoon over salmon and vegetables before serving.

**PER SERVING** *(3½ oz. salmon + ½ cup vegetables each)* **CAL** 276, **FAT** 14 g (2 g sat. fat), **CHOL** 62 mg, **SODIUM** 362 mg, **CARB** 13 g (3 g fiber, 8 g sugars), **PRO** 25 g

# Tomato Salad with Grilled Tuna and Beans

**44g**
**CARB**

**SERVES** 4
**HANDS ON** 25 min.
**TOTAL** 4 hr. 30 min.

- 1 orange
- 2 15-oz. cans cannellini (white kidney) beans, rinsed and drained
- ¼ cup snipped fresh basil
- ¼ cup white balsamic vinegar
- 2 tsp. Dijon-style mustard
- 2 cloves garlic, minced
- ¼ tsp. anise seeds, crushed
- 2 6-oz. fresh or frozen yellowfin tuna steaks, 1 inch thick
- 2 Tbsp. snipped fresh rosemary
- 1 Tbsp. lemon zest
- 3 cloves garlic, minced
- 2 tsp. olive oil
- 3 large heirloom tomatoes and/or cherry tomatoes, cut up
  Freshly ground black pepper
  Fresh basil sprigs (optional)

**1.** Remove 1 tsp. zest and squeeze 2 Tbsp. juice from orange. In a bowl

TRY THIS
Steelhead trout is an excellent substitute for salmon because it has salmon's rosy hue and rich flavor.

combine zest and the next six ingredients (through anise seeds). Cover and chill up to 4 hours.

**2.** Thaw fish, if frozen. Rinse fish; pat dry with paper towels. In a bowl combine orange juice, rosemary, lemon zest, and the 3 cloves garlic. Brush tuna with olive oil. Spread rosemary mixture over both sides of tuna, pressing to adhere.

**3.** Grill fish, uncovered, on a greased rack over medium 6 to 8 minutes or until just pink in center, gently turning fish once. Thinly slice tuna steaks.

**4.** Top bean mixture with tuna and serve with tomatoes. Sprinkle with pepper. If desired, top with additional fresh basil. Serve immediately.

**PER SERVING** *(¾ cup bean mixture + 3 oz. tuna + ¾ cup tomatoes each)* **CAL** 329, **FAT** 3 g (1 g sat. fat), **CHOL** 33 mg, **SODIUM** 509 mg, **CARB** 44 g (11 g fiber, 11 g sugars), **PRO** 33 g

# world classics

Add a little international flair to mealtime with both familiar and new recipes inspired by flavors from across the globe.

## Jerk Marinated Chicken with Caribbean Rice

**29g**
**CARB**

| | |
|---|---|
| **SERVES** 4 | |
| **HANDS ON** 25 min. | |
| **TOTAL** 6 hr. 40 min. | |

- 2  8-oz. skinless, boneless chicken breast halves
- 2  Tbsp. canola oil
- 2  Tbsp. red wine vinegar
- 2  Tbsp. orange juice
- 2  Tbsp. thinly sliced green onion
- 1  Tbsp. packed brown sugar
- 1  Tbsp. reduced-sodium soy sauce
- 1  Tbsp. fresh jalapeño chile pepper, seeded (if desired) and finely chopped (tip, *p. 250*)
- 2  tsp. Caribbean jerk seasoning
- 3  cloves garlic, minced
- ⅛  tsp. salt
- 1  recipe Caribbean Rice
   Lime wedges

**1.** Place chicken in a resealable plastic bag set in a shallow dish. For marinade, in a bowl combine the next 10 ingredients (through salt). Pour marinade over chicken. Seal bag; turn to coat chicken. Marinate in the refrigerator 6 to 24 hours, turning bag occasionally.
**2.** Drain chicken, reserving marinade. Grill chicken, covered, over medium 15 to 18 minutes or until done (165°F), turning once. Remove from grill and let stand 5 minutes.
**3.** Meanwhile, for glaze, in a small saucepan bring reserved marinade to boiling; reduce heat. Simmer, uncovered, 10 minutes or until reduced to ¼ cup. Slice chicken. Serve over Caribbean Rice with lime wedges and drizzle with glaze.

**Caribbean Rice**  Coat an 8-inch nonstick skillet with **nonstick cooking spray**; heat over medium-high. Add **½ cup each chopped fresh pineapple and chopped green sweet pepper; 1 Tbsp. seeded (if desired) and finely chopped fresh jalapeño chile pepper** (tip, *p. 250*); **¼ tsp. each salt, garlic powder, and black pepper;** and **⅛ tsp. ground cinnamon.** Cook 5 minutes, stirring occasionally. Stir in **one 8.8-oz. pouch cooked whole grain brown rice, ½ cup canned no-salt-added red kidney beans,** and **¼ cup orange juice;** heat through. Stir in **¼ cup snipped fresh cilantro.**

**PER SERVING** *(3 oz. chicken + ¾ cup rice + 1 Tbsp. glaze each)* **CAL** 286, **FAT** 6 g (1 g sat. fat), **CHOL** 83 mg, **SODIUM** 265 mg, **CARB** 29 g (5 g fiber, 5 g sugars), **PRO** 30 g

# Korean-Style Chili-Garlic Chicken Stir-Fry

**32g** CARB

**SERVES** 4
**HANDS ON** 25 min.
**TOTAL** 40 min.

- 2 Tbsp. reduced-sodium soy sauce
- 2 Tbsp. rice vinegar
- 1 Tbsp. Asian chili-garlic sauce
- 1 Tbsp. finely chopped fresh ginger
- 3 cloves garlic, minced
- 1 lb. skinless, boneless chicken breast halves, cut into 1-inch pieces
- 3 Tbsp. honey or packed brown sugar*
- 2 tsp. cornstarch
- 8 oz. fresh green beans, trimmed
- 1 Tbsp. toasted sesame oil
- 1 Tbsp. canola oil
- ½ cup coarsely chopped onion
- ¾ cup coarsely chopped red sweet pepper
- 1 recipe Quick-Pickled Vegetables, drained
- 2 tsp. sesame seeds, toasted

**1.** In a medium bowl combine the first five ingredients (through garlic). Transfer half of the mixture to a small bowl. Add chicken to the remaining mixture in medium bowl. Toss to coat. Add honey and cornstarch to soy sauce mixture in small bowl, stirring to dissolve cornstarch.

**2.** In a large wok or 10-inch nonstick skillet cook beans in just enough boiling water to cover about 4 minutes or just until crisp-tender; drain beans in a colander. Wipe wok dry.

**3.** In the same wok heat sesame and canola oils over medium-high. Add onion and sweet pepper; cook and stir 3 to 4 minutes or until crisp-tender. Remove vegetables from wok. Add half of the chicken to wok; cook and stir over medium-high 3 to 4 minutes or until chicken is no longer pink. Remove chicken from wok. Repeat with remaining chicken. Return chicken, green beans, onion, and red pepper to wok. Stir sauce well. Add to wok; cook and stir until thickened and bubbly.

**4.** Spoon Quick-Pickled Vegetables over chicken mixture. Top with sesame seeds.

**Quick-Pickled Vegetables** In a small saucepan combine **½ cup each water and rice vinegar, ¼ cup sugar,* ½ tsp. salt,** and **⅛ tsp. crushed red pepper.** Bring to boiling; reduce heat. Simmer, uncovered, 2 minutes. Remove from heat. Add **1 cup coarsely shredded napa cabbage, ½ cup each shredded carrots and thinly sliced quartered red onion,** and **1 tsp. finely chopped fresh ginger;** stir until well combined. Cover; let stand at room temperature 30 to 60 minutes. Drain before serving.

**PER SERVING** *(1⅓ cups chicken mixture + ⅓ cup pickled vegetables each)* **CAL** 342, **FAT** 11 g (2 g sat. fat), **CHOL** 83 mg, **SODIUM** 564 mg, **CARB** 32 g (4 g fiber, 24 g sugars), **PRO** 29 g

**\*Sugar Sub** Choose Splenda Brown Sugar Blend for the sauce mixture. Follow package directions to use 3 Tbsp. packed brown sugar equivalent. Choose Splenda Sugar Blend for the Quick-Pickled Vegetables. Follow package directions to use ¼ cup granulated sugar equivalent.

**PER SERVING WITH SUB** Same as above, except **CAL** 312, **CARB** 22 g (14 g sugars)

GLOBAL

This Mexican dish started as a way to use leftover tortillas. As they simmer, they soften, thickening the sauce.

# Chicken Chilaquiles

**24g CARB**

**SERVES** 6
**HANDS ON** 40 min.
**TOTAL** 55 min.

- 10 6-inch corn tortillas, cut into 1-inch-wide strips
- 1 Tbsp. vegetable oil
- ⅓ cup chopped onion
- 2 cloves garlic, minced
- 1 tsp. dried Mexican oregano or regular oregano, crushed
- 2 14.5-oz. cans diced tomatoes, undrained
- 1 to 2 canned chipotle chile peppers in adobo sauce, finely chopped (tip, *p. 250*) + 1 tsp. of the adobo sauce
- 1 14.5-oz. can reduced-sodium chicken broth
- 2 cups shredded cooked chicken
- ¼ tsp. cracked black pepper
- 1 cup crumbled queso fresco, Cotija, or feta cheese (4 oz.)
  Fresh cilantro sprigs
- ¼ cup light sour cream
- 1 Tbsp. fat-free milk

**1.** Preheat oven to 350°F. Spread tortilla strips in an even layer on two large baking sheets. Bake 15 minutes. Cool on a wire rack.
**2.** Meanwhile, in a 12-inch skillet heat oil over medium-high. Add onion, garlic, and oregano; cook about 3 minutes or until onion is tender, stirring occasionally. Add tomatoes and chipotle pepper(s) plus the 1 tsp. adobo sauce. Bring to boiling; cook 1 minute, stirring occasionally. Add broth; return to boiling. Simmer, uncovered,

5 minutes. Stir in cooked chicken and black pepper; heat through.

**3.** Set aside a few of the baked tortilla strips. Gradually stir the remaining tortilla strips into the chicken mixture; heat through. Remove from heat; sprinkle with cheese. Top with cilantro sprigs and the reserved tortilla strips. In a bowl combine sour cream and milk; serve with casserole.

PER SERVING (⅙ casserole each) **CAL** 286, **FAT** 12 g (4 g sat. fat), **CHOL** 57 mg, **SODIUM** 735 mg, **CARB** 24 g (5 g fiber, 6 g sugars), **PRO** 21 g

---

# 🍲 Mu Shu Chicken

**34g**
**CARB**

**SERVES** 6
**HANDS ON** 20 min.
**SLOW COOK** 6 hr.

½  cup hoisin sauce
2  Tbsp. water
4  tsp. toasted sesame oil
1  Tbsp. cornstarch
1  Tbsp. reduced-sodium soy sauce
3  large cloves garlic, minced
1  16-oz. pkg. shredded cabbage with carrots (coleslaw mix)
1  cup coarsely shredded carrots
12  oz. skinless, boneless chicken thighs
6  8-inch whole wheat flour tortillas
   Green onions (optional)

**1.** In a small bowl combine the first six ingredients (through garlic).

**2.** In a 3½- or 4-qt. slow cooker combine coleslaw mix and coarsely shredded carrots. Cut chicken into ⅛-inch slices; cut each slice in half lengthwise. Place chicken on top of cabbage mixture. Drizzle with ¼ cup of the hoisin mixture.

**3.** Cover and cook on low 6 hours or high 4 hours. Stir in the remaining hoisin mixture.

**4.** Heat tortillas according to package directions. Fill tortillas with chicken mixture. If desired, top with green onions.

PER SERVING (1 filled tortilla each) **CAL** 269, **FAT** 8 g (1 g sat. fat), **CHOL** 54 mg, **SODIUM** 579 mg, **CARB** 34 g (5 g fiber, 11 g sugars), **PRO** 16 g

# Turkey Kabob Pitas

**40g** CARB | **SERVES** 4
**HANDS ON** 25 min.
**TOTAL** 35 min.

- 1 tsp. whole cumin seeds, lightly crushed
- 1 cup shredded cucumber
- ⅓ cup seeded and chopped roma tomato
- ¼ cup slivered red onion
- ¼ cup shredded radishes
- ¼ cup snipped fresh cilantro
- ¼ tsp. black pepper
- 1 lb. turkey breast, cut into thin strips
- 1 recipe Curry Blend
- ¼ cup plain fat-free Greek yogurt
- 4 6-inch whole wheat pita bread rounds

**1.** If using wooden skewers, soak in water 30 minutes. In an 8-inch dry skillet toast cumin seeds over medium about 1 minute or until fragrant. Transfer to a bowl. Add the next six ingredients (through pepper) to bowl; stir to combine.
**2.** In another bowl combine turkey and Curry Blend; stir to coat. Thread turkey onto skewers. Grill kabobs, uncovered, over medium 6 to 8 minutes or until turkey is no longer pink, turning kabobs occasionally.
**3.** Remove turkey from skewers. Spread Greek yogurt on pita rounds. Using a slotted spoon, spoon cucumber mixture over yogurt. Top with grilled turkey.

**Curry Blend** In a bowl stir together **2 tsp. olive oil; 1 tsp. curry powder; ½ tsp. each ground cumin, ground turmeric, and ground coriander; ¼ tsp. ground ginger; and ⅛ tsp. each salt and cayenne pepper.**

**Tip** Curry powders in India are usually individually blended, and each family has its own combo. If you wish, use 2 to 3 tsp. of a favorite premade curry powder instead of the Curry Blend spices with the oil to coat the turkey strips.

**PER SERVING** (1 sandwich each) **CAL** 343, **FAT** 6 g (1 g sat. fat), **CHOL** 61 mg, **SODIUM** 506 mg, **CARB** 40 g (5 g fiber, 4 g sugars), **PRO** 35 g

#  Stewed Moroccan Chicken

**51g** CARB | **SERVES** 6
**HANDS ON** 30 min.
**SLOW COOK** 4 hr.

- 6 4- to 6-oz. skinless, boneless chicken thighs
- 2 cups reduced-sodium chicken broth
- 3 medium carrots, cut into ½-inch pieces
- 1 large yellow onion, halved and sliced ¼ inch thick
- 1 cup water
- ½ cup dried brown lentils, rinsed and drained
- 2 tsp. ground turmeric
- 2 cloves garlic, minced

1    tsp. ground cumin
½   tsp. ground cinnamon
½   tsp. salt
½   tsp. ground ginger
⅛   to ¼ tsp. cayenne pepper
     (optional)
1    lemon
3    cups cauliflower florets
1    14.5-oz. can diced no-salt-
     added tomatoes, drained
⅓   cup golden raisins or finely
     chopped dried apricots
2    cups hot cooked whole
     wheat couscous
3    Tbsp. sliced almonds, toasted
     (tip, *p. 102*)
     Snipped fresh parsley (optional)

**1.** In a 4- to 5-qt. slow cooker combine the first 13 ingredients (through cayenne pepper if using). Cover and cook on low 3 hours or high 1½ hours or just until lentils are tender.

**2.** Remove 1 tsp. zest and squeeze 1 Tbsp. juice from lemon. If slow cooker is on low, turn to high. Stir in lemon zest, cauliflower, tomatoes, and raisins. Cover and cook about 1 hour more or until cauliflower is tender.

**3.** Stir in lemon juice. Serve lentil mixture over couscous. Sprinkle with almonds and, if desired, parsley.

**PER SERVING** *(1⅔ cups stew + ⅓ cup couscous each)* **CAL** 391, **FAT** 7 g (1 g sat. fat), **CHOL** 106 mg, **SODIUM** 533 mg, **CARB** 51 g (9 g fiber, 12 g sugars), **PRO** 34 g

GLOBAL
Moroccan food features complex flavors created by assorted spices, so don't be scared by the long ingredient list.

# Greek Flat Iron Steaks

**6g** CARB

**SERVES** 4
**TOTAL** 25 min.

1 lemon
2 6- to 8-oz. boneless beef shoulder
 top blade (flat iron) steaks
¼ tsp. salt
¼ tsp. black pepper
1 tsp. dried rosemary, crushed
4 tsp. olive oil
2 cups grape tomatoes, halved if desired
2 cloves garlic, minced
⅓ cup pitted green olives, halved
¼ cup crumbled feta cheese (1 oz.)
 Lemon wedges

**1.** Remove 1 tsp. zest from the lemon. Set zest aside. Trim fat from steaks. Cut steaks in half and generously season both sides with salt and pepper. Sprinkle rosemary on both sides of steaks; rub in with your fingers.

**2.** In a 10-inch skillet heat 2 tsp. of the oil over medium-high. Add steaks; cook 8 to 10 minutes or until medium rare (145°F), turning once. Remove from skillet; cover and keep warm.

**3.** Add remaining 2 tsp. oil to skillet. Add tomatoes and garlic; cook over medium-high about 3 minutes or until tomatoes start to soften and burst. Remove from heat. Stir in olives and the lemon zest.

**4.** Serve steaks with tomato relish. Sprinkle with cheese and serve with the reserved lemon wedges.

**5.** Serve steaks with tomato relish. Sprinkle with cheese and serve with lemon wedges and additional pepper.

**PER SERVING** *(3 oz. beef + ½ cup relish each)* **CAL** 223, **FAT** 14 g (5 g sat. fat), **CHOL** 67 mg, **SODIUM** 498 mg, **CARB** 6 g (2 g fiber, 3 g sugars), **PRO** 20 g

TRY THIS
Use regular green olives in this dish or a pitted olive blend from the deli at your supermarket.

# Indian-Spiced Burgers with Cilantro Cucumber Sauce

**8g** **CARB**

**SERVES** 4
**HANDS ON** 25 min.
**TOTAL** 40 min.

- 1  5.3- to 6-oz. container plain fat-free Greek yogurt
- ⅔  cup finely chopped cucumber
- ¼  cup snipped fresh cilantro
- 2  cloves garlic, minced
- ⅛  tsp. salt
- ⅛  tsp. black pepper
- ½  cup canned garbanzo beans (chickpeas), rinsed and drained
- 1  lb. lean ground beef
- ¼  cup finely chopped red onion
- 2  Tbsp. finely chopped jalapeño pepper (tip, *p. 250*)
- ½  tsp. salt
- ¼  tsp. ground cumin
- ¼  tsp. ground coriander
- ⅛  tsp. cinnamon
- ⅛  tsp. black pepper
- 1  head radicchio, shredded

**1.** For sauce, in a bowl stir together the first six ingredients (through ⅛ tsp. black pepper). Cover and chill until ready to serve.
**2.** In a medium bowl mash garbanzo beans using a potato masher or fork. Add the next eight ingredients (through ⅛ tsp. black pepper); mix well. Form meat mixture into four ¾-inch-thick patties.
**3.** Grill burgers, covered, over medium 14 to 18 minutes or until done (160°F), turning once. Toss radicchio with additional fresh cilantro leaves. Serve burgers on radicchio; top with sauce.

**PER SERVING** (1 burger + ¼ cup sauce each) **CAL** 258, **FAT** 12 g (5 g sat. fat), **CHOL** 75 mg, **SODIUM** 539 mg, **CARB** 8 g (2 g fiber, 4 g sugars), **PRO** 29 g

# Lamb Fatteh with Asparagus

**39g** **CARB**

**SERVES** 4
**HANDS ON** 10 min.
**TOTAL** 30 min.

- 1  Tbsp. olive oil
- 1  medium onion, halved and sliced
- 4  cloves garlic, minced
- 12  oz. boneless lamb leg or beef sirloin steak, trimmed and cut into 2×½-inch pieces
- 1  14.5-oz. can 50%-less-sodium beef broth
- 1  cup whole wheat Israeli couscous
- ½  tsp. dried oregano, crushed
- ½  tsp. ground cumin
- ¼  tsp. salt
- ¼  tsp. black pepper
- 1  lb. thin asparagus spears, bias-sliced into 2-inch pieces

¾ cup chopped red sweet pepper
  Snipped fresh oregano (optional)
  Lemon wedges

**1.** In a 10-inch skillet heat oil over medium-high. Add onion; cook and stir 3 minutes. Add garlic; cook and stir 1 minute. Add lamb; cook 3 to 5 minutes or until browned on all sides. Stir in the next six ingredients (through black pepper). Bring to boiling; reduce heat. Simmer, covered, 10 minutes, stirring occasionally.

**2.** Stir in asparagus and sweet pepper. Cover and simmer 3 to 5 minutes more or until vegetables are crisp-tender. Fluff lamb mixture lightly with a fork. Top with fresh oregano, if desired, and serve with lemon wedges.

**PER SERVING** *(1½ cups each)* **CAL** 334, **FAT** 9 g (3 g sat. fat), **CHOL** 54 mg, **SODIUM** 390 mg, **CARB** 39 g (6 g fiber, 6 g sugars), **PRO** 26 g

GLOBAL
This Middle Eastern dish uses whole wheat Israeli couscous as a more healthful option to the usual pita pieces.

# 🍲 Pork-Stuffed Cabbage Rolls

**36g**
**CARB**

**SERVES** 8
**HANDS ON** 1 hr. 15 min.
**SLOW COOK** 6 hr. 30 min.

| | |
|---|---|
| 1 | 3-lb. head green cabbage, cored |
| 1 | lb. ground pork |
| 1½ | cups cooked brown rice |
| ½ | cup chopped onion |
| ½ | cup golden raisins |
| 3 | Tbsp. tomato paste |
| 4 | cloves garlic, minced |
| ½ | tsp. caraway seeds, crushed |
| 1 | tsp. salt |
| ½ | tsp. black pepper |
| 1 | 14.5-oz. can no-salt-added diced tomatoes, undrained |
| 1 | 8-oz. can low-sodium vegetable juice |
| 1 | 8-oz. can tomato sauce |
| 2 | Tbsp. reduced-sodium Worcestershire sauce |
| 2 | tsp. packed brown sugar* |
| ¼ | cup snipped fresh parsley |

**1.** In a large pot cook cabbage in a large amount of boiling lightly salted water 12 to 15 minutes, removing 16 leaves with long-handled tongs as they become pliable. Drain well; trim heavy vein from each leaf. Remove and shred enough of the remaining cabbage to measure 4 cups. Place shredded cabbage in a 5- to 6-qt. slow cooker.

**2.** For filling, in a large bowl combine the next seven ingredients (through caraway seeds), ½ tsp. of the salt, and ¼ tsp. of the pepper. Spoon a scant ⅓ cup filling onto each cabbage leaf; fold in sides and roll up.

**3.** For sauce, in a medium bowl combine the next five ingredients (through brown sugar) and remaining ½ tsp. salt and ¼ tsp. pepper. Stir half of the sauce into shredded cabbage in cooker. Add cabbage rolls and top with remaining sauce.
**4.** Cover and cook on low 6½ to 7½ hours or on high 3½ to 4 hours or until a cabbage roll in center of cooker registers 160°F. Serve cabbage rolls with shredded cabbage mixture and sprinkle with parsley.

**PER SERVING** *(2 rolls + ½ cup cabbage mixture each)* **CAL** 280, **FAT** 10 g (3 g sat. fat), **CHOL** 39 mg, **SODIUM** 634 mg, **CARB** 36 g (7 g fiber, 18 g sugars), **PRO** 15 g

***Sugar Sub*** Choose Splenda Brown Sugar Blend. Follow package directions to use 2 tsp. equivalent.
**PER SERVING WITH SUB** Same as above, except **CAL** 284, **SODIUM** 619 mg

# Pineapple Pork Fried Rice

**41g**
**CARB**

**SERVES** 4
**TOTAL** 45 min.

- 1 egg
- 2 egg whites
- 2 tsp. canola oil
- 1 lb. pork tenderloin, cut into bite-size pieces
- 1 Tbsp. canola oil
- 1 cup chopped fresh pineapple
- ½ cup thinly sliced carrot
- ½ cup thinly bias-sliced celery
- ½ cup sliced green onions
- 2 tsp. grated fresh ginger
- 2 cloves garlic, minced
- 2 cups cooked jasmine rice
- ½ cup frozen peas, thawed
- 3 Tbsp. reduced-sodium soy sauce
- 1 Tbsp. snipped fresh cilantro
  Finely chopped peanuts, lime wedges, and/or sriracha sauce (optional)

**1.** In a bowl whisk together egg and egg whites. In a 12-inch skillet or extra-large wok heat the 2 tsp. oil over medium-high. Add pork. Cook and stir 3 to 5 minutes or until pork is no longer pink. Remove from skillet.
**2.** Add the 1 Tbsp. oil to the skillet. Add the next five ingredients (through ginger); cook and stir 3 to 4 minutes or until vegetables are tender. Add garlic; cook and stir 30 seconds more. Add egg mixture; let stand 5 to 10 seconds or until egg sets on bottom but remains runny on top. Add rice. Turn and toss mixture continuously 1 minute. Stir in cooked pork, peas, soy sauce, and cilantro; heat. If desired, sprinkle with peanuts and serve with lime wedges and/or sriracha sauce.

**PER SERVING** *(1½ cups each)* **CAL** 386, **FAT** 11 g (2 g sat. fat), **CHOL** 144 mg, **SODIUM** 546 mg, **CARB** 41 g (4 g fiber, 8 g sugars), **PRO** 31 g

# Pork Tenderloin Dijon with Haricots Verts

**10g** CARB

**SERVES** 4
**HANDS ON** 25 min.
**TOTAL** 50 min.

**GLOBAL**
French cooking is remarkably simple. Everything for this dish, including the sauce, is made in one skillet.

- 3 tsp. olive oil
- 1 12- to 16-oz. natural pork tenderloin
- 2 tsp. herbes de Provence, crushed
- ¼ tsp. black pepper
- ⅛ tsp. salt
- 12 oz. fresh haricots verts (thin green beans)
- 1 cup thin wedges fennel bulb (1 medium)
- ¼ cup finely chopped shallot
- ¾ cup reduced-sodium chicken broth
- ¼ cup dry white wine, apple cider, or reduced-sodium chicken broth
- 2 Tbsp. heavy cream or half-and-half
- 2 tsp. Dijon-style mustard
- 2 Tbsp. snipped fresh parsley

**1.** Preheat oven to 425°F. Lightly brush 1 tsp. of the olive oil over pork. Sprinkle all over with herbes de Provence, pepper, and salt. Place pork in a 12-inch oven-going skillet.
**2.** In a large bowl toss green beans and fennel with the remaining 2 tsp. olive oil. Arrange vegetables around pork in skillet.
**3.** Roast 25 to 30 minutes or until pork is done (145°F), stirring vegetables once. Transfer pork and vegetables to a platter; cover to keep warm. Do not wipe out skillet.
**4.** Meanwhile, using hot pads, place skillet over medium. Add shallots to skillet; cook and stir about 2 minutes or until tender. Add broth and wine. Bring to boiling. Boil gently, uncovered, 5 minutes. Whisk in cream and mustard. Stir in parsley.
**5.** Slice pork. Serve with vegetables. Spoon sauce over top.

**Tip** Pork tenderloin that is not marked as natural may be injected with a salt solution. If you do choose a pork tenderloin that is not marked as natural, it may be larger in diameter and may need 5 to 10 minutes more roasting time.

**PER SERVING** *(3 oz. pork + ¾ cup vegetables + about 1 Tbsp. sauce each)* **CAL** 205, **FAT** 8 g (3 g sat. fat), **CHOL** 64 mg, **SODIUM** 301 mg, **CARB** 10 g (3 g fiber, 5 g sugars), **PRO** 21 g

## Caribbean Fish with Mango-Orange Relish

**20g CARB**

| SERVES 6 |
| HANDS ON 25 min. |
| TOTAL 40 min. |

- 2½ lb. fresh or frozen skinless sea bass, barramundi, or other whitefish fillets, about ½ inch thick
- 3 navel oranges
- 1 large mango, halved, seeded, peeled, and chopped
- ¾ cup chopped roasted red sweet pepper
- 2 Tbsp. dry white wine
- 1 Tbsp. snipped fresh cilantro
- ¼ tsp. salt
- ¼ tsp. black pepper
- ⅓ cup all-purpose flour
- 2 tsp. ground cardamom
- ¼ cup butter
  Snipped fresh chives

**1.** Thaw fish, if frozen. Rinse fish and pat dry with paper towels. For relish, juice one of the oranges. Peel and section the remaining two oranges. In a medium bowl combine orange sections, orange juice, and the next four ingredients (through cilantro).
**2.** Sprinkle fish with salt and pepper. On waxed paper or in a shallow dish stir together flour and cardamom. Dip fish in flour mixture, turning to coat.
**3.** Preheat oven to 300°F. In a 12-inch nonstick skillet melt 2 Tbsp. of the butter over medium-high. Add half of the fish; cook 6 to 8 minutes or until fish is golden and flakes easily, turning once. Keep warm in

oven while cooking remaining fish in remaining 2 Tbsp. butter. Serve with relish and sprinkle with chives.

**Tip** You can use freshly roasted or jarred roasted red sweet peppers in this recipe. Leftovers don't keep long in the refrigerator, so freeze them or use in salads, sandwiches, omelets, or soups.

PER SERVING *(1 fillet + ⅓ cup relish each)* **CAL** 343, **FAT** 12 g (6 g sat. fat), **CHOL** 97 mg, **SODIUM** 365 mg, **CARB** 20 g (2 g fiber, 12 g sugars), **PRO** 37 g

**1.** For filling, combine the first four ingredients (through soy sauce), ¼ cup of the green onions, and 2 Tbsp. of the cilantro.
**2.** Working with two wonton wrappers at a time, top each with a rounded teaspoon of the filling. Brush edges of wrappers with water; fold one corner over filling to meet opposite corner, forming triangles. Press down around filling to force out any air and to seal edges well. Cover filled wontonsi with a dry kitchen towel while filling

**3.** In a large saucepan combine the next four ingredients (through salt) and the remaining green onions and cilantro. Bring to boiling. Slowly add wontons to boiling broth mixture. Boil gently, 2 to 3 minutes or until tender, gently, stirring occasionally. Stir in spinach and sesame oil. If desired, top with additional snipped fresh cilantro. Serve immediately.

PER SERVING *(1⅓ cups each)* **CAL** 189, **FAT** 3 g (1 g sat. fat), **CHOL** 58 mg, **SODIUM** 637 mg, **CARB** 24 g (2 g fiber, 2 g sugars), **PRO** 17 g

# Shrimp and Chicken Dumpling Soup

**24g** CARB | **SERVES** 6
**TOTAL** 45 min.

- 1  6-oz. pkg. frozen peeled, cooked shrimp, thawed and finely chopped
- ½  cup finely chopped cooked chicken
- ½  cup finely chopped fresh mushrooms
- 2  Tbsp. reduced-sodium soy sauce
- ½  cup sliced green onions
- ¼  cup finely snipped fresh cilantro
- 24  wonton wrappers
- 6  cups low-sodium chicken broth
- ¾  cup chopped red sweet pepper
- ½  cup frozen edamame
- ¼  tsp. salt
- 2  cups fresh baby spinach
- 1  to 2 tsp. toasted sesame oil

# Mushroom-Farro Melanzane

**27g**
**CARB**

**SERVES** 6
**HANDS ON** 35 min.
**TOTAL** 50 min.

- 1 small eggplant, trimmed and cut crosswise into ½-inch-thick slices
- 3 Tbsp. olive oil
- 2 cups sliced fresh cremini mushrooms
- ¾ cup chopped shallots
- 4 cloves garlic, minced
- 1 8-oz. pkg. precooked farro
- 1½ cups tomato puree
- 2 cups thinly sliced, halved zucchini
- 1 cup cherry tomatoes, halved
- ¼ cup dry red wine or water
- 2 Tbsp. snipped fresh oregano
- 1½ cups shredded Italian-blend cheeses (6 oz.)
- 2 tsp. snipped fresh thyme
- ½ tsp. sea salt
- ¼ tsp. black pepper
  Snipped fresh oregano (optional)

**GLOBAL**

*Melanzane,* the Italian word for eggplant, refers to a layered baked dish. It has been translated here into this faster skillet meal.

**1.** Brush eggplant slices with 2 Tbsp. of the oil. In a 10-inch oven-going skillet brown eggplant slices, in batches, turning once. Transfer browned slices to a plate.
**2.** In the same skillet heat the remaining 1 Tbsp. oil over medium. Add mushrooms, shallots, and garlic. Cook 6 to 8 minutes or until mushrooms are tender and lightly browned, stirring occasionally. Stir in the next six ingredients (through oregano) and ¾ cup of the cheese until combined. Top evenly with eggplant slices, overlapping as needed. Sprinkle with thyme, salt, pepper, and the remaining cheese. Cover and cook about 7 minutes or until heated through and cheese is melted.
**3.** If desired, preheat broiler. Uncover skillet and broil 3 to 4 inches from heat about 1 minute or until cheese is golden and bubbly. If desired, garnish with oregano.

**PER SERVING** *(1¾ cups each)* **CAL** 277, **FAT** 14 g (5 g sat. fat), **CHOL** 20 mg, **SODIUM** 555 mg, **CARB** 27 g (5 g fiber, 8 g sugars), **PRO** 12 g

# Butternut Squash Shakshuka

**45g**
**CARB**

**SERVES** 6
**HANDS ON** 25 min.
**SLOW COOK** 11 hr. 25 min.

- ¾ cup chopped red sweet pepper
- 1 small onion, halved and thinly sliced
- 1 medium fresh jalapeño chile pepper, seeded and finely chopped (tip, *p. 250*)

- 2  cloves garlic, minced
- 1  tsp. dried oregano, crushed
- 1  tsp. ground cumin
- ½  tsp. salt
- ½  tsp. black pepper
- 1  2-lb. butternut squash, peeled, seeded, and chopped (6 cups)
- 1  15-oz. can crushed tomatoes
- 1  8-oz. can tomato sauce
- 6  eggs
- ¾  cup crumbled feta cheese (3 oz.)
- 2  Tbsp. snipped fresh parsley

**1.** In a 3½- or 4-qt. slow cooker combine first eight ingredients (through black pepper). Stir in squash, crushed tomatoes, and tomato sauce.

**2.** Cover and cook on low 11 to 12 hours or high 5½ to 6 hours. If slow cooker is on low, turn to high. Break an egg into a custard cup. Make an indentation in squash mixture and slip egg into indentation. Repeat with remaining eggs. Cover and cook 25 to 35 minutes more or until eggs are desired doneness.

**3.** Top servings with cheese and parsley.

**PER SERVING** *(1 cup squash mixture + 1 egg each)* **CAL** 315, **FAT** 10 g (5 g sat. fat), **CHOL** 203 mg, **SODIUM** 917 mg, **CARB** 45 g (6 g fiber, 10 g sugars), **PRO** 15 g

# smart snacks

Snacks satisfy in more ways than just filling you up. These options are crunchy, zesty, chewy, and tasty.

### Red Pepper-Fennel Salsa

**4g**
**CARB**

**SERVES** 4
**TOTAL** 15 min.

- ¾ cup roasted red sweet peppers, drained and finely chopped
- ¼ cup finely chopped fresh fennel bulb
- 1 Tbsp. chopped Kalamata olives
- 2 tsp. olive oil
- 2 tsp. balsamic or red wine vinegar
- ½ tsp. stone-ground mustard
- ½ tsp. snipped fresh rosemary or oregano
- 1 small clove garlic, minced
  Pinch cayenne pepper
- 1 cup sliced fresh cucumber, zucchini, and/or wide sweet pepper strips

**1.** In a bowl stir together the first nine ingredients (through cayenne pepper). Cover and chill up to 24 hours. Serve as a dip with sliced vegetables.

**PER SERVING** (¼ cup salsa + ¼ cup veggies each) **CAL** 46, **FAT** 3 g (0 g sat. fat), **CHOL** 0 mg, **SODIUM** 188 mg, **CARB** 4 g (1 g fiber, 3 g sugars), **PRO** 1 g

# Cauliflower-Stuffed Mini Peppers

**6g** CARB | **SERVES** 4 | **TOTAL** 30 min.

- 1 cup packaged refrigerated riced cauliflower
- 1 Tbsp. olive oil
- 1 Tbsp. white wine vinegar
- 1 Tbsp. finely chopped red onion
- 2 tsp. snipped fresh parsley
- 1 tsp. rinsed and drained capers
- ¼ tsp. salt
- ⅛ tsp. black pepper
- 8 desired-color miniature sweet peppers

**1.** Preheat oven to 400°F. In a 9-inch pie plate toss cauliflower with oil to coat. Roast about 15 minutes or until beginning to brown, stirring once. Cool slightly. Add the next six ingredients (through black pepper); toss to combine.

**2.** Meanwhile, cut mini peppers in half lengthwise and remove seeds and ribs. Spoon cauliflower mixture into hollow halves.

**Tip** Riced cauliflower is available in the produce section of your supermarket. You can also make your own by pulsing cauliflower florets in a food processor until they are the size of rice grains.

**PER SERVING** *(4 stuffed pepper halves each)* **CAL** 56, **FAT** 4 g (1 g sat. fat), **CHOL** 0 mg, **SODIUM** 173 mg, **CARB** 6 g (2 g fiber, 3 g sugars), **PRO** 1 g

# Toasted Carrot Chips

**8g** CARB | **SERVES** 3 | **HANDS ON** 15 min. | **TOTAL** 35 min.

- 2 to 3 large-diameter carrots, peeled (about 8 oz.)
- 1 Tbsp. olive oil
- ½ tsp. ground cumin
- ½ tsp. ground coriander
- ¼ tsp. dried thyme, crushed
- ⅛ tsp. salt

**1.** Preheat oven to 375°F. Starting at the thick end, slice carrots paper-thin (¹⁄₁₆ inch) on the bias using a vegetable peeler (about 2 cups total). Pat dry and place in a bowl. Add the remaining ingredients; toss to coat. Spread carrot slices in a single layer in a 15×10-inch baking pan.

**2.** Bake 17 to 20 minutes or until crisp, turning once. Watch closely during the last 5 minutes to avoid burning. Remove pan from oven when edges of chips are starting to brown. Cool in pan on a wire rack. Chips will continue to crisp as they cool. Serve immediately after cooling.

**PER SERVING** *(⅓ cup each)* **CAL** 73, **FAT** 5 g (1 g sat. fat), **CHOL** 0 mg, **SODIUM** 150 mg, **CARB** 8 g (2 g fiber, 4 g sugars), **PRO** 1 g

## Harissa Deviled Egg

**2g** CARB | **SERVES** 1
**TOTAL** 5 min.

1 hard-cooked egg, peeled
1 Tbsp. harissa sauce (not paste)
 Black pepper
 Snipped fresh herbs (optional)

**1.** Cut egg in half lengthwise and remove yolk. In a bowl mash yolk with a fork. Add harissa sauce; mix well. Spoon yolk mixture into egg white halves. Sprinkle with pepper and, if desired, herbs.

**PER SERVING** (2 stuffed egg halves) **CAL** 91, **FAT** 6 g (2 g sat. fat), **CHOL** 187 mg, **SODIUM** 172 mg, **CARB** 2 g (1 g fiber, 1 g sugars), **PRO** 6 g

## Ricotta Tzatziki Dip

**5g** CARB | **SERVES** 6
**TOTAL** 20 min.

1 lemon
1 cup part-skim ricotta cheese
2 Tbsp. plain whole-milk yogurt
2 tsp. chopped fresh dill
1 small clove garlic, minced
¼ tsp. salt
¼ tsp. black pepper
½ cup shredded unpeeled
 English cucumber
1½ cups assorted fresh
 vegetables, such as carrot
 sticks, celery sticks, broccoli
 florets, cauliflower florets, and
 cucumber slices

**1.** Remove 1 tsp. zest and squeeze 1 Tbsp. juice from lemon. In a bowl whisk together zest, juice, and the next six ingredients (through pepper). Wrap shredded cucumber in paper towels and squeeze to remove excess moisture. Add cucumber to ricotta mixture; stir until combined. Serve with vegetables as dippers. Store in the refrigerator up to 3 days. Stir just before serving. If desired, sprinkle with additional pepper and chopped fresh dill.

**PER SERVING** *(¼ cup dip + ¼ cup veggies each)* **CAL** 71, **FAT** 3 g (2 g sat. fat), **CHOL** 13 mg, **SODIUM** 156 mg, **CARB** 5 g (1 g fiber, 1 g sugars), **PRO** 5 g

# Crunchy Puffed Cherry Granola

**15g**
**CARB**

SERVES 9
HANDS ON 15 min.
TOTAL 30 min.

- 1 cup puffed rice cereal
- 1 cup regular rolled oats
- ½ cup walnuts, coarsely chopped
- 2 Tbsp. unsweetened shredded coconut
- 3 Tbsp. pure maple syrup
- 2 tsp. olive oil
- 1½ tsp. orange zest
- ½ tsp. ground cinnamon
- ¼ tsp. vanilla
- 2 Tbsp. dried tart cherries or dried cranberries, finely chopped

**1.** Preheat oven to 350°F. Line a 15×10-inch baking pan with parchment paper.

**2.** In a bowl stir together rice cereal, oats, walnuts, and coconut. In another bowl whisk together the next five ingredients (through vanilla). Drizzle over oats mixture; stir to coat well. Spread oats mixture in prepared pan.

**3.** Bake about 15 minutes or until golden, stirring after 10 minutes. Remove from oven. Stir in cherries. Let cool on a wire rack. Store in an airtight container up to 2 weeks.

**PER SERVING** *(⅓ cup each)* **CAL** 116, **FAT** 6 g (1 g sat. fat), **CHOL** 0 mg, **SODIUM** 2 mg, **CARB** 15 g (2 g fiber, 6 g sugars), **PRO** 2 g

# Watermelon Fruit Pizza

**25g**
CARB

**SERVES** 4

**TOTAL** 15 min.

- 1  1-inch-thick slice watermelon, cut from the center of a large watermelon
- ½  cup plain low-fat Greek yogurt
- 2  tsp. honey
- ½  tsp. lime zest
- ¼  cup unsweetened shredded coconut, lightly toasted
- ¼  cup coarsely chopped shelled, roasted, salted pistachio nuts
- ¼  cup snipped fresh mint

**1.** Cut watermelon slice into eight equal wedges; remove seeds. Place wedges 1 inch apart on a platter. In a small bowl whisk together yogurt, honey, and lime zest. Spoon over watermelon wedges. Sprinkle evenly with coconut, pistachio nuts, and mint. Serve immediately.

**PER SERVING** *(2 wedges each)* **CAL** 173, **FAT** 7 g (3 g sat. fat), **CHOL** 3 mg, **SODIUM** 49 mg, **CARB** 25 g (3 g fiber, 19 g sugars), **PRO** 6 g

# Turkey Roll-Ups with Chili-Lime Cream

**8g**
CARB

**SERVES** 4

**TOTAL** 15 min.

- ¼  cup light sour cream
- 2  tsp. chili powder
- 1  tsp. lime juice
- 1  low-calorie multigrain flatbread with flax, such as Fit & Active or Flatout
- ¾  cup fresh baby spinach
- ¼  cup bite-size red sweet pepper strips
- ¼  cup shredded carrot
- 2  1-oz. slices deli-style lower-sodium turkey breast

**1.** In a bowl stir together sour cream, chili powder, and lime juice. Spread over flatbread. Arrange spinach over cream mixture to within 1 inch of one long edge. Sprinkle red pepper and carrot over spinach. Top with turkey slices. Starting from the opposite long edge, tightly roll up flatbread. Cut roll into eight pieces. Serve immediately or cover tightly and refrigerate up to 8 hours before serving. If desired, sprinkle roll-ups with additional chili powder.

**PER SERVING** *(2 roll-ups each)* **CAL** 68, **FAT** 2 g (1 g sat. fat), **CHOL** 12 mg, **SODIUM** 212 mg, **CARB** 8 g (3 g fiber, 1 g sugars), **PRO** 6 g

## Sesame-Almond Bites

**7g**
**CARB**

| | |
|---|---|
| **SERVES** 8 | |
| **HANDS ON** 10 min. | |
| **TOTAL** 50 min. | |

- ¼ cup sesame seeds
- ¼ cup unsweetened shredded coconut
- ¼ cup slivered almonds, toasted (tip, *p. 102*)
- 2 Tbsp. honey
- 1 Tbsp. creamy almond butter
- ¼ tsp. salt
- ⅛ tsp. vanilla

**1.** Preheat oven to 325°F. Line a 15×10×1-inch baking pan with parchment paper. In a bowl stir together all ingredients; mix well. Pat mixture to ¼-inch thickness on the baking pan.

**2.** Bake 13 to 15 minutes or until golden brown. Transfer parchment with mixture to a wire rack and let cool completely. Break into ½- to 1-inch pieces.

**PER SERVING** (*¼ cup each*) **CAL** 83, **FAT** 6 g (2 g sat. fat), **CHOL** 0 mg, **SODIUM** 80 mg, **CARB** 7 g (2 g fiber, 5 g sugars), **PRO** 2 g

## Lemony Butter Bean Lettuce Wraps

**14g**
**CARB**

| | |
|---|---|
| **SERVES** 4 | |
| **TOTAL** 10 min. | |

- 1 lemon
- 1 Tbsp. olive oil
- 1 Tbsp. snipped fresh mint
- ¼ tsp. salt
- ¼ tsp. black pepper
- 1 15-oz. can no-salt-added butter beans, rinsed and drained
- 1 Tbsp. finely chopped shallot
- 4 Bibb or butterhead lettuce leaves

**1.** Remove 1 tsp. zest and squeeze 2 Tbsp. juice from lemon. In a bowl whisk together zest, juice, olive oil, mint, salt, and pepper. Add beans and shallot; stir to coat. Spoon bean mixture into lettuce leaves.

**PER SERVING** (*1 wrap each*) **CAL** 110, **FAT** 4 g (0 g sat. fat), **CHOL** 0 mg, **SODIUM** 173 mg, **CARB** 14 g (3 g fiber, 0 g sugars), **PRO** 4 g

# a little bit of sweet

Sometimes you just need a little something to finish a meal on a sweet note. These small servings do the job.

## Frozen Yogurt Bark

**9g CARB**

**SERVES** 24
**HANDS ON** 15 min.
**TOTAL** 2 hr. 15 min.

1 32-oz. carton plain whole-milk Greek yogurt
¼ cup honey or 2 Tbsp. agave syrup
2 tsp. vanilla or 1 tsp. almond extract
1 cup filling(s), such as chopped dark chocolate, berries, and/or nuts
2 cups topper(s), such as toasted raw chip coconut, nuts, or seeds; fruit; and/or cacao nibs

**1.** Line two large baking sheets or trays with parchment paper. In a large bowl combine yogurt, honey, and vanilla. Stir in filling(s).
**2.** Divide yogurt mixture between prepared baking sheets, spreading into rectangles. Sprinkle with topper(s).
**3.** Freeze 2 to 4 hours or until firm. To serve, break bark into 24 irregular pieces. Store in freezer.

**Tip** Whole-milk yogurt has a little more fat in it, but it gives the best texture. Since you can store it in the freezer up to 3 months, it's easy to treat yourself to a little bit at a time.

**PER SERVING** *(1 piece each)* **CAL** 117, **FAT** 7 g (4 g sat. fat), **CHOL** 5 mg, **SODIUM** 14 mg, **CARB** 9 g (2 g fiber, 6 g sugars), **PRO** 5 g

# Sweet Ricotta and Strawberry Parfaits

**18g**
**CARB**

**SERVES** 6
**TOTAL** 35 min.

- 1 lb. fresh strawberries, hulled and halved or quartered
- 1 Tbsp. snipped fresh mint
- 1 tsp. sugar*
- 1 15-oz. carton part-skim ricotta cheese
- 3 Tbsp. agave nectar or honey
- ½ tsp. vanilla
- ¼ tsp. lemon zest

**1.** In a bowl gently stir together strawberries, mint, and sugar. Let stand about 15 minutes or until berries are softened and starting to release their juices.

**2.** In another bowl beat the remaining ingredients with a mixer on medium 2 minutes.

**3.** To assemble parfaits, scoop 2 Tbsp. of the ricotta mixture into each of six parfait glasses. Top each with a large spoonful of strawberry mixture. Repeat layers. If desired, top with additional fresh mint. Serve immediately or cover and chill up to 4 hours.

**PER SERVING** *(1 parfait each)* **CAL** 159, **FAT** 6 g (4 g sat. fat), **CHOL** 22 mg, **SODIUM** 90 mg, **CARB** 18 g (2 g fiber, 12 g sugars), **PRO** 9 g

**\*Sugar Sub** We do not recommend a sugar sub for this recipe.

# Chocolate-Date Truffles

**19g**
**CARB**

**SERVES** 10
**HANDS ON** 30 min.
**TOTAL** 1 hr. 30 min.

- ½ cup coarsely chopped walnuts
- ⅛ tsp. salt
- 1½ cups pitted whole Medjool dates
- 3 Tbsp. unsweetened cocoa powder
- 1 Tbsp. apple juice
- ¼ tsp. salt
- Water (optional)
- Cocoa powder (optional)

**1.** In a food processor combine walnuts and the ⅛ tsp. salt. Cover and pulse until finely chopped. Transfer to a shallow dish.

**2.** In food processor combine the next four ingredients (through ¼ tsp. salt). Cover and process until mixture forms a thick paste. If necessary, add 3 to 4 tsp. water, 1 tsp. at a time, to reach desired consistency.

**3.** For each truffle, shape 2 tsp. of the mixture into a ball. Roll balls in walnuts to coat. (If dough becomes too sticky, chill 15 to 20 minutes.) If desired, dust with cocoa powder. Cover and chill at least 1 hour before serving. Store in refrigerator up to 2 weeks.

**Tip** These truffles are all about the dates. Make sure you get Medjool dates for enough moisture to hold the truffles together.

**PER SERVING** *(2 truffles each)* **CAL** 105, **FAT** 4 g (0 g sat. fat), **CHOL** 0 mg, **SODIUM** 88 mg, **CARB** 19 g (2 g fiber, 15 g sugars), **PRO** 2 g

**\*Sugar Sub** We do not recommend a sugar sub for this recipe.

## Citrus Custard

**28g** **CARB**

| SERVES | 4 |
|---|---|
| **HANDS ON** | 30 min. |
| **TOTAL** | 4 hr. 30 min. |

- ¼ cup sugar*
- 2 Tbsp. cornstarch
- 2½ cups low-fat (1%) milk
- 4 egg yolks, lightly beaten
- ½ tsp. orange zest
- ½ tsp. vanilla
- ¼ cup coarsely crushed shortbread cookies
  Orange slices and/or citrus peel twists (optional)

**1.** In a medium heavy saucepan stir together sugar and cornstarch; stir in milk. Cook and stir over medium until thick and bubbly. Cook and stir 2 minutes more. Remove from heat.
**2.** Gradually stir about 1 cup of the hot mixture into egg yolks; return to saucepan. Bring just to boiling; remove from heat. Stir in orange zest and vanilla. Pour into a serving bowl or four dessert dishes and cover surfaces with plastic wrap; cool slightly. Chill at least 4 hours before serving; do not stir.
**3.** Top custard with crushed cookies and, if desired, orange slices and/ or twists.

**PER SERVING** *(⅔ cup each)* **CAL** 212, **FAT** 7 g (3 g sat. fat), **CHOL** 192 mg, **SODIUM** 95 mg, **CARB** 28 g (0 g fiber, 22 g sugars), **PRO** 8 g

**\*Sugar Sub** We do not recommend a sugar sub for this recipe.

# Creamy Chocolate Pudding

**26g**
**CARB**

| | |
|---|---|
| **SERVES** | 4 |
| **TOTAL** | 10 min. |

- 1 ripe avocado, halved, seeded, peeled, and cut up
- ½ of a banana, peeled and cut up
- ½ cup unsweetened cocoa powder
- ½ cup milk or soymilk
- 3 to 4 Tbsp. honey or agave syrup
- 2 tsp. vanilla

**1.** In a blender combine all ingredients. Cover; blend until smooth. If desired, cover surface with plastic wrap and chill.

**PER SERVING** *(½ cup each)* **CAL** 163, **FAT** 7 g (2 g sat. fat), **CHOL** 2 mg, **SODIUM** 20 mg, **CARB** 26 g (6 g fiber, 14 g sugars), **PRO** 4 g

# Peanut Cluster Butterscotch Bites

**8g**
**CARB**

| | |
|---|---|
| **SERVES** | 45 |
| **HANDS ON** | 30 min. |
| **TOTAL** | 45 min. |

- 1¼ cups semisweet chocolate pieces
- ½ cup butterscotch-flavor pieces
- ⅓ cup fat-free half-and-half
- 1 cup unsalted peanuts
- 45 baked miniature frozen phyllo shells
- ¼ cup unsalted peanuts, finely chopped
  Flaked sea salt (optional)

**1.** In a small saucepan heat chocolate pieces and butterscotch-flavor pieces over low until melted and smooth, stirring frequently. Stir in half-and-half until smooth. Stir in the 1 cup peanuts.
**2.** Immediately spoon peanut mixture into phyllo shells, using about 2 tsp. per shell. Before mixture is set, sprinkle tops with the finely chopped peanuts and, if desired, flaked sea salt. Let stand at room temperature about 15 minutes or until set.

**PER SERVING** *(1 bite each)* **CAL** 85, **FAT** 5 g (2 g sat. fat), **CHOL** 0 mg, **SODIUM** 14 mg, **CARB** 8 g (1 g fiber, 4 g sugars), **PRO** 2 g

# Apple Dippers

Start with 1 medium apple, cut it into 12 slices. Choose a crisp, tart apple like Granny Smith or Pink Lady. Pick one flavor per apple. Each serving: 2 slices.

**1. MAPLE-PECAN** Dip apple slices halfway into a mixture of **3 oz. melted butterscotch-flavor pieces** and ⅛ **tsp. shortening or coconut oil. Sprinkle with 3 Tbsp. finely chopped toasted pecans**. Arrange on a waxed paper-lined tray. Let stand until firm or cover and chill up to 1 hour. Drizzle with **1½ tsp. maple syrup.**

PER SERVING  **CAL** 120, **FAT** 6 g (4 g sat. fat), **CHOL** 0 mg, **SODIUM** 10 mg, **CARB** 15 g (1 g fiber, 15 g sugars), **PRO** 1 g

**2. DARK CHOCOLATE-GINGERSNAP** Dip apple slices halfway into **3 oz. melted bittersweet chocolate. Sprinkle with 3 Tbsp. finely crushed gingersnaps**. Arrange on a waxed paper-lined tray. Let stand until firm or cover and chill up to 1 hour.

PER SERVING  **CAL** 101, **FAT** 6 g (3 g sat. fat), **CHOL** 0 mg, **SODIUM** 18 mg, **CARB** 15 g (2 g fiber, 9 g sugars), **PRO** 1 g

**3. WHITE CHOCOLATE-GRANOLA** Dip apple slices halfway into **3 oz. melted white baking chocolate. Sprinkle with ¼ cup granola** (crush granola if necessary). Arrange on a waxed paper-lined tray. Let stand until firm or cover and chill up to 1 hour.

PER SERVING  **CAL** 108, **FAT** 5 g (3 g sat. fat), **CHOL** 3 mg, **SODIUM** 21 mg, **CARB** 16 g (1 g fiber, 13 g sugars), **PRO** 1 g

**4. CARAMEL-PRETZEL** Dip apple slices halfway into **3 oz. melted white baking chocolate. Sprinkle with 3 Tbsp. crushed pretzels**. Arrange on a waxed paper-lined tray. Let stand until firm or cover and chill up to 1 hour. Drizzle with **1½ tsp. caramel-flavor ice cream topping.**

PER SERVING  **CAL** 104, **FAT** 5 g (3 g sat. fat), **CHOL** 3 mg, **SODIUM** 38 mg, **CARB** 15 g (1 g fiber, 13 g sugars), **PRO** 1 g

**5. PEANUT BUTTER-CHOCOLATE** Dip apple slices halfway into a mixture of **3 oz. melted peanut butter-flavor pieces** and ⅛ **tsp. shortening or coconut oil.** Arrange on a waxed paper-lined tray. Sprinkle with **3 Tbsp. miniature semisweet chocolate pieces.** Let stand until firm or cover and chill up to 1 hour.

PER SERVING  **CAL** 132, **FAT** 6 g (5 g sat. fat), **CHOL** 0 mg, **SODIUM** 29 mg, **CARB** 17 g (2 g fiber, 13 g sugars), **PRO** 3 g

**6. MARGARITA** Dip apple slices halfway into **3 oz. melted white baking chocolate.** Arrange on a waxed paper-lined tray. Sprinkle with **2 Tbsp. lime zest.** Let stand until firm or cover and chill up to 1 hour.

PER SERVING  **CAL** 93, **FAT** 5 g (3 g sat. fat), **CHOL** 3 mg, **SODIUM** 11 mg, **CARB** 13 g (1 g fiber, 12 g sugars), **PRO** 1 g

**7. STRAWBERRY SHORTBREAD** Dip apple slices halfway into **3 oz. melted white baking chocolate. Sprinkle with 3 Tbsp. crushed shortbread cookies.** Arrange on a waxed paper-lined tray. Let stand until firm or cover and chill up to 1 hour. Drizzle with **3 Tbsp. warmed reduced-sugar strawberry fruit spread.**

PER SERVING  **CAL** 121, **FAT** 6 g (3 g sat. fat), **CHOL** 3 mg, **SODIUM** 24 mg, **CARB** 18 g (1 g fiber, 15 g sugars), **PRO** 1 g

**8. DARK CHOCOLATE S'MORES** Dip apple slices halfway into **3 oz. melted bittersweet chocolate. Sprinkle with 3 Tbsp. crushed graham crackers.** Arrange on a waxed paper-lined tray. Cut up **12 tiny marshmallows** and arrange on apple slices. Let stand until firm or cover and chill up to 1 hour.

PER SERVING  **CAL** 104, **FAT** 6 g (3 g sat. fat), **CHOL** 0 mg, **SODIUM** 17 mg, **CARB** 15 g (2 g fiber, 10 g sugars), **PRO** 1 g

# Apricot Pocket Cookies

**25g** CARB

**SERVES** 24
**HANDS ON** 50 min.
**TOTAL** 3 hr. 30 min.

- ⅓ cup butter, softened
- ½ cup granulated sugar*
- ¾ tsp. baking powder
- ¼ tsp. salt
- ¼ cup light sour cream
- ¼ cup refrigerated or frozen egg product, thawed, or 1 egg
- 1 tsp. vanilla
- 2⅔ cups cake flour, sifted
- ¾ cup dried apricots (4 oz.)
- 1½ Tbsp. granulated sugar*
- 1 cup powdered sugar*
- 3 to 4 tsp. fat-free milk
- 1 tsp. almond extract

**1.** In a bowl beat butter with a mixer on medium 30 seconds. Add the ½ cup sugar, the baking powder, and salt. Beat until combined, scraping bowl as needed. Add sour cream, egg, and vanilla; beat until combined. Beat in flour. Divide dough in half. Cover and chill dough about 1½ hours or until easy to handle.
**2.** In another bowl combine apricots and enough boiling water to cover. Let stand 1 hour. Drain apricots; blot dry on paper towels. Finely chop. Combine apricots and the 1½ Tbsp. sugar.

**3.** Preheat oven to 375°F. On a lightly floured surface roll half of the dough to ⅛ inch thick (keep remaining dough chilled until ready to use). Using a 2-inch round cookie cutter, cut dough into rounds, rerolling scraps as necessary.
**4.** Arrange half the cutouts 1 inch apart on ungreased cookie sheets. Brush outer edges of cutouts with water. Spoon rounded teaspoons of apricot mixture in centers of cutouts on cookie sheets. Lay remaining cutouts over filling. Using tines of a fork, lightly press edges of assembled cookies to seal. If desired, make a small slit in tops of cookies.
**5.** Bake 8 to 9 minutes or until firm and bottoms are lightly browned. Remove; cool on wire racks. Repeat with remaining dough and filling.
**6.** For icing, in a bowl stir together the remaining ingredients; add more milk, 1 tsp. at a time, if needed to reach drizzling consistency. Drizzle icing on cooled cookies.

**PER SERVING** (1 cookie each) **CAL.** 132, **FAT** 3 g total (2 g sat. fat), **CHOL.** 8 mg, **SODIUM** 67 mg, **CARB.** 25 g, **FIBER** 1 g, **SUGAR** 12 g, **PRO.** 2 g

**\*Sugar Sub** Use Splenda Sugar Blend. Follow package directions to use ½ cup and 1½ Tbsp. granulated sugar equivalents. We do not recommend a sub for the powdered sugar.
**PER SERVING WITH SUB** Same as above, except **CAL.** 124, **CARB** 22 g (10 g sugars)

# recipe guide

## Inside Our Recipes
▶ Precise serving sizes help you to manage portions.
▶ Ingredients listed as optional are not included in the per-serving nutrition analysis.

## Ingredients
▶ Tub-style vegetable oil spread refers to 60% to 70% vegetable oil product.
▶ Lean ground beef refers to 95% or leaner ground beef.

## Nutrition Information
▶ Nutrition facts per serving are noted with each recipe.
▶ Tips and sugar substitutes are listed after the recipe directions.
▶ When ingredient choices appear, we use the first one to calculate the nutrition analysis.

## Key to Abbreviations
**CAL** = calories
**SAT. FAT** = saturated fat
**CHOL** = cholesterol
**CARB** = carbohydrate
**PRO** = protein

## Tip: Handling hot chile peppers
Chile peppers can irritate skin and eyes. Wear gloves when working with them. If your bare hands do touch the peppers, wash your hands with soap and warm water.

# index

# metric information

## Product Differences

Most of the ingredients called for in the recipes in this book are available in most countries. However, some are known by different names. Here are some common American ingredients and their possible counterparts:

**SUGAR** (white) is granulated, fine granulated, or caster sugar.

**POWDERED SUGAR** is icing sugar.

**ALL-PURPOSE FLOUR** is enriched, bleached or unbleached white household flour. When self-rising flour is used in place of all-purpose flour in a recipe that calls for leavening, omit the leavening agent (baking soda or baking powder) and salt.

**LIGHT-COLOR CORN SYRUP** is golden syrup.

**CORNSTARCH** is cornflour.

**BAKING SODA** is bicarbonate of soda.

**VANILLA OR VANILLA EXTRACT** is vanilla essence.

**GREEN, RED, OR YELLOW SWEET PEPPERS** are capsicums or bell peppers.

**GOLDEN RAISINS** are sultanas.

**SHORTENING** is solid vegetable oil (substitute Copha or lard).

## Measurement Abbreviations

| MEASUREMENT | ABBREVIATIONS |
|---|---|
| fluid ounce | fl. oz. |
| gallon | gal. |
| gram | g |
| liter | L |
| milliliter | ml |
| ounce | oz. |
| package | pkg. |
| pint | pt. |

## Common Weight Equivalents

| IMPERIAL / U.S. | METRIC |
|---|---|
| ½ ounce | 14.18 g |
| 1 ounce | 28.35 g |
| 4 ounces (¼ pound) | 113.4 g |
| 8 ounces (½ pound) | 226.8 g |
| 16 ounces (1 pound) | 453.6 g |
| 1¼ pounds | 567 g |
| 1½ pounds | 680.4 g |
| 2 pounds | 907.2 g |

## Oven Temperature Equivalents

| FAHRENHEIT SETTING | CELSIUS SETTING |
|---|---|
| 300°F | 150°C |
| 325°F | 160°C |
| 350°F | 180°C |
| 375°F | 190°C |
| 400°F | 200°C |
| 425°F | 220°C |
| 450°F | 230°C |
| 475°F | 240°C |
| 500°F | 260°C |
| Broil | Broil |

*For convection or forced-air ovens (gas or electric), lower the temperature setting 25°F/10°C when cooking at all heat levels.

## Approximate Standard Metric Equivalents

| MEASUREMENT | OUNCES | METRIC |
|---|---|---|
| ⅛ tsp. | | 0.5 ml |
| ¼ tsp. | | 1 ml |
| ½ tsp. | | 2.5 ml |
| 1 tsp. | | 5 ml |
| 1 Tbsp. | | 15 ml |
| 2 Tbsp. | 1 fl. oz. | 30 ml |
| ¼ cup | 2 fl. oz. | 60 ml |
| ⅓ cup | 3 fl. oz. | 80 ml |
| ½ cup | 4 fl. oz. | 120 ml |
| ⅔ cup | 5 fl. oz. | 160 ml |
| ¾ cup | 6 fl. oz. | 180 ml |
| 1 cup | 8 fl. oz. | 240 ml |
| 2 cups | 16 fl. oz. (1 pt.) | 480 ml |
| 1 qt. | 64 fl. oz. (2 pt.) | 0.95 L |

## Converting to Metric

| | |
|---|---|
| centimeters to inches | divide centimeters by 2.54 |
| cups to liters | multiply cups by 0.236 |
| cups to milliliters | multiply cups by 236.59 |
| gallons to liters | multiply gallons by 3.785 |
| grams to ounces | divide grams by 28.35 |
| inches to centimeters | multiply inches by 2.54 |
| kilograms to pounds | divide kilograms by 0.454 |
| liters to cups | divide liters by 0.236 |
| liters to gallons | divide liters by 3.785 |
| liters to pints | divide liters by 0.473 |
| liters to quarts | divide liters by 0.946 |
| milliliters to cups | divide milliliters by 236.59 |
| milliliters to fluid ounces | divide milliliters by 29.57 |
| milliliters to tablespoons | divide milliliters by 14.79 |
| milliliters to teaspoons | divide milliliters by 4.93 |
| ounces to grams | multiply ounces by 28.35 |
| ounces to milliliters | multiply ounces by 29.57 |
| pints to liters | multiply pints by 0.473 |
| pounds to kilograms | multiply pounds by 0.454 |
| quarts to liters | multiply quarts by 0.946 |
| tablespoons to milliliters | multiply tablespoons by 14.79 |
| teaspoons to milliliters | multiply teaspoons by 4.93 |